Emanuel Ringelblum
The Man and the Historian

This publication was supported by a grant
from the following organizations:

The Conference on Jewish Material Claims Against Germany

Claims Conference ועידת התביעות
The Conference on Jewish Material Claims Against Germany

The Memorial Foundation for Jewish Culture
The Adelson Family Charitable Foundation

Emanuel Ringelblum
The Man and the Historian

Edited by

Israel Gutman

Yad Vashem ⋆ Jerusalem ⋆ 2010

The International Institute for Holocaust Research

Managing Editor (English edition): Daniella Zaidman-Mauer
Academic Consultants: Nathan Cohen, Havi Dreifuss
and David Silberklang
Assistant Editor (Hebrew edition): Avital Saf
Translator: Chaya Naor
Language Editor: Leah Aharonov
Typesetting: Judith Sternberg

Danacode: 268-749
ISBN: 978-965-308-355-4

Printed in Israel 2010

Contents

The milk cans and three of the metal boxes containing partial documentation of the *Oyneg Shabes* Archives, Warsaw, Poland, Yad Vashem Photo Archives, 1605/17

Introduction

The hiding place in which Emanuel Menahem Ringelblum, his wife Józia Yehudit, and their twelve-year-old son Uri Jurek found shelter from the summer of 1943 to March 7, 1944, was an underground bunker at 84 Grójecka Street,[1] in a suburb of Warsaw. The idea of preparing this bunker — in which more than thirty Jews lived for over a year — its exact location, and the conditions that prevailed were described in Ringelblum's book *Polish-Jewish Relations*, which he wrote while he was in the bunker,[2] and in letters written by him and his wife. These letters were removed from the bunker, and excerpts from them are quoted in the following collection.

Orna (Grodzinska) Jagur's memoirs, entitled *The Hiding Place*,[3] is another important source with regard to the bunker. Orna and Yosef, a young couple, were the sole tenants of the bunker to survive. Orna's father, who also was in the bunker, felt at a certain stage that they were in danger there and urged them to leave. Thanks to close relations he had developed with the family who owned the bunker, they found shelter elsewhere, in a place that ultimately proved to be safe.

A short chapter on the bunker, the plans that were woven

1 According to other sources, the number of the house on Grójecka Street was 81. Apparently the number of the house and the number of the lot on which the bunker was dug were not the same.

2 Joseph Kermish and Shmuel Krakowski, eds., *Emanuel Ringelblum, Polish-Jewish Relations During the Second World War* (Jerusalem: Yad Vashem and New York: Howard Fertig, 1976), pp. 227–236.

3 Orna Jagur (Irena Grodzinska), *The Hiding Place* (Łódź: Oficyna Bibliofilów, 1997).

around it, and a description of a visit there are included in a book by Yaakov Celemenski, one of the key Bund activists on the Polish side.[4] The code name of the bunker known to those who were in on the secret was "Krysia." In Polish, Krysia is an affectionate term for a woman whose name is Kristina, and it also alludes to the Polish word for a hiding place — *kryjówka*. In the documents we possess, there is some confusion about the name of the family who owned the bunker; however, everyone agrees that the "boss," the man who dealt with all matters relating to the place and who was helped by several of his family members, was Mieczysław Wolski.

Wolski was a gardener by occupation, a daring, energetic man in his late thirties, with no family of his own. In Ringelblum's book *Polish-Jewish Relations*, he described him as an idealist, a man who constantly kept an eye on everything to do with the hide out, who was totally devoted, and who believed his mission of saving the Jews under his protection was a duty and life's work that would be properly appreciated in the future. From the description it is clear that Wolski also liked adventure and tended to tempt fate. This was an unfortunate trait, which probably led to the downfall of the bunker; thus, dooming him and those hiding there. Ringelblum's letters reveal another aspect of Wolski's personality — one that came to the fore or was heightened during the period he looked after the bunker. This was his tendency to view it as a financial venture and a means to accumulate money.

Ringelblum also writes about Wolski's mother, an authoritative woman who was involved in managing the bunker and helped maintain contacts with the outside. Since she was sensitive to the distressful situation of the inhabitants of the bunker, she also settled disputes between them and the owners, as well as those that arose among them.

Orna Jagur, in writing about the family of the owners, includes the figure of the boy Janusz, Wolski's nephew and helper, who was in charge of day-to-day security. He worked with the laborers in the garden and made sure that they did not get too close to the hiding

4 Yaakov Celemenski, *Mitn farshitenem folk* (Yiddish) (New York: Undzer Tsayit, 1963), pp. 280–284.

place. Janusz became friendly with a boy his age who was hiding in the bunker, and together they would bring the food and other items to the bunker and remove the waste each day.

Several Jewish merchants who in the past had purchased produce from the Wolski's garden, and had developed close ties and relations of mutual trust with the family, were the ones who came up with the idea of establishing the bunker in the area of the garden adjacent to the home of the Wolski family. The Wolski family home and their vegetable garden were located on the outskirts of the city, far from crowded population centers. The proposal that they provide a hiding place for Jews fleeing the ghetto was raised at a family council of the Wolskis, and, although some of those present expressed their apprehensions about the possibility of discovery, Mieczysław Wolski decided in favor of the idea. He argued that Jews should be saved in spite of the strong opposition of the occupier, who had sentenced them to death, and that "it is the duty of every Pole, a civic duty, to hide Jews."[5]

A long, narrow pit was dug under the ground, covered with a layer of earth, and above it a sloping greenhouse was built, covered with dark glass panels. In the greenhouse there was a concealed entrance and a ladder leading to the hiding place. Inside there was an air opening, rows of bunks and benches, a long table, and primitive toilets. The cooking area was separated from the living space by a cloth curtain. The bunker was 23 sq. meters wide and 1.83 meters high. The bunks and benches were prepared in the ghetto and moved secretly to the bunker. In order to supply the Jews in the bunker with their basic necessities and camouflage the large quantities of food that were hoarded and transferred to them, the Wolskis opened a small grocery store. At certain hours the inhabitants of the bunker were allowed to come up for a short while to breathe fresh air in the upper structure of the greenhouse.

The Jagurs came to the bunker at a later stage, and Orna describes her first encounter with the interior of the bunker:

5 Ringelblum, *Polish-Jewish Relations*, p. 229.

> Janusz slipped into the pavilion noiselessly. His silhouette stood out like a shadow against the darkness of the night.
> "It is quiet now, there is nobody around, we can go to KRYSIA..."
> ...and then started quietly whistling a popular tune. This was a signal for the people inside to open the flap, which was the entrance to the bunker. The flap was raised slowly and a dimly lit square became visible. Somebody inside put a ladder to the wall to enable us to get down into the bunker. I started hesitantly going down the ladder... A hot wave of stale air hit me from below. It was an odor of mold, mixed with the stench of sweat, un-aired clothes and leftover food. After the fragrant, clean air of the garden the contrast was hard to bear. After a while my eyes became used to the dim, scarce light in the bunker and slowly the shape of its inside became visible...[6]

The Jews hiding in the bunker were a random group from several families – men, women, children, and elderly. According to Jagur, "... had little in common, except for the fact that all of them were all Jews, and as such, condemned to death by the Nazis and were trying to avoid the execution of their sentence."[7]

They were totally cut off from the outside. If a voice were raised inside or outside that would mean danger and jagged nerves. Because of the tense atmosphere and the tight discipline that was constantly required, any physical disability or other unusual problem immediately meant the individual was a burden and a danger to the others. They were all united by their anxiety and the need to hide until the yearned-for liberation would come – which they were incapable of bringing any closer. As they were compelled to live under a strict regime, they had to be cut off as far as possible from everything happening up above, from normalcy. Orna tells about the friendship and the tolerance that prevailed among the people who spent their days lying on their bunks in enforced idleness – despite the annoying fleas, the depressing presence of those

6 Jagur, *The Hiding Place*, pp. 21–22.
7 Ibid., p. 24.

who had become mentally imbalanced, often because of trivialities, and the tyranny of the person in charge of all the arrangements in the hiding place.

Batya Temkin-Berman was filled with sorrow when Ringelblum and the others in the bunker were all murdered, sorrow that was bound up with her grievances about the bunker itself:

> [after] Ringelblum's wife Józia also left and was taken to one of our transit addresses…she was convinced that we would bring her into the underground bunker at 81 Grójecka, where 30 Jews were already staying, most of them wealthy people who had invested a lot of money in the place. We really did not like that idea. We knew that where there are rich Jews, there are always extortionists, and in any case it is very difficult to hide such a large group. But Józia was certain that she was very fortunate to have been accepted there. Ringelblum did not want to live there either and he postponed his departure. A few times he went out for two days or more to the ghetto to complete work on his archives. On one of these times when he was wandering about, the third *Aktion* took place, and in reaction to it — the heroic uprising.[8]

It turns out that, even while they were living isolated underground in crowded conditions, those in hiding did not accurately assess what was happening to the people who were with them there. In one of the chapters of her book, Orna Jagur writes about Emanuel Ringelblum's personality:

> At one end of the table, beside the burning carbide lamp, a middle-aged, silent man sat, always in the same place, and wrote. He wrote ceaselessly during whole days and evenings and did not leave the table, which was loaded with his books and papers. This man was Dr. Emanuel Ringelblum, a well-known historian and chronicler. In the ghetto, he wrote a

8 Batya Temkin-Berman, "'Pan Rodzewski' — Ringelblum's Last Days" (Hebrew), *Yalkut Moreshet*, II (1964), p. 13.

> chronicle, known as *Notes from the Warsaw Ghetto*. During the final liquidation of the ghetto, he was sent to the SS camp Trawniki. After he escaped from there, with the help of Polish railway workers, he returned to "KRYSIA" where he had, already before, placed his family: his wife, Yehudit and his son, Uri.
>
> During his stay in the bunker, he also wrote, among other works, an essay about Polish-Jewish relations during the Second World War, in which he stressed the help extended to the Jews by a part of a Polish society, despite the threat of the death penalty for those giving it. Dr. Ringelblum did not vegetate in the bunker, unlike most of those staying there. He had a task to fulfill and the strength of will and intellect to pursue it: to transmit in his writing to future generations, the history of the annihilation of the Polish Jews and the crimes of the Nazis [...] Dr. Ringelblum was only physically present in "KRYSIA." His thoughts were far away from there. He did not take part in the everyday life of the bunker. He showed no excitement or involvement in moments of danger or relief. He did not take part in discussions or quarrels. His intensive work and the presence of his family were, evidently, his escape from the gray monotony of the passive existence in the bunker, which was to become the last stage of his life.[9]

Mrs. Jagur's words of praise and admiration are understandable. She observed how preoccupied Ringelblum was with his heavy load of work, which grew even heavier during the months of his stay in the hiding place. The amount of writing he produced during that time – only a small part of which has come into our possession – evokes amazement and admiration. However, from the bundle of letters that Ringelblum and his wife wrote in the bunker, which was given to the Berman family, it is clear that Ringelblum did not isolate himself from daily life in the bunker, and there is no basis for her claim that he was not involved in such matters. His letters show that he was very aware of his surroundings and took an

9 Jagur, *The Hiding Place*, pp. 44–45.

active position about what was taking place in the bunker and on crucial questions that arose. Among other things, he mentions the young couple that left the bunker and the impression this left on those who remained.

Moreover, Ringelblum was the representative of a group of people who were in the bunker under the protection of the National Jewish Council on the Aryan side of the city. This was headed by Adolf Abraham Berman and David Guzik, who, in the past, had been directors of the Joint in Poland. This was a complex, responsible, and nerve-wracking position, and Ringelblum dealt with the personal problems of members of the group. Above all, he had to cope with the tension and pressure caused when there was a delay in the monthly payments to the owners of the bunker, which was meant to finance the rent, the purchase of the food, and the daily needs of the bunker inhabitants. From the letters it is clear that, despite Guzik's repeated promises, for long periods the funds did not arrive on time. The tension and anxiety these delays caused the people in the bunker are clearly palpable in the letters.

It was essential to keep the existence of the bunker secret, or the people hiding there would have no chance whatsoever of survival. Its location in an urban environment and the fact that people — who, of course, were unaware of its existence — were working in the garden above it caused many problems and created a threat to the security of the Jews in the bunker. Orna Jagur relates that one day the last man on duty in the lookout post neglected to replace the pane over the opening in the roof of the greenhouse. The following day one of the women workers chased after a hen that had run into the greenhouse through that opening. When they heard the cawing, the flapping of wings, and the unexpected steps over their heads, the people inside began to panic noisily. The worker who chased the hen later told the other workers that evidently there were demons in the greenhouse that were making noises. By a clever trick Wolski managed to cover up the incident, but it is not clear whether the suspicions of the workers in the garden were not aroused.

Another, more serious, incident was apparently not known to all the inhabitants of the bunker. Some members of the Bund on the Aryan side suggested that another hiding place adjacent to the one on Grójecka Street be prepared, or that the existing bunker be expanded. Those in the bunker who knew about this idea became very worried, and this concern was reflected in letters from the Ringelblums to the Bermans. An underground activist, Yaakov Celemenski, who describes meetings with Wolski and a visit to the bunker in his memoirs, negotiated on behalf of the Bund with Wolski.[10] The suggestion was never carried out because of the large sum of money that Wolski demanded. Celemenski writes that, when he was talking with the man, a woman suddenly appeared — apparently, Wolski's lover, and "the angel of death of the Jews hiding in the bunker." Celemenski suspected that it was this woman who informed on the bunker and its inhabitants. He believes that "the inhabitants of the bunker would certainly have been liberated if it hadn't been for Wolski's blonde lover."[11]

In January 1944, extortionists got on Adolf Abraham Berman's trail, and he was forced to disappear for a while and go deep underground. The Bermans searched feverishly for a new hiding place, where they could go on hiding as Poles. Yehudit and Emanuel Ringelblum referred to this matter in several letters. Among other ideas, they raised the possibility of taking them into the bunker, but they noted the cramped conditions and the lack of comfort. At the same time they suggested a different apartment they knew about where the Bermans could hide. In the end the Bermans found another apartment for themselves.

The Ringelblums' last letters reflect their growing uncertainty about the future of the hide out, as well as a sense of grievance. They complain a great deal about the congested atmosphere and the tensions among the inhabitants, and refer to the chances of their survival in a pessimistic tone.

In April 1956, Batya Temkin-Berman's article "On Our Archives on the Aryan Side" was published.[12] It begins:

10 For details on the negotiations and the visit to the bunker, see Celemenski, *Mitn farshitenem folk*, pp. 280–284.

11 Ibid.

12 See Batya Temkin-Berman, "On Our Archives on the Aryan Side" (Hebrew), *Yedioth bet Lochamei hageta'ot*, 2–3 (14–15) (1956), pp. 31–35.

> We regarded the archives of the Jewish underground movement, to be more precise the archives of the National Jewish Council, in the "Aryan" past, as a continuation of the secret archives established in the Warsaw Ghetto by Emanuel Ringelblum, which were given the code name *Oyneg Shabes*.

This is followed by a long list of articles, personal testimonies, and diaries written by Jews in hiding.

Along with the rescue endeavor on the Aryan side, in which much effort was exerted in dealing with individuals and families in face of the danger lurking everywhere, initiatives and energy were invested in writing memoirs, in documentation, and in commemoration. Some of those who participated in this effort were the Berman family and other *Oyneg Shabes* activists in the ghetto: Hirsch and Bluma Wasser, Rachel Auerbach, and others. Poles of good will helped the remaining Jews carry out this work and preserve the material. Temkin-Berman writes in her article:

> Through the contacts and the trustees we sent a series of brief letters to people whom we believed would be able to write something. As a result, we received dozens of manuscripts, some short, and some longer, memoirs and diaries…

In addition to composing the most important pieces of writing written then, Ringelblum urged his friends to write many items that in the future would serve as a documentary source of information about a period of unique historical significance. This activity of collecting as much documentary material as possible was reflected in many of his letters to the Bermans. In addition to articles about the history of the Jews in the cities, towns, and camps, and the deportations from the Warsaw ghetto, which were written under conditions of concealment and constant danger, the fabric of relations between Poles and Jews in those trying times was also documented. Furthermore, the activities to do with rescuing Jews and the obstacles encountered, as well as a series of letters and reports sent through underground channels to London, were recorded.

Among other things, Ringelblum stressed a full, objective survey – as far as possible – of the uprising in the Warsaw ghetto, since he regarded it as a key event that had to be precisely and systematically recorded. Material written and edited outside was also brought to him in the bunker. He pointed out the shortcomings, corrected any errors, and emphasized that it was necessary to expand the circle of writers and to deal with the subjects that had been neglected. A large part of these writings were lost, including Ringelblum's monograph on the Trawniki camp. Another part of the collection and the testimonies were saved after the Polish uprising and the overall destruction in Warsaw. Temkin-Berman enumerates places and names of Poles who, in 1944, helped preserve the material. She concludes by saying:

> We keep the "useful" archives for four days in the shelter [during the Polish uprising]; after the Germans discovered us and removed us from there, we have been carrying the bag with us, wandering with our "knapsack" until the coming of redemption.[13]

Once a plan was prepared for Ringelblum's escape from Trawniki, the Jewish activists on the Aryan side clung to their hope that he would be added to the team of rescue workers of the National Jewish Council. Temkin-Berman tells how, after Ringelblum was removed from the Trawniki camp and returned to Warsaw, they saw him alive, suntanned and gaunt from his hard labor in the camp. He spoke about his experiences there, and described to us an outline of the study he was going to write about the camp. Two days later, he left to join his wife and son, promising he would return in a week.

And as she wrote sorrowfully: "He went into the accursed hole, to the bunker, and never came out again..."[14]

After blackmailers grabbed Adolf Abraham Berman, on January 4, 1944, it was suggested again that Ringelblum should leave to continue his work on the outside, but nothing came of the sugges-

13 Ibid., p. 34.

14 Temkin-Berman, "Pan Rodzewski," pp. 14–15.

tion. The Ringelblums' letters and Batya Temkin-Berman's words indicate that there were varied, complex reasons for this.

After he returned to Yehudit and Uri, who had never expected to see him alive again, they found it terribly hard to part from him. Ringelblum himself never shook off his depression in the aftermath of his stay in the camp, or his concern for the fate of his friends who remained there – as he wrote innumerable times in his letters. But apparently, the main reason he was so hesitant and finally decided not to leave was his commitment as an historian. Temkin-Berman says: "He felt that his historical work was more important than political activity or the welfare work he could have engaged in above ground."[15]

The last bundle of the Ringelblums' letters to their friends, the Bermans, who were among the heads of the Jewish National Council on the Aryan side, constitutes a rare, unparalleled personal document. They were written from a hovel in deplorable conditions, months after the final liquidation of Warsaw Jewry. The voice that rises from these letters of farewell in occupied Europe, ruled and led by the forces of evil and terror, is a coherent, matter-of-fact and humane voice. Ringelblum, who felt the bunker was not a safe refuge and that his days were numbered, does not ask for shelter for himself and his family. His words about the bunker and the fugitives in it are a call for help for those suffering around him. He mentions his own situation and that of his dear ones only in passing. He does not forget friends and those actively involved in work on the outside; he asks how they are and hopes they are safe.

Ringelblum certainly never imagined that these personal letters would ever reach a reader in the free world or in the State of Israel. When he wrote them, he was not only thoroughly convinced that those dark days were a passing nightmare for the peoples of the world, but he directs his last thoughts and his yearning to that future that will dawn without him. He is concerned solely with the store of letters and archives that he and his friends had composed, collected, and concealed, so they might serve as a true picture of the life of a murdered people. He states to whom the material should

15 Ibid., p. 15.

be given and appoints a successor to deal with it. These letters may be the most moving and authentic chapter in Ringelblum's path, strewn with effort and torment, and the last will and testimony of the man and his life's work.

* * *

The following letters, published here for the first time in full, depict the last months in the life of the Ringelblum family. Much work and effort has been invested in deciphering obscure details, such as the identity of the people mentioned and the events described in them, since both the writers of the letters and their recipients are no longer alive, and the replies of the Bermans did not survive.

I am grateful to all those who assisted and encouraged me in my work in preparing this book, and especially to Yossi Shavit, the director of the Ghetto Fighters' House Archives, whose help and advice contributed greatly to my work.

Israel Gutman

Collection of Letters by Emanuel and Józia Yehudit Ringelblum to Adolf Abraham and Batya Temkin-Berman

November 25, 1943 to March 3, 1944[1]

Emanuel Ringelblum

25.11 [1943]

My dear ones, my heartfelt thanks for transferring the 10 [thousand] to us.[2] They will help us a great deal to cover a list of current expenses (a jacket or coat for Jurek[3] from Mrs. T.[4] was lost on its way to us).

The news in your letter interested us very much, especially about our friends. I know Mr. Jeleniogórski from CKU[5] very well. He comes from Włocławek, and was very wealthy. He ran a coop-

1 From the Ghetto Fighters' House Archives (GFHA), collections 3162. Emanuel and Józia's names are inserted at the top of the letter as an editorial addition for the reader's convenience.

2 A sum of money transferred to Ringelblum, apparently from the Jewish National Council (Żydówski Komitet Narodowy – ŻKN), which actively helped with the people under the Council's care in the bunker on Grójecka Street, on the Aryan side of Warsaw. The Council was headed by Adolf Abraham Berman, Yitzhak Zuckerman, and David Guzik.

3 Jurek-Uri was Ringelblums' twelve-year-old son.

4 Probably the Polish woman Teresa Nowakowa in whose apartment Jurek hid for six months; see Teresa Prekerowa, *Konspiracyjna Rada Pomocy Żydom w Warszawie 1942–1945* (Warsaw: Państwowy Instytut Wydawniczy, 1982), p. 166.

5 The reference is apparently to Hirshberg, who was active in Centralna Komisja Uchodźców (CKU) – the Central Committee of Refugees that functioned in the Warsaw ghetto; The Ringelblum Archives, Archiwum 1360 – Żydówskiego Instytutu Historycznego (ŻIH) – Archives of the Jewish Historical Institute.

erative on Leszno Street [in central Warsaw]. He was very active socially.

Warm[6] deserves a pill from the Blei[7] company, a scoundrel, who takes bribes. He should be treated like a leper. Mr. Marek[8] doesn't know about any others. We need to check carefully before accepting them into [our] partnership.[9] We have to deal with black sheep the way that E.R. [Emanuel Ringelblum] dealt with the Trawniki & Co. firm [the Trawniki camp].[10]

Won't we find a "star" [not clear who this refers to], a very decent man, among Jeleniog's[11] partners?

As for Mr. Horn, he is not the same man as Pawel. Dolek [Adolf Abraham Berman's nickname] saw Mr. Pawel at Bronisław's.[12] Horn, from the Budzyński[13] firm, is Edzio's [Emanuel Ringelblum] brother-in-law, a friend and co-worker of the writer Y. L. P [Peretz]. Very active in quarter 1, in the orphanage [looking after] "street children" and the like. In short – a very devoted public activist. I recommend him warmly to our friends. I should like to send him warm regards from me, Józia and Jurek. [Horn] is the brother-in-law of Rożicki, a dedicated man.[14]

6 Apparently Ber Warm, who was in the Jewish Police.

7 "Lead" in German, apparently referring to a bullet.

8 Marek is Marek Passensztein, an economist by profession, who was close to Ringelblum in the hideout. For a while he was employed by the police in the ghetto and then worked in CENTOS. In the hideout he wrote a research study on the smuggling of food and essential items from the Polish side to the ghetto. It survived and was published after the war: Marek Passensztein, "Szmugiel w getcie w-wskim," *Biuletyn Żydówskiego Instytutu Historycznego* (BŻIH) 26 (1958).

9 The reference to partnership is probably the acceptance of the auspices of the Jewish National Council on the Aryan side of Warsaw.

10 Ringelblum did not accept people who had a bad name in the ghetto into an underground group that was established in Trawniki.

11 Jeleniogórski. The reference is apparently to Hirshberg, the above-mentioned CKU activist, ŻIH, Ringelblum Archives, Archiwum 1360.

12 The reference may be to the Bund member David Klin, who had connections and was active in Jewish self-help in the ghetto and in rescuing Jews on the Aryan side. He was also known among the survivors by the nickname Bronisław.

13 The Budzyń labor camp near Kraśnik in the Lublin district.

14 His identity is unknown. Perhaps Ringelblum was referring to his underground nickname, Edward Rydzewski.

You have no idea how happy we are at the news that there is hope for Lipowski,[15] and for the friends, Wilenski, Zalmanowski and Kaczka.[16] They are very valuable people. I am worried that all of this comes too late and that very valuable people have lost the partnership and only third- and fourth-class people will be left. It would be a good idea already now to change more than one chapter in SPZ,[17] since everything has changed so radically. And to think that no one among the Lublin (Lubelskich) people wanted to accept them to the partnership.[18] After all, during the time of E.R. [Emanuel Ringelblum] there were already appeals to them for help in a new partnership organization, and nothing came of it.

I am glad that we are in total agreement concerning Dr. V. and others.[19] The idea of a connection with Mr. Węg[ry][20] is very

15 The reference is to a plan to smuggle people out of the Budzyń labor camp. Lipowski is Lipa Eliezer Bloch, an activist in the Zionist movement and the director of the Keren Kayemet in Poland. He was a member of the *Oyneg Shabes* team and was active alongside Ringelblum in the social self-help organization in the ghetto. From the Budzyń camp he arrived at the Płaszów camp and apparently perished at Mauthausen.

16 Chaim Zalmanowski, a biologist, was principal of the Dror underground gymnasium in the Warsaw ghetto. During the uprising he was deported to Budzyń and survived. Wilenski and Kaczka were active in the Budzyń group.

17 *Stosunki polsko-żydowskie* was the book on relations between Poles and Jews during World War II that Ringelblum wrote while in the bunker. The book was preserved in its original Polish version. In English, see Joseph Kermish and Shmuel Krakowski, eds., Emanuel Ringelblum, *Polish-Jewish Relations during the Second World War* (Evanston: Northwestern University Press, 1992). The book was originally published by Yad Vashem in 1976.

18 The reference is to an attempt to organize jointly an escape from the camps and to arrange for those who fled to join the partisans in the area of Lublin. "The Lublin people," the "Lubelskich" – a division of the underground organization of the Armia Krajowa (AK), an underground Polish military organization subject to the Polish Government-in-exile in London – who did not keep their promise. On the attitude of the AK toward the Jewish partisans in the Lublin district, see Adam Puławski, "Postrzeganie żydowskich oddziałów partyzanckich przez Armię Krajową, Delegaturę Rządu R.P. na.Kraj," *Pamięć I Sprawiedliwość* (Warsaw: IPN, 2003), pp. 271–300.

19 This refers to Vittel and to the affair of Hotel Polski.

20 The reference is to Hungary and is probably about the plan raised in London to save several of the Jewish leaders in Poland by smuggling them out to Hungary. Berman referred to this suggestion in his article "The Jews on the Aryan Side": "At the end of 1943, the Jewish National Council received a cable from abroad,

interesting to us. Dan [Guzik][21] promised to give us details. Do you know them [the details]? It seems to me that you are considering this matter very seriously. I have the impression that in the state of our affairs, the concept of "commitment" does not have the same importance that was ascribed it in the past. But won't it be like going from the frying pan into the fire? How does this look to you?

I thank you for the promise to send business papers. I need them greatly.[22] I regarded the SPZ [*Polish-Jewish Relations*] works as a draft that will undergo many changes from numerous aspects. Insofar as Mr. Mik is concerned — I will gladly take into account the things I omitted. Things that occurred during the war are particularly important to me. I have the feeling that Mrs. Irena[23] has suc-

through the Polish underground movement, which included a list of people for whom they had obtained a possibility of leaving the country illegally with the help of the government legation. Out of 19 people on the list there were only three still alive: Dr. Berman, Leyzer Lewin and Dr. Ringelblum. The three rejected this suggestion, because they were determined to carry out their public duties in Poland until the end." See Yitzhak Grinboym, ed., *Encyclopaedia of the Diaspora Communities* (Hebrew) (Jerusalem, 1953), p. 723.

21 Daniel David Guzik was one of the directors of the Joint during the occupation and was responsible for the institution's finance section. He was a member of the *Oyneg Shabes* team and an active member of the National Jewish Council on the Aryan side. He was killed in an airplane accident after the liberation, on March 5, 1946.

22 "Business papers" are material that Ringelblum asked to receive for the purpose of writing his books and articles in the hideout.

23 It is not clear to which Irena he is referring, but probably it is Irena Sawicka, a Polish intellectual and left-wing activist, who courageously helped Jews in hiding. Batya Temkin-Berman mentions her several times in her diary; see Batya Temkin-Berman, *A Diary in the Underground: Incidents and People from Occupied Warsaw* (Hebrew) (Tel Aviv: Hakibbutz Hameuchad, 1956); new edition: (Hebrew) (Jerusalem: Am Oved, Yad Vashem, 2008). Bartoszewski Władysłw and Lewinówna Zofia, *Ten jest z ojczyzny mojej: Polacy z pomocą Żydom 1939–1945* (Kraków: Znak, 1966), pp. 107–166. Nonetheless, there are two other possibilities: one that the reference is to Irena Sendlerowa, a Polish activist who rescued Jewish children in an early stage of the deportations; or Irena Adamowicz, a Catholic activist in the scouts' movement and a friend of the Zionist youth movements. An interview ascribed to the latter in the Ringelblum archives was published in Hebrew by Joseph Kermish; see note on p. 129 in Joseph Kermish and Shmuel Krakwoski, eds., Emanuel Ringelblum, *Polish-Jewish Relations During the Second World War* (New York: Howard Fertig, 1976), p. 129.

ceeded not too badly. I wrote whatever I know about her. Do you have any details about Mr. Bergeński's improper behavior?[24] I have the impression that the author Perelski lived with him.[25] Is that so?

I will send you the first series of biographies next week.[26] The second editing is more drastic. Maybe it will come out not too badly. I believe this is our most sacred commitment, because what is left of them? But we have to keep it in many more [hiding] places. Give my very warm regards to Zalmanowski,[27] and to the friends [in the camp].

And now I have a request to make of you. About Mrs. M.'s[28] work, her difficulties and her efforts for the sake of Mrs. Melmańska[29]

24 The reference is to Bergen-Belsen, and the affair was known as the "Polish hotel." In 1943, the Germans promised another channel of exit from Poland that was supposed to enable Jews to leave with passports and permits to enter various countries, especially in South America. In the wake of this promise, Jews began rushing around in search of suitable papers. Many of the permits that arrived then for people who were no longer alive remained in the hands of the German police. They, in turn, sold them for large sums of money to Jews with means who were hiding in Warsaw. The candidates for exit were gathered mainly in the Polski Hotel on the Aryan side of Warsaw. Many people were involved in obtaining the required papers and money, including agents that served the Gestapo and public figures, including Guzik. Among the several thousand who left in this way were the poet Yitzhak Katznelson, a member of the headquarters of the Jewish Combat Organization; Eliezer Geller; Israel Kanal, commander of the central sector in the ghetto uprising; Antoni Buksbaum, one of the main activists of the Left Poalei Zion party; and members of the Guzik family. The overwhelming majority of those who left were taken in the end to their death in Auschwitz. Only a part survived, and some of them arrived in Eretz Israel. Some of them spent some time in the Vittel camp in France as well as in Bergen-Belsen. Details of the affair have not been thoroughly clarified to this day.

25 The writer Yehoshua Perle and his son were among those leaving from the Polski Hotel and were among those who were murdered.

26 In the hideout Ringelblum was engaged in writing biographies of outstanding Jews in the Warsaw ghetto – public figures, scientists, artists, and writers who perished or were murdered. Ringelblum began this project while he was still in the ghetto.

27 From the Ghetto Fighters' House Archives (GFHA), collections 3162.

28 The mother of the hideout owner's family.

29 Mrs. Melmańska, Ringelblum's neighbor in the hiding place, who is mentioned several times in his letters, is Itka Lazar-Melman, a member of the Bund who, according to Celemenski, stayed in the hideout at Grójecka Street. See Yaakov Celemenski, *Mitn farshnitenem folk* (New York: Unzer tzayt, 1963), p. 285.

and others. She applied to us asking for a one-time sum (T1) [1,000 złoty) for medical (dental) treatment. This request should be approved, for many reasons. We will be very grateful if you can obtain this sum for Mrs. M.

From Czesława[30] we received 1,000 [złoty] that were meant for Mrs. Hentzel [probably one of the women in the hide out]. Through me, Mr. Dan [Guzik] gave them the sum of 1,500, but he had to withhold the 1,000 in the meantime. I am notifying you of that.

I have already prepared a work plan [namely, a plan for a book] on POMOC.[31] I am supposed to discuss the details with Mr. Dan. I thank you very much for your efforts for our sake. We are endlessly grateful. Stay in good health.

Jurek is returning the book and asking for the next [book]. If it's not too difficult, he would like to get Latin and Polish grammar textbooks, and others for the first [grade] of the gymnasium (he has one on history).

[Continuation of the previous letter]

27.11

I am sending the first series of biographies. Some drastic adaptation will be done during the second editing. I am asking Jelenski[32] and his friends[33] to make some comments and additions, which I will gladly take into account when I go over the characters in an appropriate manner. I have forgotten a lot, because as I've already written to you, my memory betrays me since the surgery in T. [Trawniki].

30 The reference is apparently to Czesława Herman, Józia Ringelblum's sister.

31 The reference is to the Committee to Help Jews (Rada Pomocy Żydom – RPŻ), which provided assistance to Jews on the Aryan side of the city. The Committee was known as Żegota, and it is mentioned in the letters also as "Aunt Radowska," "Rada," "Mr. Radowski," and similar names.

32 "Jelenski" is Hirsch Berlinski, a member of Left Poalei Zion. In the ghetto he was a member of the headquarters of the Jewish Fighting Organization (ŻOB) and took part in the ghetto uprising. Afterward he hid on the Aryan side, fought in the Polish uprising, and was killed. He wrote a book about his activity in the ghetto. See Hirsch Berlinski, "Memoirs," *Yalkut Moreshet*, I (1963), pp. 5–24.

33 Members of Poalei Zion and fighters in the Jewish Combat Organization.

It will be enough if they provide several details that I can take into account. I don't have a copy, because as I said, in the second editing everything will be radically changed.

At the last minute, our boss lady asked us to buy two packages of candies à la T[34] for the children. Please tell me how much they cost and whether it is possible to buy them through you.

Józia Ringelblum

25.11.1943

My dear ones, I am ill. I have an inflammation in my gallbladder. I am lying on the bunk and suffering. Today we received news about V. and B., and apparently in D., department II + 13,000 of these places were liquidated.[35] What do you know about that? Has it been verified? We understand your ordeal very well, but what you are doing gives them added strength. Here there's a terrible depression, life imprisonment. Agonizing despair. Maybe you'll console us with general news and perhaps the last of those close to us will succeed in being with us.[36]

We are very grateful for the money. You are doing so much for our sake, it's hard to grasp. How good it is to know that during a catastrophe we have friends. The greetings from afar also move me to tears. We would like it very much if Edzio would be in touch with you and discuss these matters in detail. We are only waiting for the date to be set. On our part, it's arranged. Our friends are very generous, but of course, this has to be arranged, and Edzio will discuss this seriously [the reference is apparently to the (plan) to bring people from Budzyń]. Now I am going back to Edzio's request concerning Mrs. M.,[37] who always arranges everything in a pleasant, responsible manner.

34 Meaning "like in Trawniki." Evidently the reference is to a type of weapon.

35 This apparently refers to news and rumors about the murder of the Jews in camps in the Lublin district. On November 3, 1943, during "Operation Erntefest" (the "Harvest Festival"), 42,000–43,000 Jews were murdered in the Majdanek, Poniatów, and Trawniki camps.

36 This probably refers to plans to remove those who remained alive after the November 1943 killing from the Budzyń camp and to save them.

37 The Budzyń labor camp near Kraśnik in the Lublin district.

M. has given me to understand, in a very discreet manner, that regarding the dental problem, she needs a device [?]. In short, she has a large expenditure [expects us to cover it]. She deserves it, and we want, in fact we must, arrange this as a one-time expense. I know that you are taking care of everything, even when it exceeds your capability, do whatever you can.

In the list of requests to you, another one: textbooks for Jurek, grammar and orthography for sixth grade and grammar for the first grade of the gymnasium, mathematics for the gymnasium and a beginner's book in Latin.

I don't want to burden you too much. I bless you from the bottom of my heart. Do your best to hold out. I yearn to see you and the small circle of those closest to us.

P.S. I am sending you Jurek's book. Very suitable. He thanks you wholeheartedly.

Emanuel Ringelblum

6.12.[1943]

My dear ones!

I hope that Michael [Berman] is well now, since a drawn-out illness[38] does not enable him to [look after] clients. As far as Ungarski[39] is concerned, I assume that after collecting suitable information, you have decided that this client is not reliable. In this matter, we rely completely on your information.

Our partnership [the number of people in the hide out] is expanding all the time. Recently the owner of a warehouse (24 sq. meters in area) contacted us with a proposal to accept into the partnership [apparently more people] (7 meters have to undergo a thorough renovation and reconstruction). They have some un-

38 By "illness" he means the blackmailers that trapped Berman several times and who prevented him from moving outside and helping those in hiding.

39 Escape through Hungary; The reference is apparently to Hirshberg, who was active in Centralna Komisja Uchodźców (CKU) – the Central Committee of Refugees that functioned in the Warsaw ghetto; The Ringelblum Archives, Archiwum 1360 – Żydówskiego Instytutu Historycznego (ŻIH) – Archives of the Jewish Historical Institute.

pleasantness with the competitors! Mr. Ad,[40] the representative of the "Wrona Company,"[41] (Mrs. M. has the address) will give you details about this matter, and it is necessary to apply to you with the recommendation of Mr. Zygmunt.[42] The person who applies to him must be a trustworthy man who can properly represent the firms' affairs.

Something bad is taking place regarding Mrs. Idesa's[43] warehouse. Mikołaj[44] is making efforts to rent the warehouse for himself. Is it acceptable for the two firms [organizations] that are in friendship [in hiding] to be in the same yard? It is really a disgrace, and those two firms will be forced to suffer as a result. Tell this to Miko[łaj] without relying on Ide[sa].[45]

40 This probably refers to Dr. Adamowski, who is mentioned several times in the correspondence. It seems that Dr. Adamowski rented an apartment to Jews.

41 The nickname Wrona – a crow in Polish – is also mentioned in other letters. Apparently the reference is to Jewish and non-Jewish activists on the Aryan side who were involved in rescue efforts for various reasons.

42 The reference is to Berman's brother-in-law, Zygmunt Grynberg, a doctor who hid with his wife Rita and their son Marian on the Aryan side of the city and was saved. In every contact with Dr. Adamowski, it was necessary to refer to him. Apparently the relationship between Grynberg and Dr. Adamowski was created on a shared professional basis.

43 Idesa is Józia Yehudit Ringelblum, and the reference is, of course, to the hideout where the Ringelblums were hiding.

44 Mikołaj is the nickname of Leon Feiner, a lawyer from Kraków, a leading Bund activist and its main representative on the Aryan side of Warsaw. He was a member of the Żegota directorate. Members of the Bund, including the survivors of the Jewish National Council, headed by the Bermans, Guzik, and Antek-Yitzhak Zuckerman, served as a coordinating committee for rescue activities on the Aryan side of Warsaw after the uprising and the destruction of the ghetto. Feiner was one of the survivors, but he died shortly after the liberation.

45 This means that, when clarifying matters with Feiner, the Ringelblums should not be relied upon as a source of information about the affair relating to the establishment of an additional underground hideout or the expansion of the existing hideout. Ringelblum and the other tenants of the hideout were troubled for a long time by the problems involved in this idea. They regarded it as a danger that might lead to discovery and might also encourage the owners of the hideout to raise the payment. Yaakov Celemenski, one of the important Bund activists on the Aryan side, was saved and wrote a book of memoirs. In his book he writes about his role in dealing with the problem of the additional bunker and describes in detail his visit to Mieczysław Wolski's apartment on

Józia was ill with a liver disease. It was a past illness that recurred. She needs to stick to a diet, which under our conditions is not an easy thing to do.

How does the affair of Lipowski and his friends look? When will we be able to see them? We really miss them.[46]

We seem to be having a streak of bad luck. Before the war we were a large family[47] and now Divine Providence is punishing us,

Grójecka Street, his personality, and the background to the construction of the bunker. Later on he writes: "For constructing the bunker, Wolski received a very large sum of money. In addition, for each Jew that entered the bunker he was paid a sum of 10,000 złoty. These were one-time payments, to which were added weekly payments for food and 'rent.' Although the bunker made Wolski a rich man, he was a decent, dedicated person. He did everything that was required of him, and did not try, as many other Polish 'doers of good deeds' did, to extort additional sums and to simply deal in blackmail. I asked him [during the visit] if it wasn't possible in the same area [to dig] a second identical bunker for another group of Jews. I asked him at the same time if it was not possible to place several additional Jews into the existing bunker. Wolski replied to both questions in the very same way: 'First we will go into the bunker, and you will see the place, and in that way you will get the best reply to your questions.' Celemenski describes his visit to the bunker, where he knew no one except for Itka Lazar-Melman, who was very happy to see him. He relates that there were about thirty-four men, women, and several children. He writes about the "oppressive, suffocating air inside" and that everyone "was waiting impatiently for the evening when they could go out, individually, to climb the stairs to the glass-covered greenhouse and breathe some fresh air." The day following his visit, Celemenski gave Feiner a detailed report. In it he objected to the plan, because the sum that Wolski demanded for the construction of an additional bunker — 200,000 złoty — was "a fanciful sum for us." The question again arose about arranging a place for "several more people," but nothing came of this either. Members of the Bund and the owners of the bunker considered these two possibilities. See Celemenski, *Mitn farshnitenem folk*, pp. 280–284.

46 Lipowski is Lipa Bloch, who was in the Budzyń camp in the summer of 1943. He had planned, as stated, to take Bloch and some other people with him out of Budzyń. Later, on February 20, 1944, the Ringelblums wrote a letter to Lipowski. According to the testimony of Shoshana (Emilka) Kosower — today Shoshana Rozenzweig and living in Israel — Bloch did not agree to flee from the camp. Shoshana had participated in smuggling prisoners from the camps and also took part in rescuing Ringelblum from Trawiniki. For details of the case, see Batya Temkin-Berman, "Pan Rydzewski — Ringelblum's Last Days," *Yalkut Moreshet*, II (1964).

47 The reference is to members of Left Poalei Zion.

for He has taken Antoni[48] from us. Has this bit of information been checked and is it one hundred percent certain?

Have you received the biographies? What comments do you have? You undoubtedly have a lot to add, because as I wrote to you several times, the Trawniki illness [from the Trawniki camp] has seriously impaired my memory.

Do you know whether Mr. Dan [Guzik] has handled the matter of Kristina, the granddaughter of Michelski who is well known (worked with the engineer Czerniakowski)?[49] Tell me, do you have any news from Mr. Bergeński and his friend Mr. Vi[ttel]?[50] Did the suppositions prove to be true?

Dan has been warned not to negotiate with the boss Ridz[uski] regarding the warehouse for the two partners. I don't need to explain the reasons to you.

To Wachowski [a tenant in Ringelblum's hide out] I gave 1.5 [1,500 złoty] as soon as I received them from you. I sent you a receipt. Since you did not receive this receipt, I am sending you a copy. As far as the 1 [1,000 złoty] for the engineer is concerned, I explained to them in my previous letter that Dan gave them on my behalf 1.5 [1,500 złoty] and 1 [1,000 złoty] and asked to delay it temporarily. I now have this sum for your disposal. Write and tell me what to do with it. I expect that in your letter there will be a reply regarding the two packets of candies with the irises [probably bullets] for our children, like those you sent to T [Trawniki].[51] I am reminding you of the matter of Mrs. Wisi [probably the woman who owns the hide out] and Mrs. M., which we are asking you to arrange favorably, for reasons I enumerated in my previous letter.

I am returning the book *The Prince and the Pauper* with my

48 Antoni Buksbaum, one of the main activists of Left Poalei Zion, returned to Warsaw from Lwów. For some time he was connected with the Jewish National Council. He was at the Hotel Polski with his family and was murdered.

49 Michelski is probably Rabbi Yehezkel Zvi Michelson, who was active in the Warsaw ghetto. The engineer Czerniakowski is Adam Czerniaków, the head of the Judenrat in the Warsaw ghetto.

50 The Hotel Polski affair; The reference to partnership is probably the acceptance of the auspices of the Jewish National Council on the Aryan side of Warsaw.

51 This refers to Vittel and to the affair of the Hotel Polski.

heartfelt thanks. Jurek was delighted with it and asks you to send another of the same type.

Józia Ringelblum

6.12.1943

Ed[zio] already wrote you nearly everything. What's going on with Dolek [Berman]? Is he already healthy [has the danger of his exposure passed]? I still haven't gotten over my aches, without a doctor, without medicines, on a bunk which the light of a carbide [lamp] doesn't even reach, the illness drags on. I don't take it too hard, because what is it compared to everything…[illegible] as Edzio already wrote about the recent anxieties, I asked that this be arranged discreetly. The firm [the reference is apparently to the Bund] is contributing a large sum, it probably has a lot, I assume this from what Mrs. Mel[Mánska] receives, and I fear that that can…[illegible] and that will be bad. I don't know what role Dan [Guzik] plays in that, but M. [Berman] also needs to know about that. Why does he talk so much about money with the boss, and because of that we cannot get out of Edzio's debts? It seems I did not correctly assess my tendencies. I am a collector of worries. For a long time I've been wanting to ask you about our friends: Maria and Zofia.[52] What are they doing? Do you meet with them? Haven't they recently mentioned to you Halina Domb, the daughter of [our] friend who remained alone?[53] We have a whole list of questions, but I promised myself that Edzio would arrange it orally. I hope you will meet. I would like to receive clarifications about the amounts – who will give them and how – has there been any change? What is Dan's role? I am not entirely satisfied. But in any case, Czesława[54] [unclear excerpt] will somehow be able to survive and pay reasonable sums, because here…[unclear excerpt] I'll be very grateful to you if you register me for two books at the library…[unclear excerpt] and the transfer of good books to me.
Batya, I kiss you.
Józia, regards to all of you.

52 Apparently Maria Grzegorzewska and Zofia Rożewicz, Polish women who were active in saving Jews.

53 Not deciphered.

54 Józia Ringelblum's sister.

Emanuel Ringelblum
13.12.[1943]
My dear ones!

The meeting with Dolek [Berman] was a very important event in our gray lives. It gave me a little hope and encouraged me to go on with my work. I received a list of the partners in the OB firm.[55] I have biographical details about a list of people, for example: Rozowski [Welwel], Lutek [Rotblat], Winogron [Shlomo], Arbuz [Chaim] Alek, Michał Kle[pfisz], Elek [surname missing], Różanski [Eliyahu] (I met him personally, a wonderful person), Blank [Mark], Pasmanik [Rivka], Rysia, Stangel [Moniek], Hochberg [David].[56] We ought to collect details about all of them (years of birth, place of residence, parents' occupation, education, character traits, participation in various activities, the last endeavor and the like). Time is running out, and since the partners can disappear, it would be a pity if this information was missing. What happened with [Abraham] Zandman from the SZ firm [Shomer ha-Za'ir][57]

55 ŻOB – Żydówska Organizacja Bojowa, the Jewish Fighting Organization. The organization was founded when the deportations from the Warsaw ghetto began in the summer of 1942. It was established by three Zionist youth movements: Ha-Shomer ha-Za'ir, Dror, and Akiva. The organization fought for the first time on January 18, 1943, under the command of Mordechai Anielewicz. Later it was joined by the Gordonia movement, Left Poalei Zion, Poalei Zion-ZS, the Bund, and the Communists. Afterward the Jewish National Council was established alongside the ŻOB, and its members were leading public activists in the ghetto. The ŻOB played a key role in the uprising that broke out on April 19, 1943.

56 All of them were party and youth-movement activists from Left Poalei Zion, the Bund, Ha-Shomer ha-Za'ir, Ha-Noar ha-Zioni, and Akiva. Chaim Arbuz and Shlomo Winogron were members of Ha-Shomer ha-Za'ir; Wolf Rozowski, Michał Klepfisz, and David Hochberg were members of the Bund; Lutek Rotblat was a member of Ha-Noar ha-Zioni; Rivka Pasmanik was a member of Akiva. Eliyahu (Elek) Różanski, a member of Ha-Shomer ha-Za'ir, was one of those who carried out the death sentence passed on Yaakov Lejkin, the head of the Jewish Police in the ghetto during the Great Deportation. He participated in the first battle in the Warsaw ghetto under the command of Mordechai Anielewicz, in January 1943, and was killed at that time.

57 Abraham (Abramek) Zandman, a member of Ha-Shomer ha-Za'ir, participated in the operation against the Werkschutz, the units of the Jewish Order Police that were engaged in maintaining order in the shops, which was carried out in the shop of Hallmann on Nowolipki. He was arrested but was freed by members of Ha-Shomer ha-Za'ir.

(recently with Hallmann),[58] a brave young man, one of the bravest, who was left out? What about Hela Wodniowy [from the Wasser family] and [Raphael] Kuczer?[59] Why is there no data about ŻZW?[60] Their traces must remain for history, even if we don't find them very likable.

Mikołaj's [Leon Feiner] friends have caused us much damage! If they do not install the warehouse here, and I think that is what will happen, then in any case it will cost us a great deal, because it will be necessary to pay the boss [Mieczysław Wolski, the owner of the hide out] some sum of money. In the meantime, things are constantly worsening, the money is running out, and everyone is pressuring us in their own direction. That's how it looks here! If it's not too late, we need to act resolutely to convince Mr. Mik [Feiner] to withdraw from the deal.

We could tell you a great deal about how "fortune smiles upon the fool," because the boss is not always as cautious as he should be. What will happen to us if Mik[ołaj]'s plan is implemented? That would be a great danger. And the danger is greater especially because of the location of the second warehouse.[61]

Mrs. Mel[mánska] played a despicable role here. She told us one thing, and told them something different. Their agent [an advocate] Mr. K. filled, and perhaps still fills, an unpleasant role. He wants to be an agent so that he can release his family from certain payments, although his brother-in-law is rich. He behaves like a

58 Hallmann was one of the Germans who owned industrial workshops in the Warsaw ghetto – referred to as the "shops." Most of the shops were established after the first deportation in 1942, and were generally privately owned by Germans. The Jews who worked there lived in special areas allotted them after the Great Deportation in the summer of 1942.

59 Hela Wasser and Raphael Kuczer were Communist activists in the ghetto. After the uprising Kotsher hid on the Aryan side of Warsaw.

60 Żydówska Związek Wojskowy, the Jewish Military Union (ŻZW), was a fighting organization active in the Warsaw ghetto during the uprising, in addition to the ŻOB. Its organizers, commanders, and many of its members belonged to the Revisionist movement and to Betar, although some of its members were from other streams, or were not organized. During the uprising in the ghetto, members of the ŻZW fought in one of the main battles in the Muranów area.

61 The reference is to a plan to prepare another hideout, for members of the Bund, adjacent to the hiding place of Ringelblum and his friends.

real Orenski[62] - calls us "Yids" and the like. We need to remember that, and at a suitable moment – to remind [him].

Marek [Passensztein] wants very much to clarify the matter of his work with Mr. Lekinski. He has encountered complaints against him here, and Dolek, after all, is very familiar with his work in CEN[TOS] and with Mr. Lekinski.[63]

As for the suggestion about children, there is some fear that they will be asked questions about the whereabouts of their parents.[64]

This week I am completing the first editing of the biographies. I would very much like our friends to begin at once to copy them. I recalled that Mrs. Natalia Kaczkowski (or something similar to that, in any event – her profession is the same as Emanuel's)[65] was very active in this area. It would be a good idea to contact her about keeping the material, otherwise it would be a pity to go to all that trouble. Henryk [Chaim Wasser] has an excellent technique of preservation. I know that you have a lot on your minds, but I am asking that you arrange this as fast as possible, because time is running out.

The letter to grandfather,[66] which is marvelously edited, moved me greatly. It would be good to get the two men, Radomski and Lewovski [from the Radom and Lwów districts] involved in work [providing help]; this particularly concerns an environment about which we know nothing [probably Łódź]. I sent you the question-

62 An allusion to the acronym ONR of Obóz Narodowo-Radykalny, a pro-fascist organization with extreme antisemitic positions that was established in Poland in the 1930s.

63 Marek Passensztein was employed for a time with the Jewish Police in the ghetto, and in the hideout he met with accusations regarding that position. By "Mr. Lekinski" the writer refers to Yaakov Lejkin, who was head of the police. Passensztein asks for Berman's opinion, because after he left the police he was employed in CENTOS, the Society for Jewish Child Welfare headed by Berman.

64 This is probably about the separation between parents in the hideout and their children who were given over to the care of Polish families. There was the fear that the children were likely to give away their identity and their parents' location.

65 She was a historian like Ringelblum.

66 He is probably referring to Yaakov Zerubavel and his friends in Israel.

naire [basis for a questionnaire for taking testimonies] at the time and you certainly must have it. If necessary, I can send you a copy.

In a letter to Mr. L. [London] the names of those participating from the Trawnitzka [Trawniki] firm were left out. It would be desirable to enumerate them at the next opportunity: Kielman Szapirski (a well-known figure, the rabbi from Piaseczno, a wonderful man, a noble character);[67] the engineer Dr. Kalnicki Herman; Dr. Zgierski, the musician; Arkadi Flatau; Miecio Mieczkowski, an artist,[68] his friends Kutner, Stefan Lubliner, Winogorski,[69] Bormanowa (a translator?), commander [of the underground organization] Henryk Frysz [Dr. Szyfrys][70] with friends (24), Cwikovski

67 The reference is to Rabbi Kalman Klonimus Shapira, a religious personality who embraced lofty values. The sermons he delivered in the Warsaw ghetto were preserved in the Ringelblum archives and are regarded as important Holocaust documents; see Nehemia Polen, *The Holy Fire: The Teachings of Rabbi Klonimus Kalman Shapira, the Rebbe of the Warsaw Ghetto* (Northvale, N.J.: Jason Aronson, 1998).

68 A well-known artist in the Warsaw ghetto.

69 A newspaper editor. Before the war he worked in the Polish foreign ministry; in the ghetto he was employed by the Jewish Police.

70 This probably refers to men in Trawniki who did not receive the help promised them by the AK in Lublin and were murdered. Batya Temkin-Berman writes about this: "His arrival [of Ringelblum from Trawniki] helped us create close ties with the secret leadership of the Trawniki camp, which after he left was composed of Dr. Szyfrys, Advocate Szulman and Malinowski. Ringelblum told us about the attempts to prepare an armed uprising. They lack weapons and explosives there and since we know all the concealed ways we sent them, in coordination with Antek [Zuckerman], some chemicals, some weapons and money. The next step was to ensure false papers for the activity of the men in the camp and to link it with the partisans. Unfortunately, the partisans in this area are from the AK and they deceived the Jews. No one waited for them at the fixed place, and those who fled had to return to the camp. We sent them maps, medicines (a typhus epidemic broke out there) and birth certificates for the children. So the close ties with Trawniki continued from July (when Ringelblum returned to Warsaw) until September-October. The approaching winter made it difficult to leave and go to the forest. Ringelblum and we warned against trusting the Nazis, but some of the people in the camp believed they would be given a break until the spring and then, when the Red Army would be close, they'd go out to the forest. But on November 3, 1943, the camp was unexpectedly surrounded by a huge number of cars with gendarmes and S.S. men, and within a few hours all of its inhabitants were murdered"; see Temkin-Berman, "Pan Rydzewski," p. 15.

[the advocate Szulman] whom you know from correspondence, Dr. Marienstrauss – chief doctor, Dr. Bielenski, Mr. Lubelski.[71]

[Continuation of previous letter]

13.12.1943
My dear ones,

Further to my letter of 13.12., I am strongly requesting that you buy, at our expense, a *na gwiazdkę* [for Christmas] gift for Theodor.[72] Perhaps some sort of sweets for his children; it is very important to me to express the eternal gratitude I feel for him.

As for the second warehouse, we are asking you as an exception [to arrange] for Batya to have a meeting this week on Friday too. There may be important announcements.

As a postscript to the letter to be sent to Raphael [Mahler][73] it is possible to inform [him] that his sister-in-law the teacher is alive and working. I forgot to ask if there is any news about a young, talented historian, Dr. Philip F. [Friedman][74] from Łódź, who in 1941 was in Lwów. Everything should be done to help him. My family, R. [Ringelblum] lives in Lwów. My cousin was wounded in Lorca de Vega [the Spanish Civil War]. I ask that they be remembered.

My heartfelt greetings

71 Marienstrauss was a member of the management of the kitchen organized in the Warsaw ghetto for the community officials.

72 Teodor Pajewski, a Pole, was a member of the Polish underground; together with Shoshana (Emilka) Kosower, he rescued Ringelblum from Trawniki.

73 Raphael Mahler was a historian from the circle of Jewish historians active in Poland between the two world wars and a very close friend of Ringelblum's. During this period he was in the United States. After the war he immigrated to Israel and served as a professor of history at Tel Aviv University and wrote a series of books about Polish Jewry. See letters that Ringelblum sent him and the letter signed by A. Berman and E. Ringelblum, to which Ringelblum is apparently referring and which was addressed to YIVO in New York, to the Jewish PEN club, to Shalom Esh, to Y. Leyvik, Y. Opatoshu, and R. Mahler. See also Ringelblum, *Polish-Jewish Relations*.

74 Philip Friedman was a Jewish historian from Galicia who wrote a comprehensive book about the Jews of Łódź. During the war he hid in Lwów and survived. After the war he founded and was the first director of the Jewish Historical Institute in Warsaw and was regarded as one of the pioneers of Holocaust research. After some time he immigrated to the United States and died in New York in 1960.

To complete the list [list of biographies?] we need to add Professor Marceli H. [Handelsman].[75]

Doesn't Mr. Jeleniogórski know anything about Gwiazda, who worked with them in the same firm?[76] Mr. Shimon Zaj[czyk][77] could write an interesting piece on findings that disappeared or were destroyed. He is a great expert in this field. Does he have any collections or have they been lost? For copies of them it would be worthwhile to pay even 10 [ten thousand złoty]. After the war it will be very rare. Do you know Dr. Malowist (a cripple)?[78]

Emanuel Ringelblum
16.12.1943
My dear ones!

In the warehouse [the hide out] everything is temporarily on

75 Professor Marceli Handelsman, a renowned Polish historian, was an outstanding figure at the University of Warsaw and in the world of science in Poland in the inter-war period. Ringelblum was Handelsman's student and included him in the series of biographies he wrote about well-known Jews who perished. Handelsman is the only one among the subjects of these biographies who was not interned in the ghetto, as he had converted to Christianity. Among other things, Ringelblum wrote about him: "For years he served as dean of the humanities faculty of Warsaw University and also was Rector of the University. He educated generations of historians who remained as loyal to him as sons are to their fathers...", "The Society of Promoters of Polish History," which Handelsman headed, published Ringelblum's book that was based on his Ph.D. dissertation on the Jews of Warsaw from ancient times until their expulsion in 1527. The book's publication heightened the hostility of the Polish extreme right-wing circles toward Professor Handelsman, and he became a target of attacks in the press as well as of physical violence. Handelsman joined the Polish Legion as a volunteer in World War I and was active in the Polish underground during World War II. He was among the employees in the "Office of Information and Propaganda" of the AK. Members of the right-wing arm of the Polish underground handed Handelsman over to the Germans. See Israel Gutman, Joseph Kermish, and Israel Shacham, eds., Emanuel Ringelblum, *Last Writings: Polish Jewish Relations, January 1943-April 1944* (Hebrew) (Jerusalem: Yad Vashem and Bet Lochamei Hageta'ot, 1993), pp. 107–108.

76 Not deciphered.

77 Shimon Zajczyk, an art historian and owner of important collections, perished while he was in hiding on the Aryan side of Warsaw.

78 Marian Malowist, a teacher and scholar in the Warsaw ghetto; after the war he was a professor at Warsaw University.

hold. We do not know whether Mikołaj's friends [members of the Bund] have given up. But in any case, those irresponsible persons have gotten what they wanted. They have made our lives miserable. Please "thank" them from the bottom of our heart in the name of all those working with us.

In keeping with your instructions, Mrs. M. [the mother of the family that owns the hide out] has made contact with Mr. Dan [Guzik]. In my next letter I will inform you of the results. In case of a journey to the previous address of Szapirski and Holenderski,[79] I can help with names of people who merit the trust of the group of Mr. Lipowski's [Lipa Bloch], Sakowski [Józef Sak], Tartakower [Aryeh Tartakower].[80] In a letter to L. [London] it would be a good idea to add the name of Professor Marceli [Handelsman]. The former senator Suchecki [Trockenheim][81] recently stayed with Lubelski [Budzyń], and that should also be mentioned.

As for Szymon Zajczykowski [Zajczyk][82] – he has a wonderful collection of photographs of objects that no longer exist. It is worth paying in order to obtain these photographs or alternately to make a copy. How do things look for Mr. Lipowski and others?[83] I cannot forget them even for one minute. I thank you very much for Mr. Radeczki's letter,[84] I read it several times. But why so few concrete numbers according to months, etc.? Are there no such fig-

79 The reference is probably to a letter that arrived from the Polish Government-in-exile in London that included a list of Jews they planned to smuggle out of Poland to Hungary. The Żegota organization did make contact with Łódź. However, in that city, which was annexed to the German Reich, so that its ghetto was hermetically sealed, there was no ongoing, regular activity. The names that are mentioned alluded to Leo Holender and Baruch Szapira, who were activists of Left Poalei Zion and before the war were members of the Łódź city council.

80 Lipa Bloch, Józef Sak, and Aryeh Tartakower were members of various Zionist streams.

81 Senator Yaakov Trockenheim had been a representative of the Agudat Israel party in the Polish parliament in the inter-war period.

82 Shimon Zajczyk, an art historian and owner of important collections, perished while he was in hiding on the Aryan side of Warsaw.

83 The reference is to Budzyń and the other camps near Lublin.

84 The reference is to Żegota.

ures? Mr. Pilichowski,[85] from L. [London] also will need them. In the letter to Raphael [Mahler in the United States] it would be a good idea to insert a sentence about the cemeteries and the schools *à la* Tłomackie.[86]

I have begun documenting [events] from the beginning of the war; for this purpose I need the reports from July, which I sent at the time to Dolek [Berman]. I am very grateful for the [material] that you sent me. I have finished the biographies, now I am beginning to finally edit them. If Henryk [Wasser],[87] Jelenski [Hirsch Berlinski][88] and Polinska [Pola Elster] have any additions on Saganski [Shakhna Sagan][89] and other members of PL [Poalei Zion], I will be very grateful if you can provide me with them. My memory betrays me quite often, and hence I am forced [to turn] to others for help. Especially since I was not active in everything. I also wrote on L. Szymek.[90]

My warmest regards,

E.

I just received money for December. I am paying for my neighbors [who are under the protection of the Jewish National Council] and I sent the receipt to Mr. G. [Guzik]. It is also necessary to confirm Wisi's request. I am therefore asking you to send us the money for December, as we arranged with Dolek through Mrs. M.

85 Pilichowski; the reference is apparently to people in the Polish government-in-exile in London.

86 The reference is to the Institute of Judaic Studies on Tłomacka Street. The building, one of the very few in the ghetto that survived, now houses the Jewish Historical Institute.

87 Hirsch Wasser, one of the major collaborators on the *Oyneg Shabes* archives, was responsible for the administrative side of the work.

88 Hirsch Berlinski was a member of Left Poalei Zion. In the ghetto he was a member of the headquarters of the Jewish Fighting Organization (ŻOB) and took part in the ghetto uprising. Afterward he hid on the Aryan side, fought in the Polish uprising, and was killed.

89 Shakhna Sagan, one of the heads of Left Poalei Zion and a leader of the party in the ghetto, was sent with his family to Treblinka during the Great Deportation from the Warsaw ghetto.

90 This may be a reference to Dr. Shimon Lubelski, an educator and member of Ha-Shomer ha-Za'ir and the youth group of Left Poalei Zion.

Emanuel Ringelblum

20.12.[1943]

My dear ones,

Thank you so much for intervening on my behalf with Mr. Mik[ołai]! It achieved certain results,[91] although it also caused me some unpleasantness. P.C.[92] recently came to Mr. W. [apparently Wolski] and said that something is ruining the deal with his friends, that E.R. [Emanuel Ringelblum] is opposed to opening a second warehouse. In my previous letter I asked that no one mention to Mr. W. that any of us is intervening with Mik[ołai]. But apparently Mr. C. [Celemenski] is no gentleman. We are considering whether you should inform Mik[ołai] about this. Because it is possible that the [matter] will "start over from the beginning." As for Mr. Lubelski, I have learned that he stopped 50 checks. The remainder (there were 15,000 beforehand) he sent to Leon R. We should take an interest in this remainder, because it may be valuable merchandise. There may be some things lying there that belong to Mr. F.Z., or Mrs. Dobrzyńska or others.[93]

I recalled that for some time the Senator Trok. lived with Mr. Lubelski.[94] I am sure of that, because I met his nephew at T. [Trawniki]. My friend Dr. Philip F. [Friedman],[95] an excellent historian, lived in the previous apartment of Antoni [Buksbaum].[96] We must remember him. My uncle whose son was wounded short-

91 This refers to the Bund's plan to expand the hideout where Ringelblum was staying, or to prepare another one adjacent to it.

92 Probably refers to Yaakov Celemenski, Pan Celemenski, an active Bund member on the Aryan side.

93 The reference is apparently to sums of money transferred to certain Jews but which did not reach those for whom they were intended.

94 Yaakov Trockenheim.

95 Philip Friedman was a Jewish historian from Galicia who wrote a comprehensive book about the Jews of Łódź. During the war he hid in Lwów and survived. After the war he founded and was the first director of the Jewish Historical Institute in Warsaw and was regarded as one of the pioneers of Holocaust research.

96 This refers to Lwów; Antoni Natan Buksbaum, one of the main activists of Left Poalei Zion, returned to Warsaw from Lwów. For some time he was connected with the Jewish National Council. He was at the Polski Hotel with his family and was murdered.

ly before the war (1936) with Mr. Lorca de Vega [the Spanish Civil War] also lived there. They unquestionably deserve help if they are still living there.

In case of a trip to Mr. Rumk.,[97] I have several addresses of loyal friends. I have enlisted a new member into our business. Beforehand he worked for Mr. Wrona. He gave me several interesting details about friends.[98]

Is there any news about K. Kazia?[99] It is probable that Paprocki[100] knows something about that.

I am very glad that the letter to Raphael [Mahler] is going to be sent. What about the contents, can you make any changes, for example about providing help. You know better about that than I do.

Józia and Jurek have asked me to give regards to L. [Lipa Bloch].

Several warm words should be written about Henryk Friszows-

97 This refers to making contact with the Jews in the Łódź ghetto, where Mordechai Chaim Rumkowski was the head of the Judenrat.

98 It is hard to know what this refers to. Apparently a member of the Bund who Ringelblum had enlisted to work on his research joined the others in the hideout.

99 The full name has not been deciphered.

100 This apparently refers to PPR, the Polish Communist Party since 1942 (Polska Partia Robotnicza). Between the two wars the Polish Communist Party (KPP) was illegal; in 1938, the Communist Internationale decided to disband it, because many of its members were deviating from the mandatory ideological-political line, and agents of the Polish government had infiltrated its ranks. The PPR, which acquired a relatively small number of supporters and members, was regarded by the institutions of the Polish underground, which were subordinate to the Polish Government-in-exile in London, as a body that served foreign political interests and was impairing Polish nationalism and its plans. The Communists, who obeyed orders from Moscow, established a military branch of their own as well as partisan units who were to act immediately against the German forces and, as far as possible, make things easier for the Soviets in their military campaign. The Jewish Communists were organized in a separate small cell and founded the "anti-fascist bloc." This also included the Zionist left-wing organizations, and, through them, the first small quantities of weapons arrived in the ghetto. The Communists did not take part in the Council for Aid to Jews, Żegota, as a separate body, but there were people among their members and supporters who helped rescue Jews and played an active part in this endeavor.

ki[101] and his friends [in Trawniki]. They deserve that, they were wonderful compared to friends of Lub. [the Lublin district] who did not meet the challenge of the task.[102]

Since I have I have finished the biographies and am copying them, I would like to start on the subject we talked about at the time: Obr[ona] G[etta] [defense of the ghetto]. In this connection, I am writing a letter to Antek [Yitzhak Zuckerman] and am asking you to speak to him about this matter. Marek [Edelman] certainly will not give. I am asking you to turn to him [to Antek] on this subject. Tell them [the members of the Bund] that at the time I gave them everything [all the material] (to Maurycy [Orzech] and others).[103] So it is only right that I should receive the necessary materials from them. And I am asking you to send me the material that you possess on this matter.

Why doesn't Kuczerski appear on the list if you know about him?[104]

I know the life stories of more than ten people on the list.[105] It has to be completed. I suggest we conduct a survey on the living, and not only on those who died. I am attaching the text. It is our obligation to do this for them!

101 The reference is to Dr. Zeev Szyfrys, a public figure who stayed in Trawniki and was head of the underground cell there after Ringelblum left. See Temkin-Berman, *Diary in the Underground*, pp. 254.

102 This probably refers to men in Trawniki who did not receive the help promised them by the AK in Lublin and were murdered.

103 The reference is to Maurycy Orzech, leader of the Bund in the Warsaw ghetto.

104 Raphael Kuczer was a Communist activists in the ghetto. After the uprising he hid on the Aryan side of Warsaw.

105 The reference is apparently to a list prepared by Yitzhak Zuckerman and Marek Edelman of those members of the Jewish Combatants Organization who were killed. The list is flawed, because those who prepared it remembered mainly the members of their own movements and their own friends. In addition, only a few activists of the underground and combatant organizations in other cities, who were not in Warsaw, were mentioned; those, too, were according to their movement affiliation. Melekh Neusztadt notes the difficulties and problems involved in this endeavor and the impossibility of arriving at a full, exact list; see Melekh Neusztadt, *Churban vamered shel Yehudey Warsha* (Hebrew) (Tel Aviv: Vaadat HaGolah fun der algemeiner Yiddisher arbeter-Organizatzie in Eretz Yisroel, 1948), pp. 323–326.

In my previous letters, I had confirmed the receipt of a letter from Mr. Radowski [apparently Żegota]. I wrote that I wonder why there are no numerical data on developments according to months, data on occupations, etc. Perhaps that's deliberate!

Today I learned some more details about Mr. C.'s matter. They looked for guilty parties. The suspicion fell on E.R. [Ringelblum] but it was rejected, because when he met with Dolek [Berman], nothing was known yet about the second warehouse. P.C. [Celemenski] said: "What a mess you have, everything that's inside gets out." Refe[rent] [apparently on behalf of Żegota] threatened that he would prevent any contact [with us]. You understand what that means for us. All of this because of one irresponsible man.

As for the warehouse of Jeleniogórski,[106] it seems the help is not sufficient. According to Dr. A.'s opinion,[107] some even starved, and perhaps the money does not reach the needy. Dr. A. asks to get in touch directly with these people. He was here not long ago and that is his opinion. His address is: Dr. Adamowski, 39 Chłodna Street, and to mention Mr. Zygmunt.[108] I do not want to accuse anyone, but Jeleniogórski was not a public employee before the war and he is a **merchant** [emphasis in original] by profession.

I think that Mik[ołai] has done better than we have in collecting commercial papers [a list of testimonies about resistance in the ghetto], and that is a pity. We did everything from the start, and someone will take that for himself. If it's possible, it would be good to hurry up this work, and so I suggest that the Messrs. RAD [Żegota], Antoni's friend [Left Poalei Zion] and Marian's friend [one of the code names of Mordechai Anielewicz] report on themselves in detail. I sent the questionnaire [to you] at the time. If you don't have it, I can send the expanded second copy.

Mrs. I[rena],[109] since she has many clients, could "exploit"

106 The reference is apparently to Hirshberg, who was active in Centralna Komisja Uchodźców (CKU) – the Central Committee of Refugees that functioned in the Warsaw ghetto.

107 Dr. Adamowski.

108 Zygmunt Grynberg, Batya Temkin-Berman's brother-in-law.

109 There were several Polish women who were active in the rescue mission whose first name was Irena.

them at an opportunity when she is arranging other matters[?]. I know that you are overloaded with work, but I feel obliged to comment to you about that.

Regarding the extra expenses that Y.Z.[110] is asking about, they relate to two matters: to the boss – another new 3 [a sum] (for the day I arrived we have already given him 7) and a coat or jacket for Jurek that costs 2.5 – 3. These are extra expenses (or 5.5 – 6) in addition to the regular [expenses]. I sent Mr. Dan [Guzik] receipts for the sums I received for my neighbors, and as far as I am concerned, I confirmed what we agreed upon. After the payment 3 to the boss [Wolski], the account will be finally in order, although [he] would like to receive more from us. Z.M. [for the apartment] we paid like the others.

Józia does not feel well at all, but at the moment there is no other choice. Rydz[ewski] [Ringelblum] asks if don't need to extend his paper.[111] It is valid until September, and perhaps [to prepare] an *Arbeitskarte* [a work card].

In my previous letter I asked you to buy, at our expense, a gift for the holidays for Theodor [Pajewski] and Emilka [Kosower].[112] I am very grateful to them and I'd like them to know that.

I bless you,

Józia Ringelblum
20.12.1943
My dear ones,

We bothered Basia [Batya Temkin-Berman] on Friday, because something was hovering over us and somehow things calmed down. About the behavior of our friend Mr. Mik[ołai], Edzio has already written to you and there's no need to add anything. A great deal of sorrow, threats of breaking all contact [with the outside world] – he is a total cretin, an idiot. I leave it to you to settle this, but remember it is very hard to get along with such idiots – they

110 It is not clear who this is, perhaps Yitzhak Zuckerman.

111 Ringelblum is alluding to the possibility that he might be part of the rescue work on the Aryan side.

112 Shoshana (Emilka) Kosower and Teodor Pajewski smuggled Ringelblum out of Trawniki.

are very dangerous. And I helped common acquaintances, while her greed knows no boundaries.

Now contact Knopf Daniel [Guzik], he also should be informed of this matter, because he is supposed to be here at the end of the month. That's what he wrote, so he ought to know everything. We asked for help for Wisi, Dan sent 1,000 [złoty]. She did not want to take it, because for a year the boss has been keeping her. Now he believes it is no longer his obligation, and she has done a lot for the firm – we need to concretely support her. It has been two weeks since I have heard from Czesława [Józia's sister]. I sent her 250 złoty [and] a women [sent] two scarves for sale, but I do not know if they were given to her. Please let us know.

I am asking you, although I know how hard it is and perhaps at this moment it is not urgent, to think of some locum [another place]. Recently something has gone wrong. Now it is Christmas, a nice gift, but "something" is hanging in the air. Hopefully it will only be money. I bless you with all of my heart. What about Dolek, is he still sick?[113] I wish you good health. Kisses. If you have any textbooks, send them.
Józia.

Emanuel Ringelblum
27.12.1943
Last week we received a package of sweets from you and we thank you very much.[114] As to what is happening in the warehouse, there are no changes. Around the first [of the month] we expect some complaints of a monetary nature [monthly payment].

Next week, I will send you a thick notebook of biographies. I hope that within ten days I will finish them all. In this connection, for my next project, I urgently need the books I asked for in my previous letters.

I read Paprocki's [115] letter with great interest, but I was sur-

113 She is referring to one of the blackmail attempts that prevented Berman from moving around freely.

114 This time the reference is apparently to sweets sent to children in the hide-out.

115 Apparently this refers to a PPR publication.

prised by his apathy regarding the Częstochowski family [a code name for Jews in hiding]. After the tragedy that the family suffered, not one word of condolence; it's unbelievable. Maybe he's afraid that Maciek [a code name for Poles] will suspect that his origin [of the letter writer] is from Częstochowa [namely, that he's a Jew]. I am curious to know whether you also noticed this.

I have recently learned that Mr. Bielak[116] has traveled to L. Pilichowski [to London] to discuss some urgent matters of his firm with him. Wouldn't it be possible to arrange for our firm [Jewish organizations] to travel the same way? After all, our matters are no less urgent.

What about the Budzyński family [the prisoners at the Budzyń camp and in the Lublin district]? Is there still hope that they will remain alive? As for Rewiz,[117] I have no information on them. At T.[Trawniki] I spoke with Mr. Cwikovski.[118] He was very dissatisfied with their work. His criticism was similar to ours, but despite that, we have to try to complete the list [the list of fighters in the ghetto uprising or of witnesses]. I have only two names: Rodalski [Leon Rodal] and Frenklowski [Paweł Frenkel]. The latter (dark-haired) was the manager of the firm.[119] We need to find one of them or their friends.

I already have a piece written on the Częstochowa branch of Mr. Wronski [apparently members of the Bund in Częstochowa] by a man who has recently come here. I will send it next week. It clarifies the April mystery,[120] which I knew about more or less. Has Raphael's [Mahler] letter been sent already, and if not - when will it be? I thank you for the promise to send Mr. Ob[rona]'s novel [Ob-

116 It is not clear to whom this refers. Most likely, Ringelblum learned that a courier of the underground had left for London, and he is asking whether members of the Jewish underground can be taken out through the same route.

117 The reference is to the Revisionists and members of the Betar movement who were members of the Jewish Military Union and their role in the Warsaw ghetto uprising.

118 Apparently this refers to Advocate Szulman, a Revisionist journalist before the war, who was a member of the underground organization at Trawniki.

119 Commanders of the Jewish Military Union.

120 Apparently refers to an event connected with the ghetto uprising in April, but it is not clear which event.

rona, namely the Jewish defense in the ghetto]. I am very curious about it.

I bless you all, yours,

P.S. I heard that friends of ours are working with Częstochowa [Jews].[121] Would it be possible with their help to contact Borokh (68)?[122] This is about a warehouse [a place where archives material is hidden] and the workers in it (Świetlicki) and Smolarski [Smolar].[123]

We are returning the book along with Jurek's heartfelt thanks. We are asking for more. I have nearly settled [the possibility] of arranging with E.R. [Emanuel Ringelblum] a branch of the O.S. [*Oyneg Shabes*] archives. I have already written to Henryk [Wasser] who will submit the technical details. Of course I will give you the exact address.

29.12
Since Basia [Batya Temkin-Berman] was not here on Tuesday, I am sending the letter today.

I am attaching the first series of biographies. Mrs. Melm[124] asks that you tell Mr. Mik[ołai] [Feiner] that she would like to send something and that he enable her to do so.

Józia Ringelblum
30.12 [1943]
My dearest ones!

You weren't here – something important must have happened. Not an illness?[125] Write. For a number of days Mr. Dan [Guzik] gave

121 Apparently Jews hiding in the city.
122 The reference is to a school named after Borochov, which was on 68 Nowolipki Street. Ringelblum may have been asking about people connected with the school or about material of the *Oyneg Shabes* archives that was hidden in the school building, or he may be asking if through them it would be possible to obtain material that should be preserved.
123 One of the principals of the school was Natan Smolar. Świetlicki is probably Lichtenstein, another principal of the Borochov school.
124 Mrs. Melm, or sometimes Melmańska, is Itka Lazar-Melman.
125 An encounter with blackmailers or those who handed over Jews.

2,000 for Krysia, Rabbi Michelson's granddaughter, through Mrs. Mar [Merenholc]; I want you to know about that.

If Dolek [Berman] has no difficulties, then the matter is arranged here so that Edzio can meet him next week. Coordinate that, because I'd like to know about that a day beforehand so I can organize it. Edzio is already happy at the thought of meeting with you. It strengthens our will to live for a while. Do you see Czesława [Józia's sister]? I have had a bit of news from her recently. Will Danielski [Guzik] come to us? He promises all the time.

Kisses – Józia.

What about Lipowski [Lipa Bloch] and the friends [in Budzyń]?

Write.

Emanuel Ringelblum

3.1.1944

My dear ones!

I was very worried because Basia [Batya Temkin-Berman] did not arrive on Friday. According to your letter from some time ago, if Basia did not appear on Tuesday, then we should expect her on Friday. I suppose there must have been some important things [that delayed her coming]. The engineer Kozłowski[126] has asked me to arrange an *Arbeitskarte* [work card] for him. I am attaching a note with [his] details. In addition, to change the date on the attached *Bescheinigung* [approval] from 1943 to 1944 (in three places). I wrote at the time that he has a first-class occupation.

It is interesting that Mr. Brandowski's[127] friend, an acquaintance of our boss [Wolski], estimates the number of trees in the Częstochowa garden [the number of Jews in hiding] at 1,000 in W. [Warsaw].[128]

126 Batya Temkin-Berman mentions in her diary that she was trying to arrange papers for Kozłowski, one of the tenants in the hideout.

127 The reference is apparently to Karl Georg Brandt, a member of the Gestapo who was deputy director of the IVB4 Department of the Security Police in Warsaw.

128 It is difficult to know in what context this remark appears. The number of all the Jews who remained on the Aryan side of Warsaw in the peak period is estimated as 15,000–20,000.

The boss [apparently Wolski] who recently returned from Częstochowa [the city] told us that work is being carried out there as in Warsaw with Mr. Leszinski and Mr. Nowolipski.[129] Several weeks ago, Mrs. Krysia [a hide out, perhaps bunkers] was there, but they didn't like her and they ousted her. I am waiting for a reply regarding the affairs of the firm that I wrote about in my previous letters.

Yours,

Mr. Marek [Passensztein] is very ill because of a toothache. If you can, help him with the matter I wrote about in my letter.

Józia Ringelblum

3.1.1944

My dearest ones!

We didn't receive a letter last time, and that seems a bit strange to us. We waited. How did the holidays pass? How is Dolek's [Berman] health? Is he well already? At our place, there was a festive atmosphere. We generously handed out gifts to our nice bosses, and the younger ones spent the holidays with us.[130] Mr. Danielski [Guzik] has told us he will come, but until now he hasn't arrived. He arranged [the matter] with Mrs. Wisi and Mr. Mel[Melman] – it is not really clear to us, but it's his own affair.[131]

I wrote to you about Krysia, Rabbi Miche[lson]'s granddaughter,[132] but you didn't reply about that, and now we are told that Dan [Guzik] is asking us for an accounting in relation to the money. You certainly recall that the little one is in the village, Father was in Poniatów, and the one-time increased payment has already been spent. The attitude of those looking after us has worsened as a result, the

129 The reference is to main streets in the ghetto, Leszno and Nowolipki streets, where the workshops were concentrated. The shops in the Częstochowa ghetto were liquidated in 1942, and this probably refers to labor camps in the vicinity.

130 The members of the bunker owners' family maintained close ties with the Jews hiding there and spent a lot of time in their company; see Orna Jagur (Irena Grodzinska), *The Hiding Place* (Łódź: Oficyna Bibliofilów, 1997).

131 Guzik belonged to the Jewish National Council, and Józia does not understand why he is transferring funds to the Bund.

132 Probably Rabbi Yehezkel Zvi Michelson, who was active in the Warsaw ghetto.

girl apparently has no shoes, and the like. In any case, I am asking you to understand that the most important thing is to take the little one and to maintain direct contact with her, and what happened out of necessity, is only for a very short time. The girl is 12 and looks "very good,"[133] and is with relatives of those who are looking after Mr. Marek [Passensztein].

Possibly as far as they are concerned the matter is arranged through Mrs. M.[134] In this regard, it will be as Mrs. M. arranged it. However, we are asking [that you] speak with Dan [Guzik] and as far as possible arrange [the matter] as we requested.

Several times I have asked you for news of Maria and Zofia.[135] Where are they and how are they? What is happening with the Wodnitzki [the Wasser family]? Haven't they moved?

Recently two gentlemen have come to live here with the recommendation of Doctor A. [Adamowski],[136] after leaving an excellent, but expensive place for financial reasons. Here there is a real struggle over this locum [place], and I won the struggle and it is now at your disposal. You should know that I am the only one who will receive the address. Metznes[137] fought, but in vain. Write to me what your opinion is about this, do you need it. We are asking for the reply, affirmative or negative, only in writing.

Heartfelt greetings and [I] am requesting textbooks for Jurek. Everything, but not all at once, except history and grammar. That's very important to me. In the past as a pupil in a public school, I apparently should be able to get some help.

I heard something about that. If it's not difficult, look into the matter. I even have a friend in Warsaw from the same school. Do I have to apply to get information? What do you advise?
Kisses, Józia

133 Apparently this means the girl "does not look Jewish."

134 Apparently Helena Merenholc, a Jewish woman who was active in saving Jews on the Aryan side.

135 Apparently Maria Grzegorzewska and Zofia Rożewicz, Polish women who were active in saving Jews.

136 This probably refers to Dr. Adamowski, who is mentioned several times in the correspondence. It seems that Dr. Adamowski rented an apartment to Jews.

137 Probably a reference to the advocate K., one of the tenants of the bunker, who had an interest in the apartment.

Emanuel Ringelblum

6.1.1944

My dear ones!

Your letter shocked us deeply.[138] Until now you were fortunate and we believed that would go on like that until the end. We are glad that you are not despondent, which is what usually happens in such circumstances. We are with you with all our hearts. As for Mrs. Krysia [the hide out], we have an excellent locum [place] for you. Our friends have left the place after eight months because of financial difficulties. We paid 5 [5,000] per person, including food. Mrs. Krysia [the owner of the place] lives with us; they are very decent people, it's only that they really like money. It would be better to make [an agreement] only for the living quarters, because they are very stingy with the food. However, it is possible that our friends

138 The letter told about the attempt to blackmail Berman on January 4, 1944. This was extremely serious because it happened immediately after he left a meeting on matters concerning Żegota and near the meeting place. Three armed men of the Secret Police participated in the blackmail. There was a suspicion that the informer was a member or someone associated with a body that was active in rescue endeavors, and this would mean that the entire project could be endangered. After an investigation, suspicion fell on a Polish woman who had acted as a courier several times for the Jewish National Council and had engaged, among other things, in transferring money on its behalf (some discrepancies were also discovered in this regard); she was apparently responsible for informing on Berman. The entire incident caused much anxiety and led to a series of resolute steps. Berman was released by the Secret Police after large sums of ransom were paid. The Bermans, who lived in an apartment whose tenants did not know they were Jewish and were involved in underground activity, were forced to seek another safe place immediately. Berman discontinued his work for a while, and also considered the need to appoint someone else to head the activity of the Jewish National Council. The candidate to replace Berman was Emanuel Ringelblum, and in the following letters there are references and allusions to these two matters: the search for a suitable safe place for the Bermans; and the question of Ringelblum taking over the position. According to Berman, "after several months the underground movement got its hands on two out of three agents." About the entire affair, see, in addition to the following letters, a letter from Berman to the Polish underground and to Żegota in the Ghetto Fighters' House Archives; Temkin-Berman, " "Pan Rydzewski," pp. 18–19; Temkin-Berman, *Diary in the Underground*; Adolf Abraham Berman, *From the Days of the Underground* (Hebrew) (Tel Aviv, 1971), pp. 142–144.

exaggerated, but from the safety point of view, the situation there is excellent. The recent incident has proven, no matter what the price, there must be a reserve locum, because any one of us can find himself in a situation like yours. As for Mrs. Krysia,[139] her situation is as follows: in an area of 28 square meters — 38 people. There are 14 bunks, and 34 people sleep on them. Which means, on some of the very narrow bunks, three people [sleep] (we and Jurek who sleeps at our feet). The other four sleep on folding field beds and on stretchers that are put up between the beds. If you came here, we'd have to find some space, and we would, but it would not be comfortable. One would have to sleep on the table, and one with us or with Pas. [Marek Passensztein] or with Melm [Itka Melman]. The food is not bad, but the congestion, it is hard to describe. In addition, fleas and bedbugs. I am writing all this to you because the boss will ask for a large sum in advance, probably between 20 to 30 [thousand złoty], and there is no chance of any refund of the money.

It is a big advantage to be able to stay [for a while] during the day in the fresh air of snow [in the greenhouse in which the opening to the hide out is camouflaged]. It is an enormous advantage that makes up for the disadvantages and the overcrowdedness. I spend 8–10 hours a day in the free air. I am giving you this information in great detail, so that you will know everything exactly. We would very much like you to be with us, that would give us much encouragement. And you would also get used to our conditions within a few days. Only the first days are terrible, but afterwards everyone gets used to them and there is even humor here.

The possibilities for communicating are known to you. If you or Wodnitzki [the Wasser family] decide on Krysia, write at once, and Mr. G. [Guzik], who has very friendly feelings for you, will make contact with the boss [Wolski] the same day and will try to obtain a reasonable price. As for the other apartment, I am attaching a letter written by the gentlemen who lived there for eight months. The letter is addressed to the wife of one of these gentlemen who is in the apartment of Dr. A. [Adamowski], about whom I wrote to you in

139 Here the reference is to the hideout where Ringelblum was staying; for a detailed description, see Jagur, *The Hiding Place*.

my previous letter. I stress that the entire arrangement – regarding us – must be only through letters and not oral. Write what you have chosen and what we should do.
I send you my greetings,
...[illegible]

P.S. The older woman[140] - strange, very devout, goes off to church at 6:30. She's a teacher, you need to avoid conversations with her. Her eldest daughter seems trustworthy. Very few people visit the apartment. The matter can be arranged immediately.

I am going back to what I wrote about the letter. The final settlement of the matter of the locum [hiding place] seems to me to be as follows: tomorrow, Friday or Saturday, someone will come in your name as a patient of Dr. Ad. [Adamowski] (Chłodna 39)[141] between 4 to 12. He will mention Zygmunt's[142] name and ask to contact Maria, the wife of the man who has recently been living in that locum. Tomorrow, on Friday, [she] will be [there] again in order to arrange the matter of the apartment. And perhaps that same day it will be possible to go into [the apartment]. I am glad that we can repay you in some way for all the favors you have done for us, and we hope you will be satisfied with the apartment. For certain reasons, it is necessary to apply to Dr. A. as a patient.
(in the margins of the letter: confirms receipt of 10 [10,000 złoty]. Thank you very much).

Józia Ringelblum
6.1.1944
My dear ones! I do not want to express my feelings, this is no time for words – we need to act. You must disappear at any cost until you are fully recovered.

Edzio has told you all about the Krysia sanatorium [the bun-

140 The reference is apparently to the owner of the recommended apartment.
141 At 17 Chłodna Street there was an apartment where members of the Bund hid, but these are apparently two unrelated addresses.
142 Zygmunt Grynberg, Batya Temkin-Berman's brother-in-law, a doctor who hid with his wife Rita and their son Marian on the Aryan side of the city and was saved.

ker], but how different it looks in reality. Quarrels, struggles over a place, dirt, etc., have corrupted these people, who in any case were not so noble. I want you to know all this. An illness can be cured and it is possible to overcome all the obstacles...when you let us know...there is one last lifeline. I do not like to waste words, understand, there is no sacrifice we would not be willing to make to arrange [a place] for you at this [critical] time. But I don't want you to suffer, and just now Krysia's cousin [a hide out similar to the one where the Ringelblums were staying] has turned up with help. There were struggles here over it, and I kept my ear to the ground and obtained it for our own people. The place is great, 100 per cent convenience, but it costs 5 [thousand] for one person [a month]. But that is of no importance when it's a matter of life or death. We can find a way and there is Krysia. Those who lived there before have nothing but words of praise for the place. Their money ran out, and the place they got now is financed for them by Dr. A., because no one knows when this [the war and the need to hide] will be over, and it may be preferable to arrange a place for them where they have friends. Our boss [Wolski] will take at least 30 [30,000 złoty – an entry fee and payment for several months], but I am convinced that [the other place] I described is extraordinary. I would gladly go there. Be healthy, hold on bravely; keep in touch so that we won't be cut off even for a minute. Instruct Wanda[143] - that is the only thing that keeps us all going. I kiss you and wish you all the best. It pains me that there is so little I can do to help, but I will do everything I can. Again, my greetings, keep your spirits up – Józia

Warm regards from Jurek.

Józia Ringelblum

12.1.1944

My dear ones!

I am greeting you with tears in my eyes, but be brave. It is hard

143 Wanda Elster (today Rotenberg), a courier of the Jewish National Council who served as a liaison in the exchange of letters between the Bermans and the Ringelblums and also had close ties with the owners of the bunker. Wanda's sister, Pola Elster, was one of the leading activists of Left Poalei Zion. Wanda Elster lived in Israel.

for me to express [things] in a few words: the locum [place] is really wonderful – here again there was a struggle, Mr. K. [a lawyer who is a tenant of the bunker] really fought, but I was…[illegible] and I succeeded so that it may be for Budzyńskis [prisoners of Budzyń who would flee and come to Warsaw] and so we are fortunate that there is [a way out] for Edzio's best friends…[illegible]…Krysia…[illegible] I recommend Dr. A. [Adamowski], a detailed letter on the transfer.

Thanks, in friendship,

Józia

Emanuel Ringelblum

17.1.1944

My dear ones!

A few words from Henryk [Wasser], about a certain improvement in your health, we have been somewhat relieved. We agonized over what kind of illness you might have come down with,[144] and whether the pause in your work would continue. I hope that in your letter to us you will write about everything at length. We are urgently asking you to stay healthy, and that you go outside [out of the hiding place] only when that will not endanger your health. In addition, for a week we had no contact with D. [Guzik]. It turned out that the telephone was not working and we attributed too much importance to the pause in telephone communication. We thought that maybe he too had become seriously ill [namely, was also being blackmailed].

In my letter to him, I raised the matter of the supply [payment] directly to the patients or to those caring for them – from the reserve – for a longer period. I reminded him of the ill-fated experience of ZZ and Mr. Gep[ner],[145] who did not want to let go of the public property [that was at his disposal] and finally the dogs devoured it all. The lack of communication with D. made our

144 Ringelblum wonders about what type of blackmail the Bermans fell victim and on whose behalf the blackmailers were acting.

145 Zakład Zaopatrywania was a supplies' office that acted on behalf of the Judenrat in the ghetto. It was headed by Abraham Gepner, head of the merchants' organization and a well-known public figure in Poland.

neighbors panic-stricken. Very hard times will soon be upon us, and hence we have to think in advance. We also have to think about another locum from the side. Do you have any possibility to think about that and to do something concrete in that direction? As for Dr. A., Mrs. Maria [it is not clear who this is], who arranges the matter of the locum we are recommending, now knows the precise details of the place I am warmly recommending as a reserve, and she is authorized to arrange this matter. The matter continues to be pertinent.[146] The meeting [to arrange the apartment] – as [I noted] in my previous letter.

The booklet *Na Oczach* [*świata*][147] made an enormous impression on the listeners, despite the errors and the mistaken outlook on certain issues. I am attaching some comments we wrote down the day after the reading.[148] I am writing on the catacombs of the twentieth century,[149] about Holenderski, and in fact about his native city.[150]

I am adapting Gutkowski's[151] material, and am waiting for ma-

146 This excerpt from Ringelblum's letter, like similar hints in his other letters and in Józia's, attest to a threat they felt was intensifying. It is reasonable to assume that this feeling resulted from several events in the area of the hideout during this period (such as the suspicion among those employed in the vegetable garden regarding the greenhouse above the hideout; see Jagur, *The Hiding Place*), as well as the logical conclusion that, with time, the danger increased, particularly in view of the large number of those in hiding and the growing number of people outside who knew about the hideout. It is also reasonable that the blackmail of the Bermans added to the heightening anxiety. This anxiety caused Orna Jagur and her husband to leave the hideout and look for another hiding place – and to be saved as a result. The fact that they left also added to the growing fear.

147 The writer Maria Kann, who was active in the underground and engaged, among other things, in helping Jews on the Aryan side, prepared the booklet "Before the Eyes of the World" while in the underground and published it in 1943. Kann described the Warsaw ghetto and its liquidation – in particular, the struggle and the uprising – based on testimonies and documents and on the Polish underground press. Kann was recognized as a Righteous Among the Nations by Yad Vashem.

148 These comments were preserved and are in the Berman section of the GFHA.

149 The reference is to the bunkers in the ghetto.

150 Holenderski was the head of the trade unions in Łódź.

151 Eliyahu Gutkowski, from Łódź, was a member of the underground in the Warsaw ghetto and an active member of the *Oyneg Shabes* group. He perished in the sewage canals.

terial promised by Antek in order to begin on [Ż]OB [history of the Jewish Combat Organization]. You did not confirm receipt of the second notebook of biographies. How is Budzinski [the prisoners in Budzyń]? It seems it is too late for the rescue, since Mrs. Wojeńska [the war] has drawn very close to it. I fear that the same fate awaits [illegible] and Kielczynski [the Kielce area].

Has Mr. Lewinski[152] already decided on the surgery recommended by Dr. Węgrzynski?[153]

I bless you, regards to the Wodnitzkis, Jelenskis, and Polinskis [to the Wasser family, to Hirsch Berlinski and to the sisters Pola and Wanda Elster].

P.S. Marek [Passensztein] will send his comments to Ber [Berman]. If you have anything – send it. I did not read "O likwidacji."[154]

Józia Ringelblum

17.1.1944

You surely are not surprised that we are not calm. For a short time we lost all contact. From what is implied in Mrs. M.'s[155] reply, I have concluded that Dan [Guzik] has also fallen ill. In any case, something is wrong. I even thought of some infection caught from you [being grabbed by blackmailers]. Now we are a little calmer, but we are constantly thinking about what will happen to you and if you are staying healthy enough. We have made all the arrangements with the locum [place] for you. Will you take advantage of it? In any event, we would like to have Wodnitzki's [Wasser] address presented in a proper manner [in secret codes]. We need to know about one another and how to find one another. Write to us about everything. Don't allow yourselves to become depressed. I know it is hard to get to that [standing], especially after such attempts.[156] It

152 The reference is apparently to Lazer Levin, whose name appears on the list of those who are designated to leave through Hungary.

153 Apparently the suggestion to leave through Hungary.

154 "On the Liquidation" was a booklet that was in preparation but was not published.

155 The mother of the owner of the bunker.

156 The reference is to rescue activities on behalf of the Jewish National Council and Żegota.

won't take long, and [the work] will start again, and now you need to rest. But I implore you to write. In general, I ask that we all keep in touch with one another and write to one another.
Here there is unrest. For example, today, Domb-bo…ski [name is illegible; probably one of the tenants in the hide out] is organizing force etc. Write, that keeps our spirits up. Edzio can meet with Wanda [Elster], but we must know about that in advance. In case of the transfer of money that Dolek spoke about, it is best to do that indirectly through Wanda and to make an appointment with [Mrs.] M.

I bless and kiss you all. Give the Wodnitzkis [Wasser], Wanda and the others our warmest regards.

Emanuel Ringelblum
20.1.1944
My dear ones!

We are very worried because Wanda [Elster] did not arrive on Friday to the place we had set. Czesł[awa] [Józia's sister] called Dan [Guzik] yesterday and no one answered. Maybe everything is all right. I hope that everything has been settled. But you have no idea what we went through during several days of worry, and worst of all – not knowing anything. What is actually happening? Was Mr. Szantażysta [blackmailer] angry with Dolek [Berman], or perhaps it is his friendship with Paprocki[157] that is to blame? You have no idea how distressed we were by this matter. As you know from previous letters, we arranged the matter of the locum [place] in the best way possible. I think the best way to take advantage of this locum is as a reserve. We need to get there between 4 and 12. I am not raising other matters, because we are waiting for a clarification regarding

157 This may refer to Berman's ties with the Polish left-wing party. Members of the Jewish National Council had ties with members of the Polish Communist Party, PPR. At an early stage, members and supporters of the party helped transfer weapons to the ghetto and participated actively in rescue operations. Berman, Aryeh Willner, and Yitzhak Zuckerman were among those who maintained these contacts, and Ringelblum evidently wonders whether these contacts may be the cause for blackmail attempts by Polish circles hostile to the left-wing movements in Poland.

Dolek. We are strongly urging you to act with great caution. The sick man must not leave his room until he is completely healthy.

I send you my warmest greetings.

Emanuel Ringelblum

24.1.1944

My dear ones!

From your letter we understand what grave danger D. [Dolek Berman] was in because of the attack of the illness. We [are happy] along with you that it is behind us and that he is recovering and feels better. From now on, he must be careful that the illness does not recur. I hope that if Mr. Pelnicki[158] will investigate and properly diagnose the reasons for the attack, that you will let us know what the diagnosis is. I am curious to know the results of the examinations that have been conducted thus far, which Dolek promised to send us.

Here the last few days were very tense because Mr. D. [Guzik] did not transfer the payment. He has already given us two dates, and now we are waiting for the new date – Tuesday, the 25th of this month.

Our situation is that if the money is not received, people are doomed to starve to death. We had a very unpleasant experience when one of our friends, Mr. Wachowski [a man in the hide out] was forced to sell his winter coat because he couldn't wait any longer for the money from Mr. D. What happened? Dol[ek] told me that there is no lack of money. If so, why doesn't D. pay, but [instead] from time to time sets new dates? Is this a specific "illness" of Guz[ik]'s, or is it a general phenomenon?[159]

Is it impossible to borrow [the money] until Mr. D. has enough – 9.5 [9,500 złoty] for January and an equal sum for February? The matter is very urgent! We are imploring you to look into the financial situation and the chances in this regard. Hasn't Mr. L. [London] sent new money? Have the reserves run out? We are ask-

158 A representative of Delegatura in Żegota.

159 On the financial sources of the organizations to rescue Jews, see the Introduction to this book.

ing for a clear answer and a loan in the event that Mr. D. does not pay on Tuesday. We wanted to turn to you on this matter a few days ago, but we didn't know how to do that. We are urgently requesting that you give us a possibility to make contact in emergency situations. Is Mrs. Miodowska a possibility (B)?[160] If not – give us a different possibility.

In my letter before the last, I sent you a document for Kozłowski.[161] Can this matter be arranged?

E.R. [Ringelblum] asks if he can send a third notebook of biographies dedicated to Marian's [Anielewicz] friends, through W. [Wanda Elster].[162] It is about Lutek [Rotblat] and ten friends I know personally. If Antek [Zuckerman] would send me his material, I could also complete it and begin working on the biography of Mrs. [Ż]OB [the Jewish Fighting Organization].

I am curious to know when Dolek will be able to meet with his brother and it the meeting will take place without any friction.[163] I know that they very much love one another, but I would like to know what you have to say about his neighbor Mrs. A.K. Polkowski.[164]

Polinski's [Pola Elster] letters ...[a signature is missing. Probably another unsigned letter] moved me greatly. From what they wrote about Saganski,[165] I concluded what [they] think about Mrs. Partowski's[166] position. It has turned out that she is a personality

160 Probably refers to Janina Bucholz, whose office on 11 Miodowa Street served as a contact address for help to Jews hiding on the Aryan side. For details on her activity, see Temkin-Berman, "The Good Soul," *A Diary in the Underground*, pp. 84–92.

161 Batya Temkin-Berman mentions in her diary that she was trying to arrange papers for Kozłowski, one of the tenants in the hideout.

162 Wanda Elster (today Rotenberg), a courier of the Jewish National Council who served as a liaison in the exchange of letters between the Bermans and the Ringelblums and also had close ties with the owners of the bunker.

163 Adolf Abraham Berman's brother, Yaakov Berman, was an active communist and during the war was in the Soviet Union. Here the reference is to news about the situation on the Eastern front.

164 Armia Krajowa.

165 Shakhna Sagan.

166 The reference is to a party – *Partia* in Polish – and here to Left Poalei Zion, which was led by Sagan.

that has many rights, that has undergone much in her life, and has survived. I have special sentiments and a close feeling for her. I felt that the first time at Mr. Tr. [Trawniki], when they said to me: Mr. R. [Ringelblum], I know you from the old days. These words gave me encouragement for many months. They induced me to [carry out] many actions. A future sociologist will find it interesting to look into this subject. I am asking you for an answer about Lewinski [Lewin – an exit through Hungary] and Budzyński [the Budzyń camp].

My warmest greetings, regards to the whole family.

Emanuel Ringelblum

27.1.1944

As I wrote to you in my letter on Tuesday, since the month of January was not paid for, our situation seems to be at its worst. I am sure that you are doing everything to provide our neighbors with money. We are asking as far as possible that you hasten the payment. As for the payment for two-three months, I wrote [about that] for two reasons: our neighbors asked us for that, especially Mr. Wachowski who strongly requested that we do that, and [also] the information we received from Mr. Dan [Guzik] during his visit to us and that he told us that there is money for a longer period of time. Of course, I didn't tell all of that to our neighbors. Under normal conditions, the policy of ZZ[167] to create reserves seems a good idea to me. In the present conditions that is not desirable. I was amazed that you found an insult in comparison to ZZ. I have the impression that I said many times about your work that it is sacred [work], and hence it is difficult to accuse me of an analogy with an institution like ZZ.

The words about a locum [place] were erased and we could not decipher them.

Something has gone wrong here. Maybe we need to change the locum. At the moment, there is no immediate danger. The internal matters are in a boiling state. Two people have left, etc.

167 Zakład Zaopatrywania was a supplies office that acted on behalf of the Judenrat in the ghetto.

Hence, we are asking to find a way of making contact in sudden cases.[168]

I confirm receipt of Mr. Kozł[owski]'s document; I have pictures of Mic[hael] [Berman] and others. I will send them on Tuesday. I am waiting for an answer as to where to send the third notebook of biographies.

Mr. Poznański [a friend of Wroński] is working on [shop] Szczotkarze,[169] a very interesting [piece of writing] that is well-written. The work on Wroński in Częstochowa is ready.[170]

I thank Antek [Zuckerman] and Henryk [Wasser] for the letters. I will reply to them on Tuesday.

We were very sorry to hear about Budzyński and Tausio [Theodor Pajewski]. Have they already arrived?[171] You must write to us [about that]. Mikołaj's friends [Bund members] have caused internal relations to worsen so much that they are ruined from the inside. Now Mr. Cel[emenski] has offered 10 [thousand złoty] to a boy who serves us for a trip to Krynica.[172] Such offers, as well as earlier ones, demoralize the people being looked after here, and leave their imprint on us. I understand that it is impossible to "install a new head" on an idiot, but is there no solution? [He] now suggests that the warehouse [the bunker] be expanded for another ten people. We really have no more strength to wage this struggle. And on the other hand, we fear that whatever you write or say to Mikołaj [Feiner] will come back to me and will be turned against me as it was in the past. Really, I do not know what to do in this situation. My nerves are betraying me. Your letters have encouraged us somewhat; despite everything, there is someone who thinks about us and is with us.

168 The reference is to the fact that Orna and Yosef Jagur (Grodzinska) left secretly. See Jagur, *The Hiding Place*.

169 The history of the brushmakers' shop in the Warsaw ghetto.

170 The activity of the Bund in Częstochowa.

171 The reference is apparently to an attempt to smuggle prisoners form the camp; in the end the prisoners refused to leave, and Pajewski and Shoshana (Emilka) Kosower returned alone.

172 Mrs. Melman wanted very much to meet with her daughter, who was in Krynica. Celemenski offered a very large sum of money to the boy, apparently the son of the hideout owners, to arrange the meeting.

Józia Ringelblum
27.1.1944
My dears,

I do not know if this letter will reach you by tomorrow. Wanda [Elster] said that in an urgent case...[thus in the original] but I am writing nonetheless. I want you to know that here we are extremely distressed. It is clear to me that you have your own [affairs], but I cannot do otherwise. You are the only ones. Here we are regarded as representatives [of the Jewish National Council and the channel through which the money is transferred]. Our list includes many people, and non-payment has grave implications. The management [apparently the internal management of the bunker] has simply forbidden [us?] to order [food] and the like. We can come to the management with various complaints, but after all, we are in a situation that was imposed upon us. Hence [the tenants of the hide out] take advantage of the crisis and the result is a commotion. This flared up suddenly when two people left [secretly] after secretly talking with the boss [Wolski].[173] An atmosphere of panic has been created, strained nerves, and those few who have weak nerves are in a state of extreme despair. In brief – very, very difficult.

I find it very unpleasant to write [this], but I must. I am imploring you to arrange these matters [and] to give us "information" about Wod[nitzki] [Wasser] so that we can [contact them] in any event, and that is essential. Think about us personally. Write [and tell us] how this looks and what the perspectives are.

With thanks,
Kisses, Józia

Emanuel Ringelblum
7.2.1944
My dears!

Now we are sending you two letters: one from Friday, Mrs. M. [the mother of the owner of the bunker] waited for Wanda [Elster], and another from today [this excerpt erased in the original]. We hope you have arranged the financial matters of January, and

173 An allusion to the departure of the Jagurs.

perhaps also of February. We know that this requires much effort on your part, but I hope you have succeeded in overcoming the difficulties and have obtained the money for our neighbors. There are no changes here. Józia's liver is bothering her more and more, and it is really a problem to stick to a diet.

I'd like to remind you that the anniversary of an important family event will take place soon (April 19).[174] We need to remind L. [London] and Raphael [Mahler in the United States] of this anniversary, as well as the whole family. Our uncle deserves to have the whole family that has remained remember him forever. Write to him soon and suggest that he mark this special day in the family history.

Koninski's[175] brother-in-law has informed me that he is very dissatisfied with his landlords, who have been mistreating him recently (making it difficult for him to make any contact, and the like). We have no way of knowing if that is a deliberate act against him personally or it's a family illness that hangs in the air (that can happen too). Maybe it will end – Kon[inski]'s brother-in-law writes to me – in money, and maybe he is sick and tired of his sub-tenants. They wrote about that to Czesława,[176] who has some capability in this domain.

Write to me [to tell me] how Michael [Berman] has settled into his new apartment. Is he living there with Krysia?[177] And in general, how are they getting along?

The mood here is at its lowest. There's no end to the suffering, and the neighbors are adding fuel [to the fire]. We are asking you, write to us about what happened with Theodor and Budzyński.[178]

174 The anniversary of the outbreak of the uprising in the Warsaw ghetto.

175 Apparently relatives of Józia Yehudit Ringelblum.

176 Here this probably does not refer to Józia Yehudit Ringelblum's sister, but to the historian Lotta Wagmeister, who was called by that name. Wagmeister was a member of the PPR and had strong connections with the Polish intelligentsia. She left the ghetto and was active in the underground. During the Polish uprising in Warsaw in August 1944, she was captured by the Nazis and took her own life.

177 Namely, without the landlord knowing he is Jewish.

178 The reasons for the failure of the attempt to smuggle prisoners out of the Budzyń camp.

Did you send a letter to Raphael? Did you receive a proposal regarding Turczynski's brother?[179] And AR.R.?[180]

Józia Ringelblum

7.2.1944

My dear ones!

Wanda [Elster] did not arrive and the letter that was prepared is lost. Since I learned that at the last minute and had no other way – I will write the main points.

You are surely asking what the Koninskis wrote. They wrote that now it is necessary to help them. Their landlords claim they have various proposals, and they need to know how to appease them. Their mood is extremely low, and therefore I am asking you for instructions at a crucial moment; it is question of life for them. Although [we] know you [are loaded] with worries, [we are asking] that you arrange that for them.

I have also written on this matter to Józia's niece, but I do not know what she can arrange. At the moment, she is living under difficult conditions. She also has not received from Dan [Guzik] payment for the month of January. That is also true of the sister, the mother and the brother-in-law. If you can, I am asking you to arrange the payments for them. If you cannot, then perhaps they will turn to Mrs. M., [181] who they see sometimes. If there is no other way, because they simply do not have a cent.

What's new with you? Write to us more often, and a lot. If W. [Wanda Elster] wants to meet with Edzio, she should arrange that with Mrs. M. [the mother of the owner of the bunker]. How are our

179 Turczynski is Jonas Turkow, a well-known actor. He was in the ghetto, escaped from the camp, spent some time on the Polish side, and survived. He wrote books about the ghetto and that period. Jonas's brother, Mark Turkow, lived in Argentina, and Ringelblum thought it might be possible to obtain material help through him for the underground and the rescue operation. After the war Mark Turkow established the publishing house Tsentral farband fun Poilishe Yidn in Argentine in Buenos Aires. The publishing house was devoted to the history of Polish Jewry and has published more than 100 books in Yiddish.

180 Arbeiter Ring was a Jewish professional organization active in the United States; apparently Ringelblum was also asking for it to try to obtain help.

181 Apparently Helen Merenholz.

friends? The last news we received caused [us to be in] a despondent mood.

I am asking you, please write.

Yours, Józia

Emanuel Ringelblum

20.2.1944

My dear ones!

Mrs. W. [Wanda Elster] must have told you about all the affairs of the firm[182] that I touched on in our conversation. I really appreciate her work [Wanda's] for the good of our firm. She is modest [and acts] as if everything she does is nothing out of the ordinary.

We thank you for your wishes on the occasion of the 25th anniversary of our firm. W. told us by mistake that it was only twenty years. According to our calculations it's 25 years.[183]

We thank you very much for the 9.5 [thousand złoty] for our neighbors. The situation of some of them has considerably worsened. Mr. Kozł[owski]'s wife [tenants of the hide out] is very ill and she cannot be cured. Wachowski's [tenants of the bunker] condition is very bad. Mr. Poznanski, who recently came here, is a friend of Mr. Wronski [the Bund] from before the war.

I am writing the history of the brush according to the model of Faraday [history of the match]. The piece is spread over 160 pages. It will be an interesting contribution to the history of Czę[stochowa].[184]

I should like to remind you that Mr. Micha[el] [Berman] dealt with these people before Mr. D. [Guzik] received them at his personal initiative. This proposal did not come from me. Because of the reasons I mentioned to you. We are strongly requesting that you send [money] for February, since the situation of our neighbors is

182 Apparently a group of Left Poalei Zion members.

183 The reference is to the establishment of Left Poalei Zion.

184 The reference is apparently to Jews in hiding and to the activity of the owner of the brush factory, a Jew who for a long time enjoyed the protection of the Germans and also maintained contacts with the underground, especially with Bund members.

very bad. Mrs. Wanda must have told you about Czesława.[185] She remained with her family on the ice. She wrote us a shocking letter, we sent her 500 zł[oty], that's how desperate her situation was. In addition, Mr. Dan left her with a burden of 50 kilograms[186] that she has to carry on her shoulders. Something has to be done for her neighbors, because these people can find themselves in extremely difficult conditions. Czesława will be at Mrs. M.'s place [apparently Merenholz] on Wednesday. It would be good if one of you could meet her and look into the matter.

In regard to Węgrowski,[187] Józia is afraid of the saying "from the frying pan into the fire." Won't that same Mr. Yeke[h] [the Germans] be angry at Wę[gry] [Hungary] and then[188]...we are curious about more information from you on this matter.

We were very sorry to read Paprocki's letter on [illegible] and [on] Konicki. What a miserable end. Isn't something similar awaiting his daughter W-L? Do you have any more information from up close?[189]

We thank you for putting us in touch with Stasia.[190] But is the number of her house 25 or 27? We were sorry to read the letter from Teos [Theodor Pajewski] Budzyński. They are people permeated with solidarity, and that is the source of the difficulties.[191]

This week I am finishing the biographies. What do you hear from Kielczynski [the Kielce area], Radomski [the Radom area] and our other friends?

Mrs. Melm [Melman] is asking that Mr. Mikołaj [Feiner] or someone else contact her. The landlords will agree, since her health has improved.

185 Czesława (Cesia) Herman was Józia Ringelblum's sister.

186 The reference is apparently to Czesława's pregnancy.

187 The reference is to the idea of crossing into Hungary, which was mentioned several times in the letters.

188 It turns out that Ringelblum, from his hiding place, knew about what was awaiting Hungary and the Jews there.

189 Not deciphered.

190 The reference is apparently to Helena Merenholz.

191 Some of the prisoners who were offered a chance to flee refused to do so out of a sense of solidarity with the other prisoners. This is confirmed by the testimony of Shoshana Kosower.

I should like to know if Mr. Węgrowski [those staying in Hungary] has better possibilities to contact Mr. L. [London], Mr. Raphael [United States] and others. Have you tried to obtain anything through his mediation? Mr. Mieszkaniec [a tenant in the hide out] has a rich son-in-law there and he is in touch with him all the time.

Your letters have explained a lot to me, but I admit that I do not understand why Mr. Raphael [United States] is relating [to us] differently than L. [London]. At first I thought it was because of a lack of information, but it now seems that is no longer true. If so, why? From far away, many things look different. Probably they have explanations for this. As far as your controversy with Krysia[192] is concerned, don't forget her rights. I don't know if you should think so lightly of her. Isn't [a situation] of maximum [the best conditions] at the cost of health sometimes preferable to a safe [place] with minimum conditions?

We are strongly requesting news about our relatives, those close and those faraway.

We bless and kiss you, thanks for everything.

21.2.1944

P.S. Of all the urgent matters, I am reminding you of the matter of Kristina, a relative of the well-known KS. MICH.[193] Mr. Dan [Guzik] has allocated for her support [of] 2 [thousand]. She is asking for this help to continue. Mr. M. [Merenholz] knows about this matter very well.

Józia Ringelblum

My dear ones!

The personal regards from you overjoyed us. Perhaps in this way it will be possible to arrange the matter [the contact] more often. It's hard for me to describe how it affects us. To get away, at least for a short while, to relatives – what a refreshing [experience] in the hopeless state we are in. I want to write to you more, but [I will do that] next time, since I am waiting for news. I kiss you,

192 Reference apparently to the owners of the hideout.

193 Refers to the granddaughter of Rabbi Michelson.

thank you very much and ask you to write letters to me. Regards to our friends, Józia.

I am sending you a jar of real honey from the mountains, which was sent to us directly. Write, and tell me if you find it tasty.

Letter from Emanuel Ringelblum to Lipowski [Lipa Bloch]

My dear friend!

Through our common friend Mr. Ber[man], thanks to whom I have been saved from a serious problem, I learned about your ordeals. About your and Mr. Koninski's trip to L. [London] I learned through Mrs. M. [Merenholz?]. I was full of hope that I'd see you soon. Do you remember the proverb *audaces fortuna iuvat* [fate helps the audacious]? It's hard for me to explain how many times my wife and I mentioned the moments we shared at Mr. H. [Hallmann]'s [place].[194] We are tenants in Krysia [hide out], our landlady is not particularly nice, which is not so favorable to our well-being. Józia's hair has gone white, she suffers from all manner of aches. I as usual am engaged in writing diaries. I mention you frequently. I am dreaming of seeing you. Our friend Mr. Ber[man] thinks about you endlessly and would like to meet you as fast as possible. I would be prepared to go to him on foot, but fortunately there was a different opportunity. I would like to tell you a lot and to talk to you. Perhaps nonetheless I will have an opportunity to talk to you. I bless you with all my heart. Regards to Falkowski and Zalmanowski.[195]

Rydzewski[196]

Letter from Józia Ringelblum to Lipowski (Bloch)

My dear Mr. Lipowski!

I can only write a few words to you. We are trying with all of our strength to have you with us as we planned. We talk about you often. [You are] in our thoughts and our feelings.

194 The carpentry shop of the German Hallmann, where families in the ghetto stayed during the last stages of the ghetto's existence.

195 They are all apparently prisoners in Budzyń. Falkowski is Israel Falk, a Bund activist; Zalmanowski is Chaim Zalmanowski, a teacher in the secondary school in the Warsaw underground, who survived and settled in Israel.

196 One of Ringelblum's code names.

You must take yourself in hand and mobilize all of your energy. I bless you wholeheartedly and believe we will see each other.

Give [our] regards to your friends. We bless you.

Józia

Emanuel Ringelblum

1.3.1944

My dear ones!

On Friday, Mr. M. [Merenholz] waited with our letter to you. Since Mrs. Wanda [Elster] did not appear, you will now get two letters. As for the financial difficulties, I suggest you turn for help to Og Czest Kom,[197] to Arb[eiter] Rin[g][198] (Raphael [Mahler]) [United States], and also to Turczynski's [Marek Turkow] brother[199] (his brother [Jonas] has the address), who has much influence in Arg[entina]. It is possible that Mik[ołai] actually gets his income from Arb[eiter] Rin[g] through L. [London], in our name as well. Thanks to Aunt YIVO,[200] I am well known to all those mentioned above. You can sign in my name whenever you find that necessary. Have you already made some attempts in the directions I suggested to you? I have learned that Mr. D. [Guzik] will be away for a while.[201] I suggest that you receive the list, and no one else.[202] I hope that your present letter will be an answer about the contact [between us] in urgent cases. To my regret, the irresponsible behavior of several partners can have a very bad effect on the existence of the warehouse [the hide out], which was in danger of liquidation. In this context, the transfer of the merchandise [the people in hiding]

197 Ogólny Częstochowski Komitet; namely, the overall committee of Częstochowa. Here this is a code name for the World Jewish Congress.

198 A Jewish professional organization in the United States.

199 Marek Turkow in Argentina.

200 YIVO – Yidisher Visnshoftlekher Institut, the center of the Institute for Jewish Research, was transferred from Poland to New York early in the war; Ringelblum had been active in this body before the war.

201 At the end of January, Daniel Guzik was forced to hide because the Gestapo was following him.

202 The list refers to those being cared for. The job of handling Jews in hiding was divided among several active agencies: the Jewish National Council, the Bund, and the Joint, of which Guzik was apparently one of the directors.

to another place may turn out to be a very urgent matter. As we informed you, two people left the warehouse secretly, and despite the opinion of the others, took their merchandise. This adversely affected the cohesiveness of the warehouse and changed the attitude of the owners of the asset to the business.

I am waiting for a reply whether to send you more notebooks of biographies. Antek [Zuckerman] interested me greatly. It is essential that Jelenski [Hirsch Berlinski] record[203] his comments on [Ż]OB in parallel. The idea is to be able to emphasize the function and position of Mr. Stolarski [Left Poalei Zion]. Unquestionably, Mr. Cha[lutz] played a key role in all this, but if Mr. Stolarski will not mention his role in all this, the entire picture of the reality will be distorted.

Hence I am asking you to induce Jelenski to describe the discussions of Saganski[204] with Paprocki [PPR], and in general, all the attempts, before OB [before the establishment of ŻOB][205] and to tell about our role and that of our friends in the OB.

Has the matter of preservation been finally arranged?[206] I would inform Raphael of the addresses of our warehouses [the place where the archives are hidden]. It would be good already now to appoint Raphael and Aunt Yivo[207] as heirs, in case none of us stay

203 Berlinski's list has been preserved and was published in Hebrew. See Berlinski, "Memoirs"; the original is in the archives of the Jewish Historical Institute in Warsaw.

204 Shakhna Sagan, a leader of Left Poalei Zion.

205 The reference is to the establishment of the "Anti-Fascist Bloc." This organization was established in the Warsaw ghetto in the spring of 1942, and adopted the way of armed resistance, but was disbanded after several months after someone informed on it. It preceded the Jewish Combat Organization, which was founded when the deportations began in the summer of 1942.

206 The reference is to hiding places of the *Oyneg Shabes* archives, two of which were found after the war. The original is now kept in the Jewish Historical Institute in Warsaw. Some of the material has been published in Polish, and some also in Hebrew and English, and it serves as the most important basis for Holocaust research. This part of the letter originally appeared in Israel Gutman, "Emanuel Ringelblum's Last Request, March 1, 1944," *Yad Vashem Studies*, vol. 31 (2003), pp. 7–9.

207 YIVO – Yidisher Visnshaftlekher Institut, the center of the Institute for Jewish Research, was transferred from Poland to New York early in the war.

alive after the war. At least it will remain after us, and here I am of course including the warehouse at 68.[208]

I hope that you will think about that in advance and inform Raphael in time, so that in the worst case he can be our heir. By the way, is the letter to Raphael already on its way?[209] Perhaps what I write is sad, and it isn't easy for me to bring up such gloomy thoughts, but it is best to foresee everything so that everything will not be lost without any traces of it being left.

I am curious to hear about the additional material. I have thoroughly "digested" the earlier ones.[210]

I have received the document for Mr. Kozł[owski]. Is this only a temporary pause? Has Mr. Leg[alisatsia] actually come into effect and has this affected Dolek [Berman]'s health?[211] How do you feel now? Have you found a suitable warehouse for Dolek [the Berman family]? Have you arrived at a financial settlement with the warehouse of Dr A. [Adamowski]? Write to us if you were there.

We feel really terrible. Have Teodor Paje[wski] and Emilka [Kosower] already returned?[212] What news did they bring? Did Lewinski [apparently Lewin] stick to his decision? Is there anything new in this regard? At this opportunity, I am asking to [send my] heartfelt regards to Mrs. Wag[meister].[213] I have just learned that Mr. D. [Guzik] will no longer pay anything for January. So I am asking you to pay our neighbors for the months of January and February according to the attached list. I want to add that Dan has

208 68 Nowolipki Street; two parts of the *Oyneg Shabes* archives were hidden at this address and were discovered there after the war under the ruins of the house.

209 See Ringelblum, *Last Writings*, pp. 328–323.

210 This refers to material written by those hiding on the Aryan side and which came into Ringelblum's possession.

211 Ringelblum here is apparently referring to the collapse of a network that forged documents under Weiss's management; see Temkin-Berman, *A Diary in the Underground*, pp. 64–67.

212 Teodor Pajewski, a Pole, was a member of the Polish underground. Together with Shoshana (Emilka) Kosower, he rescued Ringelblum from Trawniki.

213 Lotta Wagmeister was a member of the PPR and had strong connections with the Polish intelligentsia. She left the ghetto and was active in the underground. During the Polish uprising in Warsaw in August 1944, she was captured by the Nazis and took her own life.

already noted dates **four times** [apparently payment dates]. I am asking you to pay for two months at the same time, since the situation of the neighbors is very grave, and some have even been forced to sell their belongings. I bless you.

Emanuel Ringelblum
3.3.1944
My dear ones!

I received your letter at the time when Mr. G.[214] was creating a whole commotion here and "spoiled a lot of blood" [caused us much heartache]. I would therefore more readily accept your suggestion [to leave and to take up work on the Jewish National Council], if it were not for these hesitations – whether in view of the disputes between Aunt Radomska [Żegota] and Uncle Paprocki,[215] should **we** [members of Poalei Zion] be the ones now to represent **our** candidates for the position of acting [director] of the firm?[216] Won't Paprocki be angry with us because of that and hold it against us? And as for the state of E.'s [Ringelblum] health, it is extremely bad.

E. is now in a deep depression caused by the fact that there is no way out of the situation. Józia is strongly opposed to the plan to leave, based on the assumption that in his present mental state, E. is not suitable for the position offered him. I have already written to you about Józia's state of health. Her hair turned white because of the Trawniki worries, pains in her liver, etc. In another situation, I would find it very hard, because of the importance of the matter, to agree with Józia's view.

Janina's news is truly shocking. Mr. Trawniki always said good things about her and now such horrible information about her

214 This may be a reference to Shimon Gotesman, a major activist of the "Et livnot" ("time to build") faction of the General Zionists from Kraków. He hid in Warsaw and at the last stage replaced Berman in his position on the Jewish National Council. After the war he immigrated to Brazil.

215 Probably the PPR party, which Żegota and the leadership of the Polish underground did not recognize.

216 The Jewish National Council. Ringelblum apparently is referring to a proposal – never realized – that he replace Berman as head of the Council. On this matter, see Temkin-Berman, "Pan Rydzewski."

morals.[217] Now your cautionary measures are clear to me, which in the case of Rada [Żegota] seemed exaggerated.

Mr. P.'s [not deciphered] literature was very interesting and we thank you for it. We must admit that the writer has ideas and is persuasive. It would only be interesting to know whether he has many subscribers. You have no idea how delighted we were by the news about Lipowski [Lipa Bloch]. I believe you are doing everything to get him out of the clutches of the epidemic, and we hope you succeed.[218]

How are things with Wilczynski and Zalmanski [prisoners in the Budzyń camp]? Has Mr. Bogucki[219] received Wachowski's [a tenant in the bunker] letter? He is having a hard time, until now he lived only on the support [money], and for him the non-payment for February is really a catastrophe. If there is no possibility now to pay the whole sum of the support money, wouldn't it be possible to approve the most urgent needs (Kozłowski, Wiesja, Wachowski)?

Warm regards to you and your family.

P.S. Remember Czesława [Józia's sister] and her family; they are having a very difficult time. Mrs. Melmeanska [a tenant in the bunker] is asking to notify Mr. Mik[ołaj] that she would like to meet with his friends. The landlords will gladly host them.

Józia Ringelblum

3.3.1944

Edzio has already written to you at what time your letter arrived. He wrote one sentence, but so much pain and so much sorrow, that we feel awful, totally broken. An irresponsible person who is registered here and recently has been pestering us [tenants of the bunker].

217 Janina is Janina Lakutowicz, and the shocking news is that she was behind the blackmail to which Berman fell victim in January 1944. Ringelblum was so agitated by the news, because she had undertaken missions on behalf of the Jewish underground and also had a part in preparations for the release of Ringelblum from Trawniki.

218 At a certain stage there apparently seemed to be a chance to persuade Bloch and to take him out of the camp.

219 Shimon Gotesman.

Marek [Passensztein] is standing at the side. He is brave, but in an indirect way [in personal relations] — less so. I admit that I simply do not know what to do. Is there any agreed upon decision? I know and you know what you are for us. You saved Edzio. We owe you his life, and as a result my life and Jurek's life as well. If you believe that Edzio has to go,[220] I will not refuse. I am absolutely broken. You can surely imagine how the Tr[awniki] period destroyed me. The awful atmosphere here, the poisoned air because of the despicable company, have tormented me. You certainly remember how since my youth I was connected to work, hard work. How work enthralls me and gives me added strength, and how much energy it gives me. The recent period has affected me terribly, and I don't know how I would now be affected by uncertainty regarding Edzio, although the [closeness] between me and Edzio is now far from 100%. So I repeat: if the reason in principle that Edzio gave and your proposal will be that Edzio has to go — I will not object despite everything. You are everything for me. It is very hard here. We marked the anniversary too soon — we are already paying [for that], which will be a huge burden on the budget. Second, regarding the recent events in the air [the bombardments] — this house here, [built] of cards, needs to be fixed, because in fact its foundations are shaking. If so, we will build…[illegible].

I hope things will be settled, and as for the most important matter, I have expressed my sincere view as if to a mother and to the only and closest friends.

I bless with all my heart and ask for long letters. Write about everything. We live with that from one day to the next. I am asking you, remember Czesława, her mother, her sister. They have nothing from which to live. We sent them a little, but it's beyond my strength.

I kiss you, Józia.

* * *

220 Namely, to leave the bunker and take a position on the Jewish National Council.

The last letter was written by Józia Ringelblum on an unknown date, and it is apparently the last sign of life from the Ringelblum family. At the time the letter was written, Józia Ringelblum and the other tenants of the bunker were in a state of extreme stress and great anxiety. Most of the things she wrote (in the last letter) are not clear and cannot be deciphered, and hence we have decided not to print it.

Emanuel Ringelblum: A Historian and His Time

Israel Gutman

To which personality or historian in the past can we compare Emanuel Ringelblum and his life work?

When I consider this question, I find it difficult to suggest a suitable comparison. Since the beginning of historical writing, there have always been reservations regarding the value of writing about current events. As far back as the Greek and Roman periods, however, this reservation was less substantial. For example, both Jews and non-Jews are aware of the power embodied in *The War of the Jews* by Joseph ben Mattathias, better known as Josephus Flavius. He played a prominent role in the battles of the revolt and witnessed the destruction of the Temple and the fateful reversal in Jewish history. As an author he was well-versed in the sources of both adversaries and combined their claims in his powerful descriptions. Yet we cannot ignore the fact that Josephus wrote his books under the protection of the Roman Empire and that his positions, name, and identity underwent far-reaching changes.

If we turn to another historian, closer to our own time, to the Belgian Henri Pirenne, we find that he wrote the first version of his book, *A History of Europe: From the End of the Roman World in the West to the Beginnings of the Western States*, while he was imprisoned in Germany during World War I. This was after he was expelled from his home country, and wrote without access to libraries or any archival material relevant to his subject. However, the conditions in which Pirenne wrote his book would seem like time spent in a comfortable *pension* compared to the Warsaw ghetto, the Trawniki camp, and the confined underground hide out in the Polish quarter of Warsaw.

Emanuel Ringelblum, known as Munio to his friends, was born in 1900, in Buczacz, in eastern Galicia, S. Y. Agnon's native city. The first information about Jews there dates from 1500. In 1848, when the city was under the rule of the Habsburg Empire, many of the restrictive laws relating to the Jews were abolished, and the Buczacz community grew, becoming a regional center of trade in grain. In the year of Ringelblum's birth, 6,730 Jews lived there, constituting 57 percent of its population. Ringelblum's father, a grain merchant, was influenced by the Enlightenment movement and did his best to provide his children with both a Jewish and general education. At the height of World War I, many of the Jews of Buczacz fled from the advancing Russian soldiers into the Austro-Hungarian state. In their wanderings, the Ringelblum family reached the city of Nowy Sącz (Tsanz) in western Galicia, in the Kraków district. This city, where Hasidism exerted a great influence, absorbed the refugees from the East, but also suffered from the Russian invasion. There the young Emanuel completed his secondary-school education, became an eager reader of fine literature and reference books, and expanded his studies of Judaism and the Yiddish language. At the same time he was influenced by socialist ideas and was among the founders of the "Borochov youth" circle in the city.

In 1919, Ringelblum moved to Warsaw, the capital of the reviving Polish state. He enrolled there in the university, and, after much deliberation and overcoming the many obstacles he encountered, he chose to specialize in history. During his studies at the university – far from his home and with no chance of receiving any help from his impoverished family, like many students who flocked to the city from the provinces – he lived from hand to mouth, barely earning a living by giving occasional lessons. His doctoral dissertation was on the first chapter of Jewish life in Warsaw, until the Jews were ousted in 1527. The full approval for the resettlement of Jews in Warsaw, which, in future would be the largest urban concentration of Jews in Europe, was given in the transitional period between the eighteenth and the nineteenth centuries. His work was based on unknown archival material and was published in 1923, by the Warsaw branch of the Society for the Promotion of Polish History. The historian Raphael Mahler defined it as a "classic work in the study of Jewish history in Poland."[1]

Ringelblum belonged to the third generation of historians of Polish Jewry, whose scientific acumen developed in the inter-war period. The first group of history writers focused mainly on outstanding religious figures in Poland and on the history of a select number of communities. The three scholars in the next group – Moshe Schorr, Meir Bałaban, and Yitzhak Schiper, natives of Galicia – worked in Warsaw from the last decades of the nineteenth century until the outbreak of World War II. They are considered the greatest historians of Polish Jewry, as it was they who paved the way for a scientific study of this history. These scholars were also the models for the third generation of historians. Ringelblum was a member of this young generation and, according to Raphael Mahler, was its "standard bearer." Its three leading members perished during the war years: Bałaban died in the Warsaw ghetto; Schiper was murdered in Maidanek; and Schorr was lost in a Soviet prison.

The relatively large group of members of the third generation acquired their professional training and theoretical maturity in Polish universities between the wars. In addition to Ringelblum, some of the promising, outstanding men in this group were Philip Friedman, Jacob Shatzky, and Raphael Mahler. Ringelblum, who did not survive, was the only one of the four who persisted in his writing in Poland under the occupation and showed the others a way of writing historical and documentary material under the conditions of the war and the ghetto. After the war, survivors among this third generation, as well as some who were younger than the members of this large group, were among those who laid the foundations for Holocaust research, particularly from a Jewish vantage point: Philip Friedman, Artur-Aaron Eisenbach, Isaiah Trunk, and Joseph Kermish.

1 Raphael Mahler, "Dr. Emanuel Ringelblum – The Historian of Polish Jewry," in *A Symposium in Memory of Dr. Emanuel Ringelblum* (Hebrew) (Jerusalem: Yad Vashem, 1964), p. 9.

Ringelblum the historian earned his living by teaching in secondary schools and from occasional jobs. "Jewish history" was not considered a separate subject of study in Polish universities; for example, Meir Bałaban was able to find a post in this field only on the academic staff at Warsaw University. The young historians therefore earned their living teaching at private Jewish secondary schools. Ringelblum taught in Warsaw and for some time in Vilna. Even then he was already engaged in organizing circles of historians, editing journals, and public activity. He was closely involved in the activities of the youth movement of Left Poalei Zion and edited articles for the movement's newspapers.

According to his close friend Raphael Mahler, after a hard day's work, Ringelblum would rush to archives in order to take advantage of the last hour before they closed so as to keep up with his research work. He apparently did his writing in the late hours of the evening and night. Mahler's descriptions conjure up the image of an optimistic, energetic man, and an initiator. His physical description is that of a tall, blond young man, with fine facial features, who always charmed people with his smile, "his blue eyes expressing joy of life and generosity."[2]

Nonetheless, he did manage to write a series of books and articles, which earned him the status of a well-known, highly appreciated historian. His works – published as books and articles by many publishing houses in Poland and in the United States, in Yiddish and in Polish – included some on attempts to productivize the Jews at the end of the eighteenth century; Jewish autonomy; various classes in Jewish society, particularly the poor; and the attitude of Polish society and its institutions to Jewish affairs.

His book on the Jews during Kościuszko's 1794 revolt proves that, contrary to what is generally known, not only did a Jewish regiment under the command of Berek Joselewicz take part in the campaign, but also that many ordinary Jews fought alongside the rebels or helped them in various ways. He published an important original monograph on the early stages of the appearance of print-

2 Raphael Mahler, "Emanuel Ringelblum," *Yalkut Moreshet*, *2* (Hebrew) (1964), p. 8.

ing and books among the Jews. Another original work deals with the contribution of Jewish physicians to medicine in Poland. A thoroughly researched work described the colorful figure of Samuel Zabitkower, the progenitor of one of the wealthiest Jewish families in Poland (printed in 1938, in *Zion*, in Jerusalem). Several of his articles dealt with the economic status of the Jews, the custom of early marriages, and the image of the Jews in the Warsaw press in the eighteenth century. He published a series of articles on the Jews in Warsaw from the revival of the Jewish community there, including one on Hasidism and the Enlightenment in Warsaw. He intended to write a second volume on the history of the Jews in the Polish capital and its environs – and apparently he worked on it during the war – but this material was not among the papers he left behind. The three volumes of the history of Warsaw Jewry written by Jacob Shatzky, published in Yiddish and English, draw extensively on Ringelblum's research.[3]

Ringelblum's methodology stems from his choice of subjects from among a number of areas that interested him and his meticulous use of the original documentary material on which he based his writing. A separate text on Emanuel Ringelblum and a complete bibliography of his publications is appended to Shatzky's book on Polish Jewry, published in Yiddish in 1953 in Buenos Aires. In it Shatzky listed 134 titles of books and articles by Ringelblum, most of which were in the field of his research work.[4] In a biographical note from the book published on the symposium devoted to Ringelblum, Mahler stated:

> In September 1939, with the outbreak of the World War, Ringelblum was not yet 39. But he had managed to do so much in the field of research that this "young historian" had already become one of the most eminent historians of Polish Jewry.[5]

3 Jacob Shatzky, *Geshikhte fun Yidn in Varshe* (New York: Yidisher Visnshaftlekher Institut Yivo, Historical Section, 1947–1953).

4 Idem, *Kapitlen geshikhte* (Buenos Aires: Tsentral farband fun Poilishe Yidn in Argentine, 1953, special edition), pp. L–LIX.

5 Mahler, "Emanuel Ringelblum," p. 9.

Another matter that interested several writers after the war was how Ringelblum's ideological and political positions were reflected in his work as a historian. Isaiah Trunk notes in an article on Ringelblum that the two important historians in the inter-war generation, Raphael Mahler and Emanuel Ringelblum, "were faithful to the historical-materialistic method. Ringelblum more in his descriptions of it than in actually putting it into practice."[6]

What Trunk meant by this was that Ringelblum refrained from making any historiographical generalizations and tended to rely on the real picture as it unfolded before him. As an outstanding student of Schiper, he focused on concrete social problems, the product of reality in changing times, and developments and tensions against the background of the interests of various classes in society. We find a similar evaluation, from a different vantage point, in Jacob Shatzky's book on Ringelblum:

> In Ringelblum's writing we can hardly find a trace of Marxist interpretation of Jewish history. Certainly, he presents the facts: there were rich and poor among the Jews, men of authority in the communities and the submissive masses. A few patricians and many plebeians. There were social levels, social differences. There was oppression against this background, and injustice as an outcome, but there were no classes in the classic sense of the Marxist approach. The social dynamics do not in the slightest resemble the dynamics that took place among the non-Jews. The struggle did not have the same character or wield the same influence as it did among "normal" peoples and classes...His philosophy of history was a product of a social orientation based on a subjective interpretation of Marxism which was linked to the idea of national liberation of the Borochov version. Even before he was a historian, he had his own philosophy of history.[7]

6 Isaiah Trunk, *Geshtaltn un geshikhten* (Tel Aviv: Farlag Y. L. Peretz, 1983), p. 152.

7 Shatzky, *Kapitlen Geshikhte*, pp. XXXV-XXXVI.

Mahler had a different commentary on this point. He notes that Ringelblum learned his methodology from his Polish teachers at the university and that the monographic method he applied to his writing aligns him more closely with Bałaban. But Mahler also underscores Schiper's dominant influence:

> His guide, teacher and mentor in the historical method was the eminent historian, Dr. Yitzhak Schiper, whom he admired and remained faithful to throughout his life, although their ways parted insofar as their political views were concerned, especially after the tragic controversy in July 1942 [it is more correct to speak about disagreements rather than a tragic controversy] about whether the time was fit for an uprising in the ghetto...Just as in his political-socialist view Ringelblum was more consistent than Schiper, so too did he tend in his historical view to place more emphasis on social disparities.[8]

In this case Mahler cites as proof Ringelblum's incisive views on the Judenrat. It is doubtful whether one can use controversies under the ghetto conditions as evidence of differences in political and historical positions, but the comments that attest to Ringelblum's objection to Schiper's abandonment of the socialist camp unquestionably reflect the factual situation.

The commentators who analyzed nuances and unique aspects in Ringelblum's historiographic or ideational approach based their conclusions on a short article he published in the party newspaper, *Der Nayer Dor*, in 1924, at the start of his career as a historian. In the article Ringelblum tried, along very general lines, to grapple with a cardinal historical question in Jewish life: Why is it that the Jewish people did not assimilate and disappear during its dispersion among the nations? The major reason, in his view, was that the Jews lived as a minority among other majority peoples, and, as a minority, filled special, separate economic roles at different times, while isolated and leading their own communal lifestyle. Hence the economic factor plays a major role. However, in this argument, he

8 Mahler, "Emanuel Ringelblum," pp. 15–16.

took exception to those who, in their firm adherence to materialism, totally rejected the influence of religion and the spiritual streams in Judaism: "It is clear to every observer that religion played a colossal, if not an exclusive role in Jewish history, in the existence of the Jewish nationality."[9]

Israel M. Biderman, who believes that all of Ringelblum's early activity bore the stamp of Borochovism, although he himself did not at all share views of this kind, wrote about Ringelblum in his book on Bałaban and Jewish historians:

> By the time he was thirty, however, Ringelblum was well respected as a historical researcher. The studies he produced are free of homiletics or political bias. His monographs are factual. His political affiliation finds expression only in his choice of subject matter for research. He lets the sources speak for themselves; he does not burden them with his own exegesis. At the same time he was quite successful in combining his intellectual work with his public activity.[10]

Of course, one can query whether the praise and favorable views voiced by people who are far from the political views that Ringelblum advocated are not dictated by the status and credit he earned during the war. I do not believe that is the case – and perhaps even the opposite is true. It seems that Ringelblum's independent thought and his aspiration to achieve objectivity, based on the material and the facts, enabled him to analyze soberly the critical wartime situation and to do his utmost to unite the Jewish public. His friends' words suggest that he was not a man lacking in moral courage, who was ready to give in easily. When it came to matters of principle or people whom he judged harshly, his position was assertive and unwavering, but, thanks to his easygoing nature and his interest in people with varying political views, many placed their trust in him.

9 A quotation from Trunk, *Geshtaltn un geshikhten*, from Ringelblum's article published in *Nayer dor*, 1 (1924).

10 Israel M. Biderman, *Mayer Bałaban, Historian of Polish Jewry* (New York: I.M. Biderman Book Committee, 1976), p. 286–287.

It is easier to separate Ringelblum the historian from his functions as a public figure in the period preceding the war than it is to premise such a division in the years of the destruction. However, even in his youth he was strongly attracted to social activity. His public work before the war was concentrated mainly among his own age group, his professional colleagues, and his co-members in the movement. Already then he had remarkable organizational skills and original ideas for new initiatives. He was the driving force of the historians' circle of Yivo in Poland, with which the Department of Jewish History at Warsaw University was affiliated. At its meetings the circle discussed subjects on which students and scholars were working. According to Trunk, at that time it was "the only institution of its kind in the Jewish world."

Trunk believes that Ringelblum's zeal and enthusiasm were the driving force behind the publication of two collections of the work of two of these young historians – Ringelblum and Mahler: *Yunger Historiker* ("The Young Historians") and *Bleter far Geschichte* ("Pages of History"). A significant project that he initiated, in 1933, drew special attention. That year, the year of Hitler's rise to power, an international conference of historians was held. Prof. Marceli Handelsman, a convert to Christianity and an eminent historian at the University of Warsaw – who also took a particular interest in Ringelblum – was, to a great extent, in charge of planning and organizing the conference. Only delegations representing various nations attended, but Ringelblum succeeded in convincing the organizers that Jewish historians merited recognition as a separate division. Although they did not represent a state, they were creative scholars in their field in different countries. The participation of young and more well-established [Jewish] historians at the conference was an impressive and unexpected achievement at the time.

In 1933, Ringelblum was given a part-time position with the Polish branch of the Joint and, in 1938, became a permanent employee of that institution. He edited the paper *Folkshilf* of the CKB [Centrala Kas Bezprocentowych], "The Center for Non-Interest Loans." The purpose of this organization was to aid Jews adversely affected by the economic depression and the wave of antisemitism that took the form of an economic boycott. The close relations that developed through his work there with Yitzhak Gitterman, director of the Joint, turned into an ongoing, stable friendship until Gitterman's murder in January 1943.

In the autumn of 1938, Gitterman sent Ringelblum and several other employees to the town of Zbąszýn on the Polish-German border to set up an improvised absorption camp for the thousands of Jews expelled from Germany (the number of Jews who went through Zbąszýn is estimated at 10,000, out of a total of 17,000 deportees). The deportees in Zbąszýn were citizens of Poland, holders of Polish passports – even though some of them had been born in Germany – and most were deeply integrated into the cultural and economic life of that country.

The Polish authorities had decided to check the passports of its citizens in foreign countries and to cancel the citizenship of those who, in their view, and according to the interests of the Polish state, had no justification for staying in foreign countries for more than five years. It was clear that this decision was primarily directed against the Jews, and nearly all of them would lose their civil status. Nazi Germany took advantage of this opportunity even before the matter had been officially decided. In the evening hours of October 27, 1938, they suddenly and cruelly expelled from Germany Jews with Polish citizenship according to a pre-prepared list. Consequently, in the bitter winter cold, thousands of destitute deportees – families and individuals who had lived in Germany for many years – were thrown into an open area near the border. Nazi Germany did not want them, and the Polish state refused to let them into the country despite their citizenship and the fact that either they or their fathers had been born there. This expulsion had indirect implications for the *Kristallnacht* pogrom that was carried out by the Nazis in November throughout the entire German Reich.[11]

Ringelblum remained in Zbąszýn for five weeks, and, with his characteristic empathy, he identified totally with the thousands of

11 On the expulsion of the Jews and the Zbąszýn camp, see Jerzy Tomaszewski, *Preludium Zaglady: Wygnanie Żydów polskich z Niemiec w 1938 r* (Warsaw: PWN, 1998).

miserable refugees. The catastrophe that had engulfed these unwanted Jews may be the first act of deportation that marked the beginning of the period of terror and trampling of human rights that was to ensue. In December 1938, Ringelblum wrote to his friend Mahler in the United States:

> I haven't got the strength or the patience to describe what I went through in Zbąszýn. In any case, I think that the Jewish collective has never known such a savage, merciless expulsion…such brutality, unknown throughout history… Zbąszýn struck a moral blow at the Jewish population in Poland…Consequently, everything leads from the masses of Jews to Zbąszýn and those suffering there…[12]

Meir Korzen, a Joint employee who was also in Zbąszýn and closely observed Ringelblum and his work there, wrote in his memoirs:

> In an atmosphere of strained nerves, depression and tension, Ringelblum worked tirelessly about twenty hours a day. He organized schools for the children, devoted much energy to the youth, many of whom had been in pioneer training camps in Germany, initiated cultural activities and the like… Zbąszýn was an important landmark in Ringelblum's life. There he acquired much experience in public work, which served him later in his activities in the ghetto. Incidentally, from Zbąszýn, Ringelblum brought crates full of documentary material, which he certainly hoped to edit and publish at some future time. In October [1939], when the Germans were already in Warsaw and everyone had destroyed the material that might seem "suspect," I asked Ringelblum what he had done with the material from Zbąszýn. He replied quietly, as if it was the simplest, most natural thing: "It's in my home."[13]

12 Raphael Mahler, "E. Ringelblum's Letter from Zbąszýn and about Zbąszýn," (Hebrew) *Yalkut Moreshet*, II, 1964, p. 24.

13 Meir Korzen, "Emanuel Ringelblum – Before the War and During Its First Days," *Yedioth Yad Vashem* (Hebrew), 23–24 (May 1960), p. 19.

Unfortunately, all that material was lost and was not among the papers that Ringelblum left in the archives of *Oyneg Shabes*.

I think it is correct to say that the underlying pattern of Ringelblum's future activity during the war did, to a great extent, begin to take shape in Zbąszýn. There he witnessed the human catastrophe, the crime of uprooting a person from his home, his work, his native landscape, his property, his relatives. That person was robbed of the essence of his life, his dignity was crushed, and like an unwanted object, he was thrown onto the rubbish heap. There he learned what German Nazism embodied and what one could expect from it — and Ringelblum never forgot that lesson.

In August 1939, he traveled to Geneva on behalf of his party to attend the Twenty-first Zionist Congress. The deliberations of the Congress were held in the shadow of anxiety and uncertainty. Later Chaim Weizmann, president of the Congress, wrote in his book, *Trial and Error: The Autobiography of Chaim Weizmann:*

> On the evening of the twenty-fourth, a day before the closing, I took my leave of the Congress. It was a painful leave-taking in which personal and general forebodings were mingled and hopes expressed that these forebodings might come to naught. I turned to the Polish delegates in particular, saying: "God grant that your fate be not that of the Jews in the neighboring land" — and all of us felt that this indeed was the only prayer we could offer up for them. Most of our Polish friends we never saw again.[14]

Ringelblum returned to his home on the eve of the outbreak of World War II. A few days later, in view of the disquieting news about the breakthrough on the front and the destruction from the air and on the ground, hundreds of thousands of Polish Jews moved eastward. Their hope was that in the eastern area a front would be fortified that would block the German forces. They also wanted to

14 Chaim Weizmann, *Trial and Error, the Autobiography of Chaim Weizmann* (New York: Harper & Brothers, 1949), p. 414.

move as far away as possible from the areas occupied by the Nazi enemy, which was approaching the gates of Warsaw.

Ringelblum wrote in his diary: "More than a hundred telephone calls: Are you leaving?" His brother-in-law, the historian Artur Eisenbach, tried in vain to convince him to join him on his journey.[15]

Ringelblum was enraged when the head of the Warsaw community and prominent figures in the political, general, and municipal areas left, and he denounced them for that. In a September 1939 entry in his diary, he expressed his position in one brief sentence: "The chairman of the community has fled."[16]

Meir Korzen wrote about those days:

> During the siege on Warsaw, under the heaviest bombardments on the city, Ringelblum never missed a day at the office. With a small group of employees of the institution and volunteers he dashed from place to place, under a deluge of falling shells in the burning city, to give help to those who needed it.[17]

In the chaos that prevailed with the beginning of the occupation, the Jewish philanthropic aid agencies collapsed, and the public social help in Warsaw no longer provided any aid to the Jews. There was no solution for the terrible distress of the refugees who poured into Warsaw, those left without a roof over their heads when their homes were destroyed by bombs, or the city's impoverished Jews. In his survey on social aid during the war, Ringelblum stated:

> The Joint earned the right to be acknowledged by history be-

15 Artur Eisenbach's introduction to the Polish edition of Ringelblum's chronicle, Emanuel Ringelblum, *Kronika getta warszawskiego* (Warsaw: Czytelnik, 1983).

16 Israel Gutman, Joseph Kermish, and Israel Shacham, eds., Emanuel Ringelblum, *Diary and Notes from the Period of the War: The Warsaw Ghetto September 1939-December 1942* (Hebrew) (Jerusalem: Yad Vashem, 1992), p. 6 (in most cases the citations from this book are given only with dates).

17 Korzen, "Emanuel Ringelblum – Before the War and in Its First Days," p. 19.

> cause its management remained in place and was always at the head of aid operations while the managements of other institutions such as the community, TOZ [Society for the Protection of the Health of the Jews], CENTOS [Children's Welfare Society] and others fled and left everything behind.[18]

In addition to a fairly large staff of Joint people, its financial resources were also left intact, and, as an institution based in the United States, a country that was not engaged in the war until early 1942, the Joint was still able to receive aid legally. The ŻSS (Żydówska Samopomoc Społeczna), the Jewish self-help organization, was also established under the aegis of the Joint. Later the ŻSS was combined with the RGO (Rada Główna Opiekuńcza), the Central Council for Social Aid, an overall organization for social aid in the *Generalgouvernement* under the aegis of the Germans, located in Kraków. Poles ran the RGO, but it also helped Jews and Ukrainians.

The Jewish branch of this organization in Warsaw actually operated for years as an autonomous unit of the Joint and as a Jewish public council independent of the Judenrat. The aid that came directly from both the Joint and other aid agencies, officially or otherwise, was transferred to ghettos throughout the occupied country. Aid from this source ceased almost completely when the United States joined the war against Germany at the end of 1941.

In the spring of 1940, Ringelblum was appointed head of the social sector of the Jewish Self-Help, which, under his leadership, developed into a department that operated a system of public kitchens, provided care for refugees, and organized a society of "House Committees" that had more than 1,000 public cells in homes often occupied by many hundreds of tenants. Rachel Auerbach, a writer who was also associated with the *Oyneg Shabes*, described how, at Ringelblum's initiative, she ran a kitchen intended for writers and journalists that provided them with a daily portion of soup and a slice of bread. Since she had no equipment for this facility, she and

18 Israel Gutman, Joseph Kermish, and Israel Shacham, eds., Emanuel Ringelblum, *Last Writings: Polish Jewish Relations, January 1943-April 1944* (Hebrew), (Jerusalem: Yad Vashem and Bet Lochamei Hageta'ot, 1993), pp. 1–4.

one of Ringelblum's staff went out to find each item of basic furniture, cooking utensils and food for the empty kitchen.[19]

Dozens of those kitchens, where an equal daily portion of food was distributed, unofficially served as gathering places for groups disseminating culture and for political bodies in the underground, as well as hostels for the youth movements. The children's kitchens had a special function. Many teachers who were unemployed because of the prohibition against Jewish schools were able to teach there. In addition to a more nourishing portion of food, the children also received hours of study, education, and play.

The early curfew required the Jews to shut themselves up in their homes in the evening. As a result, religious and cultural groups were formed, along with a society that disseminated culture and arranged lectures and other activities in the homes. Ringelblum and his friend, the sociologist and demographist Menahem Linder, organized a group of people who loved the Yiddish language and culture. This was called YIKOR (Yidishe Kultur Organizatsye), and the members organized lectures and evenings devoted to Yiddish literature and popular writers. Promoters of Hebrew organized their own group, called Tekumah.

Hundreds of people, mainly intellectuals and artists, were active in the self-help organization. In his memoirs, Jonas Turkow, a well-known actor, relates how intellectuals considered failures in practical life and who had no employment or means of livelihood proved to be effective, devoted men of action in their self-help activity.[20]

The House Committees were headed by ordinary people or businessmen who in the past had never engaged in public activity. Now they were eagerly working in public service and inducing many others to share in providing help to the weakest among the tenants – refugees, orphans, the ill, the impoverished. The committees in houses that were still in a tolerable state sometimes extended a helping hand to those in houses that were in more dire straits.

19 Rachel Auerbach, *Varshever Tsavoes* (Tel Aviv: Israel Buch, 1974), p. 64.

20 Jonas Turkow, *Azoi iz es geven* (Buenos Aires: Tsentral farband fun Poilishe Yidn in Argentine, 1948), pp. 65–67.

The House Committees operated kindergartens, held parties on the holidays or for special events, and were an active public element that frequently stood up to the Judenrat and demanded the rights of the poor and disadvantaged.[21]

However, all the initiatives and achievements of all the branches of the self- help organizations were shattered in the face of the growing hunger and rampant epidemics that were crushing the Jews. In this critical hour many Jews were forced to exchange their private property, the fruit of a lifetime of labor, for basic foodstuffs that were smuggled in through the ghetto wall from the Aryan side of the city at exorbitant prices. But these supplies were also depleted all too quickly.

The Joint funds were running out as well. At the 1940 Passover *seder*, there were still *matzot* on the table along with some of the traditional foods that were distributed in Joint packages. But the financial aid from the Joint and the packages from private people that Jews were permitted to receive (they arrived in considerable quantities from the areas under Soviet control) dwindled rapidly. The shipment of packages from the eastern regions ceased totally with "Operation Barbarossa," the German attack on the Soviet Union in mid-1941. Many of the kitchens closed down, and in the few remaining ones the food that was served had little nutritional value — it was really only a stimulant and an illusion. Starving refugee and poor families were a common sight in the streets.

In May 1941, Ringelblum wrote in his chronicle: "The mortality rate has reached such dimensions that death is wallowing in all the streets. The children no longer fear death…"

Added to the chronic hunger, typhus began to spread rapidly. The congestion, the disintegrating clothing, the lack of fuel for heating, and the lack of soap precipitated the epidemic. The Jews, who for a long time had been resolute, filled with hope that the German evil would have to disappear, now gave up; their spirits broken, they sunk into apathy.

The Polish underground, which was connected to the Pol-

21 Ruta Sakowska, "Komitety domowe w getcie warszawskim," *Biuletyn ŻIH*, no 61 (1967), pp. 59–68.

ish Government-in-exile and which had secret headquarters in an enormous building, had considerable means at its disposal. It ran a network of newspapers and an administrative apparatus proudly called "a state in the underground"; however, it had no presence at all in the Polish ghettos nor did it lift a finger to alleviate the fatal physical and mental suffering of the Jewish citizens. If there was any minute help from the Poles, it was a result of personal connections or an expression of compassion and solidarity by private persons.

In 1941, the situation worsened. That year in the Warsaw ghetto, which the Germans had turned into an "ark of death," 11 percent of all residents slowly perished. Under these circumstances, the self-help organization could do nothing. In an entry from the end of August, Ringelblum bemoaned the fact that:

> the hospitals have for a thousand reasons lost their therapeutic character and have become houses of death…because other than a little soup and some other minor nourishment the patients get nothing to eat…The patients don't die from typhus, really, but because of their weakened condition.

And, in December, he wrote that children in the street "were begging for alms or whining that they have nowhere to sleep…Children weep bitterly at night. Although I hear this weeping every night, I cannot fall asleep until late."

However, shortly before the Great Deportation from the Warsaw ghetto – the deportation that put an end to a period of daily suffering and opened a phase of murder and struggle that lasted less than a year – Ringelblum made the tragic final reckoning of the Self-Help. In his entry for May 26, 1942, he wrote:

> Relief doesn't solve the problem. It only keeps people going a little longer…Relief only lengthens the period of suffering, but is no solution, for in order to really accomplish anything, the relief organization would have to have millions of złotys a month at its disposal and it has no such sums. The well-established fact is that the people who are fed in the public kitchens are all dying out, subsisting as they do only on soup and dry

> rationed bread. So the question arises whether it might not be more rational to set aside the money that is available for the sole use of certain select individuals, those who are socially productive, the intellectual elite and the like. However, the situation is that, in the first place, the elite themselves constitute a considerable group and there wouldn't be enough to go around even for them; and in the second place, why should laborers and artisans, perfectly deserving people, who were productive in their home towns, and whom only the war and the ghetto existence have deprived of their productive capacity – why should they be judged worthless, the dregs of society, candidates for mass graves? One is left with the tragic dilemma: What are we to do? Are we to dole out spoonfuls to everyone, the result being that no one will survive? Or are we to give full measure to a few – with only a handful having enough to survive?

The members of the Self-Help and the Judenrat were divided not only by imposed obedience, on the one hand, and Jewish public considerations, on the other, but also by marked mutual revulsion. According to Ringelblum, the "egalitarianism" practiced by the Judenrat applied only to uniformity in the tax they collected from the meager portion of bread distributed equally among all according to official food cards. These were given to the many beggars and to the few Jews of means who managed to hold on to some of their property, or were among the leading smugglers or workers in the secret workshops. On the other hand, in order to fill the quotas for forced labor in the camps, the Jewish police under the Judenrat chased mainly after the starving and the refugees, those in the worst physical condition. Later, following pressure brought to bear by the Germans to exploit most effectively the Jewish work force, the Judenrat supplied additional food to the forced laborers.

The Jewish Self-Help, in contrast, concentrated on helping children and the chronically hungry. The optimistic, easy-going Ringelblum was strict and meticulous when it came to moral principles that guide human beings. He regarded Abraham Gancwajch, who openly collaborated with the Nazis, and also tried to gather a circle of people around him – including public figures who benefited from his benevolence – as a "leper." Czerniaków, the head of the Judenrat, was, in his view, "a good for nothing," indifferent to the suffering of the masses, an assimilationist who surrounded himself with people of his own kind.

In a diary replete with innumerable details, meetings, and names of Jews, Germans and Poles that Czerniaków kept for nearly three years, Ringelblum's name is not mentioned even once. In a semi-laconic derisive sentence and a half, the head of the Judenrat surveyed one meeting out of many. This was held at Czerniaków's place on May 10, 1941, where the two certainly were present: "The activists of the Self-Help J.U.S. [Jewish Self-Help Organization] and others were here. They are asking us to take 30 percent of the bread cards from the rich and distribute them among the poor, etc."[22]

Ringelblum's reaction to Czerniaków's suicide is also marked by condemnation, although he once said with a trace of charity: "Czerniaków's suicide – too late, a sign of weakness, [he was] too divided internally to resist, but a decent man."

As a matter of fact, it is clear from Czerniaków's diary that many of the accusations made against the head of the Judenrat were not justified. He was forced against his will to acquiesce to the manipulations of the Germans, who cynically depicted the head of the Judenrat as the one who was imposing the baneful decrees on the inhabitants of the ghetto. In any event, while, at the start, Czerniaków seemed to care little about the common people in the ghetto, later he changed. He became sensitive to their fate and felt responsible for it, and tried to gain the esteem of the Jewish public. His suicide should be understood in this light, despite the fact that Ringelblum and other leaders in the ghetto disapproved of him. [23]

This was not the case with regard to the behavior of the Jewish policemen in the ghetto. During the first months that Jews were made policemen – a totally new occupation for Jews – Ringelblum commended them for the restraint and patience with which they

22 Raul Hilberg, Stanisław Staron and Josef Kermisz, eds., *The Warsaw Diary of Adam Czerniaków* (Chicago: Ivan R. Dee, 1999), p. 233.

23 See documents appended to Israel Gutman's article, "Adam Czerniaków – The Man and the Diary," *Yalkut Moreshet*, 10 (1968), pp. 144–155.

carried out their duties. But due to the corruption and arrogance that soon spread through their ranks, as well as their role in abducting Jews to be sent to the forced-labor camps, the ghetto inhabitants grew very hostile toward them and denounced them as criminals and as an alien element.[24]

Ringelblum, who engaged in relief and aid activities, maintained close contacts with people from different political streams on the public council in charge of this activity. The cultural projects that he initiated, in particular the establishment of the underground archives, earned him a prominent place in the underground circles. He believed the various bodies within the underground ought to unite in view of the threat posed by the Nazi regime, and he expressed this opinion both through his activities and his writing. In the biographical sketch that Ringelblum wrote about Shakhna Sagan, the leader of the Poalei Zion underground, he stated:

> The war waged by Nazism against the Jewish population has taken on the nature of physical extermination...For Nazism there was no difference between Zionists and Bundists...They wanted to annihilate both of them. Hence it was necessary to establish a line of struggle in the Jewish society, a uniform Jewish front...of to be or not to be. The [underground] advisory institution from all partisan directions...acted as a permanent body that instructed the Joint, the social self-help, and quite often, the community as well.[25]

David Wdowinski headed the Revisionist stream in the ghetto and was considered the political and spiritual leader of the Jewish Military Union established by the members of Betar close to the time of the uprising. In his memoirs he wrote about Shakhna Sagan, a member of Poalei Zion – from the opposite end of the political spectrum: "He was a very fair and just person, and we always worked together in great harmony in the ZYTOS."[26]

24 Ringelblum, *Diary and Notes*, pp. 391, 407, 428–432.
25 Ringelblum, *Last Writings*, p. 73.
26 David Wdowinski, *And We Are Not Saved* (New York: Philosophical Library, 1963), p. 38.

Nathan Eck, who was also politically far removed from the camp to which Ringelblum belonged but worked in the ghetto with the House Committees, wrote in a book that contains chapters from his memoirs:

> On more than one occasion, I heard complaints about Ringelblum from members of Left Poalei Zion, that he "doesn't look after his friends," that he is "excessively" objective, decent and honest; and not only that, but that the "problem" is that that's his nature and the way he was brought up, and it's very difficult to change it...what they thought was a fault, I considered praiseworthy...[27]

A separate chapter, albeit one that is connected with his overall activity, is that of the *Oyneg Shabes* archives that Ringelblum established and of his own writing, which never ceased, even in his last days in a bunker on the Aryan side.

On November 22, 1939, Ringelblum, together with a small group of friends, established the archival project *Oyneg Shabes*.[28] From the outset the occupiers in Poland conducted their anti-Jewish campaign through the publication of orders and raging violence. Ringelblum and his friends got together to come up with some ideas about how to follow what was taking place and to collect the information and papers that would document the events and prevent the criminals from denying their deeds and responsibility in the future. This mission was the force that drove Ringelblum, the members of his circle, and the many writers of diaries in Warsaw and other places in the midst of the Holocaust. The documentary record, which they regarded as their mission, had to be as full and accurate as possible.

Hirsch Wasser, Ringelblum's close friend, who was the secretary of the archival project, said at a symposium held in memory of Ringelblum at Yad Vashem in 1964:

27 Nathan Eck, *The Lost Ones on the Way to Death: Life and Thought in the Days of Annihilation* (Hebrew) (Jerusalem: Yad Vashem, 1959), p. 25.

28 See "*Oyneg Shabes*," Ringelblum, *Last Writings*, pp. 3–22.

> The most important rule was: to record and collect everything – it was not the right time for adapting and synthesizing. The material received had to be faithful to the truth. It was essential that the future historians receive accurately recorded material about the past. We were obligated by the very fact of our being there – namely, the Jews in the occupied areas – in a situation that had no historical precedent.[29]

Among the list of names of members of the expanded directorate of *Oyneg Shabes* in early 1941, Wasser enumerates people from various public and political streams. Ringelblum was not content to gather material on Warsaw alone. Since the Jewish Self-Help had ongoing contacts with couriers from the provinces, who were permitted to visit Warsaw in order to arrange relief matters, methodical information was also accumulated on what was happening to the Jews in many remote communities. Over time the core of people active in the archives was expanded, and an appropriate team of writers and supporters from diverse sociopolitical groups in the underground and cultural workers from the ghetto joined.

As reflected in Ringelblum's essay on *Oyneg Shabes*, two types of employees were engaged in the work on the archives: dozens of full-time people, who devoted all their time to the archives; and those who were temporarily engaged to work on a one-time basis. In addition to collecting current material on decrees and persecutions, the workers found time to write about a series of singular events caused by the war, such as wandering and deportations, the situation of the refugees, attempts at adjustment, and the search for means of existence. One section investigated the changes that took place in sectors of Jewish society (women, children, and youth), the labor camps, health problems, and the hunger. On the internal Jewish scene, public and cultural activity was researched, as well as the later, unprecedented social phenomena such as the Judenrat, the Jewish police, and the prison.

29 Hirsch Wasser, "The Ghetto Archives – E. Ringelblum's Undertaking," in *Symposium in Memory of Dr. Emanuel Ringelblum* (Jerusalem: Yad Vashem, 1964), p. 18.

In order to cover the various aspects of the developments, surveys were conducted, and monographs by people who had acquired specific knowledge on various issues were commissioned. Prizes were also awarded to writers of outstanding monographs. At home after an exhausting workday, Ringelblum would read the items that flowed into the archives – and, according to Wasser, they all passed through his hands. At first the archives team nearly singlehandedly concentrated on collecting material from non-official Jewish sources, and only after they made progress on this work did they also begin collecting Judenrat and German documentation. The sheer quantity of the material led Ringelblum to write, "It seems to all of us that the time has come to arrive if not at a synthesis, then at least at summaries of certain subjects and important phenomena in Jewish life."[30]

This project was called "two and a half years," and a series of people undertook to work on separate subjects that, when compiled, would provide as complete a picture as possible. However, the project was never implemented. "When many writers were on the verge of completing the entire job or half of it, and the work on 'two and a half years' was about to become work on 'three years of ghetto,' a new disaster descended on the heads of Warsaw Jews." During the *Aktion* and the deportation to Treblinka in July-September 1942, the writers, along with the overwhelming majority of the Warsaw Jewish community, perished.[31]

Ringelblum also attempted to collect diaries written by many Jews during the war years for the *Oyneg Shabes* archives. He regarded these as immensely important documentary sources and tried to persuade the writers to hand over their manuscripts to the archives. The writers, who did not record only the "litany of tribulations" but also exposed their private lives in their recollections, found it difficult to part with their diaries. However, Abraham Lewin's important diary was given to the *Oyneg Shabes* archives, along with others and some excerpts. But only a few pages from the multi-volume diary of Shmuel Vinter, a member of the Judenrat and a public figure

30 Ringelblum, *Last Writings*, p. 6.

31 Ibid., p.7.

with close connections to the underground, was found among the ghetto ruins. Yet a unique diary written in Hebrew by Chaim Aaron Kaplan, a teacher and principal of a Jewish school in Warsaw, was preserved despite the vicissitudes of the war.[32] In an entry dated October 26, 1939, he wrote:

> ...in our litany of tribulations, not even a small detail is missing. Even though today we are in terrible distress and we are in darkness in the noonday sun, we have not lost hope that the time of light will indeed come. Our existence as a people will not become extinct. Individuals will be lost: the Jewish collective will go on living. Hence – every note is more precious than gold, on condition that it is properly recorded, based on facts that contain no exaggerations or hyperbole.[33]

Kaplan completed his last entry a day or two before the deportation to Treblinka, at 8 in the evening of August 8, 1942, with the words: "If my end should come – what will be the fate of my diary!"[34]

Issues of newspapers printed by the various factions of the ghetto underground were also handed over to the archives and preserved. These newspapers, in three languages (Yiddish, Polish, and Hebrew), were printed on a hectograph, distributed in the Warsaw ghetto, and sent to the provincial cities through secret channels. They dealt with the underground activities of the various ideological streams, the political positions that were taking shape in the isolation of the ghetto, and detailed debates and discussions. This material was translated in its entirety into Hebrew and published in six volumes by Yad Vashem.[35]

Ringelblum's own writings from the war years are varied. His best-known work is the diary he wrote in Yiddish in chronological

32 Abraham I. Katsh, ed., *Scroll of Agony: The Warsaw Diary of Chaim A. Kaplan* (Bloomington and Indianapolis: Indiana University Press, 1999).

33 Ibid., p. 57–58.

34 Ibid., p. 399–400.

35 *The Jewish Underground Press in Warsaw*, vols. 1–6, May 1940–July 1944 (Hebrew), Joseph Kermish and Israel Bialystotzki, editors of vols. 1–5, and Israel Shacham, editor of vol. 6 (Jerusalem: Yad Vashem, 1979–1995).

order from September 1939 until the last days of the deportation in the summer of 1942. In their content and style, these notes are actually more of a chronicle than a diary. The writer meticulously followed the events that inundated daily life in the ghetto, took in conversations and rumors passed by word of mouth, recorded his own musings and those of others, and described events that reflected the conduct of the Poles and Germans. Occasionally, his observations contradict one another; the author was not striving for uniformity, but merely describing the reality, absorbing and immediately documenting news, daily life, and diverse and shifting moods. It is reasonable to assume that he had intended to collect raw material and then edit it later into a comprehensive, faithful description of life in the ghetto. Only in rare cases did Ringelblum write about himself and his family, and even then he usually referred to matters that supplemented public knowledge and feelings.

The chronicle was miraculously discovered in its entirety after the war among the ghetto ruins, concealed in one of the two subterranean hiding places in which the archival treasure was stored. Today the material serves as the most important authentic historical source that was left on the life of the Jewish collective in Poland during the war years. The chronicle is a primary source for scholars and readers and has been published in Yiddish, English, Polish, and in a complete, annotated edition in Hebrew. Ringelblum also wrote in the ghetto, and later in the bunker on the Aryan side, an anthology of biographies of prominent Jewish figures who perished and of key activists in the underground during the war. In addition, he wrote, during his stay in the bunker, an extensive essay on Polish-Jewish relations during the war. This essay, written in a place from which he had no access to a library or to newspapers, is actually the basic work for understanding this complex subject.

Among the works that were lost was a monograph by Ringelblum that he wrote about the Trawniki forced-labor camp in the Lublin district, where he was interned for several months. From the bunker in which he and his family, along with about thirty other Jews of various ages, spent the last chapter of their lives, Ringelblum corresponded with Adolf Abraham Berman and his wife Batya Temkin-Berman. Along with details about life in the bunker, he wrote to them about his work plans and urged others to write and collect material from the last Jews still in hiding. The project, conducted on the outside, at constant risk, in hide outs and hiding places in Polish homes, with Batya Temkin-Berman's active participation, was actually a continuation of the work on the *Oyneg Shabes* archives in the ghetto.

In his chronicle Ringelblum occasionally speculated about what percentage of the Jews had a chance to survive under the conditions of occupation and the ghetto. Neither he nor the groups active in the underground could have imagined the horror or the enormous scope of the killing until the mass murder of Jews by the Einsatzgruppen in Operation Barbarossa. Until then he wondered how starving families could reconcile themselves to their fate without rising up against those who still had food and money. In one of his entries he wrote that, "Perhaps the pessimism brought on by hunger leads the Jewish public to go on starving in silence, without voicing any protest."[36]

The first time anyone said that the murder of the Jews in the areas captured from the Soviets was not a one-time outburst of riots against those considered loyal to the hostile regime was in a handbill written by Abba Kovner. In it was also written that Hitler was "plotting to annihilate all the Jews of Europe." This handbill was in the name of a group of underground activists in Vilna and was read out on the last evening of 1941, after the murder of most of the Jews of "Jerusalem of Lithuania." It went on to say: "The Jews of Lithuania have been singled out to be the first in line...true, we are weak and defenseless, but the only answer to the enemy is resistance!"[37]

From then on more and more dreadful news reached the Jews – of terrible deportations and killing in the eastern regions of Poland and the Baltic countries that fell to the Germans; the opera-

36 Ringelblum, *Diary and Notes*, p. 307.

37 "Proclamation by a Jewish Pioneer Youth Group in Vilna, Calling for Resistance, January 1, 1942," in Yitzhak Arad, Yisrael Gutman, and Abraham Margaliot, eds., *Documents on the Holocaust: Selected Sources on the Destruction of the Jews in Germany and Austria, Poland and the Soviet Union and Austria* (Lincoln, NE, London, and Jerusalem: University of Nebraska Press and Yad Vashem, 1999), p. 433.

tion of death camps in Chełmno in the west and in Bełżec in the east; and of deportations from ghettos in occupied Poland.

For a long time Ringelblum believed that the Germans were unhesitatingly sacrificing the lives of the Jews. They were providing meager food to the Jews who were working for them, and others were fated to disappear.

Thus, Ringelblum and his friends were convinced that the self-defense efforts and work had to focus on the weak sectors: the refugees, the intelligentsia who lacked a base of support, and the children. The self-help organization adopted these principles, as well as the slogan "*iberleben*" – to survive. In June 1942, someone who knew what was happening in the Sobibor death camp asked him bitterly:

> Until when will we go "like sheep to the slaughter," why are we keeping silent? Why are we not calling on Jews to go out into the forest, to resist?...And Ringelblum replies in a dialogue with himself that Jews have been doing this in order to enable others to live, because each one knew that to lift a hand against a German means endangering [everyone as well as] brethren in another city or perhaps in another state...It was probably an existential instinct imprinted in the masses that dictated to all how to behave in one way or another. And it seems that no propaganda, no explanation will be of any avail here. It is impossible to fight against the position of the masses. We have to come to terms with it.[38]

In a bulletin *Oyneg Shabes* reported on the course of the murders and deportations throughout the occupied country, but it did not call for an uprising. In the underground press, in contrast, these tendencies recurred often. In January 1942, a Jewish prisoner who had fled from the first death camp in which Jews were gassed arrived in Warsaw. That camp was operated at the end of 1941, in Chełmno, a Polish village west of Łódź annexed to the German Reich. The witness, who worked in the camp, gave *Oyneg Shabes*

38 Ringelblum, *Diary and Notes*, pp. 382–383.

a detailed report of the structure of the place and the method of killing. His testimony was sent on to London through the Polish underground.

On June 26, 1942, less than a month before the beginning of the Great Deportation from the Warsaw ghetto, Ringelblum agitatedly wrote in his chronicle:

> Friday, June 26, has been a great day for O.S. [and until that date he did not mention *Oyneg Shabes* in his chronicle even only by its initials]. This morning the English radio broadcast about the fate of Polish Jewry. They told about everything we know so well: Slonim and Vilna, Lemberg and Chełmno, and so forth. For long months we had been suffering because the world was deaf and dumb to our unparalleled tragedy. We complained about Polish public opinion, about the liaison men in contact with the Polish government-in-exile. Why weren't we reporting to the world the story of the slaughter of Polish Jewry? We accused the Polish liaison men of deliberately keeping our tragedy quiet, so that *their* tragedy might not be thrown into the shade. But now it seems that all our interventions have finally achieved their purpose. There have been regular broadcasts summarizing the situation: 700,000 the number of Jews killed in Poland, was mentioned. At the same time, the broadcast vowed revenge, a final accounting for all these deeds of violence. The O.S. group has fulfilled a great historical mission. It has alarmed the world to our fate, and perhaps saved hundreds of thousands of Polish Jews from extermination (Naturally only the immediate future will prove whether or not the last is true)...We have run a line through his [the enemy's] calculations and have exposed his cards. And if England keeps its word and turns to the formidable massive attacks that it has threatened — then perhaps we shall be saved.[39]

The note that Ringelblum found so stirring contained fresh infor-

39 Ibid., pp. 386–387.

mation broadcast from London, but none of it surprised the British authorities. The intelligence information about the mass murder had been received a bit late and with a certain degree of skepticism, but the reports on the situation in Poland transferred by the Polish underground at set times to the government-in-exile in London had included information on the murder of the Jews on Polish soil. And even if the figures about the Jews were given as part of one lump number relating to the fate of all the Poles – with the stress, generally, on the non-Jewish Poles, it was still enough to make it very clear that the Jews were being exterminated.

In May 1942, the underground of the Jewish socialist party, the Bund, in Warsaw managed, through its Polish friends, to send to London a detailed, chilling picture of the catastrophe that was engulfing the Jews. This document described the wave of mass killings that had begun early in the war between Germany and the Soviet Union and was sweeping across cities and towns in the eastern regions of Poland and Lithuania on its way to the center of the country. It reported on the transport of tens of thousands of Jews to an "unknown destination" and on what was happening in the Chełmno death camp. Until the date when the document was sent, its authors stated, 700,000 Jews had already been exterminated, and, by the end of the war – whenever that might be – the Germans intended to liquidate all of European Jewry. The writers of the document called on the Polish government-in-exile to take immediate steps to prevent the destruction of the Jews and demanded that the Germans who were within the Allies' reach be mercilessly punished.[40]

Ringelblum, and probably the writers of the Bund's letter as well, were deluding themselves by thinking that once the Allies fully internalized the information they would immediately react. It is, of course, impossible to know whether any deliberate acts of punishment and deterrence, if taken, would have stopped the murder. In any event, except for threatening that a reckoning and ret-

40 "In di yorn foon Yidishn khurbn," *Di shtim fun unter erdishn bund* (New York, 1948), pp. 20–23. The author has a copy of the letter that is in the archives of the armed forces in London.

ribution would take place after the war, in actual fact, they took no immediate steps.

The marked contrast between the positions of the two sides is all too clear from what we know today. In all the occupied countries, Hitler and the German state moved full speed ahead with the implementation of the "final solution of the Jewish problem," as the *Fuhrer* declared in his January 1939 speech.[41] The Jews were designated as an enemy in the war, and, with Operation Barbarossa, the pan-European mass murder and deportations began. These were planned and executed by the Germans, along with the auxiliary forces they mobilized. However, from the standpoint of the Allies, the extermination of European Jewry was classified as a civilian matter, outside the domain of the war; that is, it was an issue that ought to be postponed and dealt with only in the days following the Allied victory. The fact that the victims of the unprecedented total murder were Jews in deeply antisemitic Europe, which was being exposed to vociferous Nazi propaganda, may also have contributed to the no-action policy – despite the cries of alarm and the urgent suggestions that the railways leading transports of families doomed to death in the camps should be destroyed.

During the Great Deportation, which began in the last week of July 1942, Ringelblum and his family found temporary shelter with workers in the Hallman shop, a carpentry shop under German ownership at 68 Nowolipki Street. Two parts of the *Oyneg Shabes* archives were later buried in the cellar of that house. Abraham Lewin, who belonged to the small nucleus of archives workers, wrote in his Hebrew diary that, in the midst of the deportation, on August 24, there was:

> A meeting of *Oyneg Shabes* in the house of the guards[42] attended by the members R-m [Ringelblum], G-n [Yitzhak Gitterman], G-k [David Guzik], B-Ch [Eliezer Lipa Bloch], L-n [Abraham Lewin], G-ski [Eliyahu Gutkowski], V-r [Hirsch

41 *Documents on the Holocaust*, p. 132–135.

42 The reference is to the place where the shop workers lived on Milo Street; Lewin also worked in that shop. One of the owners was Alexander Landau.

> Wasser], Shmuel [Breslau], Yosef [Kaplan] and L [Alexander Landau]. Rabbi Huberband, who was caught in the brush-making shop, was absent. The place, the hour and the appearance of the people attending underscored the special tragic nature of the meeting.[43]

The deportation from the Warsaw ghetto led to a radical shift in Ringelblum's view of the world. He concluded that "economic criteria do not apply to the Jews" and that an "*Aktion* of extermination" is all-inclusive. The hopes he had clung to earlier – that self-help, the details of what was taking place being transferred to the Allies, or a reversal on the eastern front would assist in bringing about a large-scale rescue, or would even bring the Jews salvation from the Nazis – were dispelled. During the tense days of the deportations, he participated in deliberations about specific plans of rescue – of children and of an elite group – by moving them to the Polish side of the city. When there seemed to be a chance that some Poles would save a certain number of children, the heart-rending question arose whether it was right to take these children away from their families and their Jewish roots.[44] Individuals who went over to the Polish side, activists of the National Jewish Council, especially the couple Adolf Abraham Berman and Batya Temkin-Berman, who were friendly with Ringelblum and with the Bund activists, suggested the possibility of setting up a rescue channel for a certain number of children.

However, the loss of the people, the terror and the hopelessness of the situation were the major, decisive elements in the metamorphosis that Ringelblum underwent. It expressed itself in his call for resistance and his resolute support of armed revolt. This approach replaced his view of the underground as an endeavor for material aid, protecting human values, and fostering clandestine

43 Abraham Lewin, *A Cup of Tears: A Diary of the Warsaw Ghetto* (Oxford: Basil Blackwell, 1989).

44 Jonas Turkow tells about a special meeting of activists held in Ringelblum's home in the area of the shops, where the issue of saving children was discussed; see Turkow, *Azoi iz es geven*, p. 370; Emanuel Ringelblum, "Priests wish to rescue Jewish children," *Notes from the Warsaw Ghetto*, p. 336.

cultural and socio-political activities. Even earlier Ringelblum had drawn closer to the pioneering Zionist youth movements. The lack of any hope finally won him over to the idea they advocated in the face of the destruction. He also expressed these feelings in writing: "Why didn't we resist when they began to resettle 300,000 Jews from Warsaw? Why did we allow ourselves to be led like sheep to the slaughter? Why did everything come so easy to the enemy?"[45]

He pointed to the cynical deception of the Germans, who sowed confusion and uncertainty and misled the Jews into completely misunderstanding what was going on, "We taught our youth political economics instead of strategy – the people of the book. The education of the young to books, not to daggers. To shoot, to shoot!"[46]

His discerning eye picked up on the rapid reversal taking place. After initial hesitation, the members of the pioneering youth movements reached a decision. At the start of the deportation, they founded the Jewish Combat Organization (Żydówska Organizacja Bojowa – ŻOB). It is not clear whether Ringelblum knew when it was established, but he wrote: "The role the youth played – the only ones who remained on the battlefield, the romantics, the ones with imagination…Shmuel [Breslaw; one of the founders of ŻOB] couldn't bear the catastrophe of the ghetto."[47]

After the attempt to set fire to the warehouses in Hallman's shop on September 6, and after the deportation, Ringelblum felt that it was not only the young people who were changing their views. After the period of enduring such horrible experiences and

45 Ringelblum, *Diary and Notes*, p. 407.

46 Ibid., p.402.

47 Shmuel Breslaw, an *Oyneg Shabes* activist, was one of a group of pioneers discovered on a train from Warsaw to Hrubieszów. This is described only in a note in the book *The Wars of the Ghettos* (Hebrew) (Bet Lochamei Hageta'ot, 1954), p. 106. For a description of the incident, which cost the lives of Breslaw and Yosef Kaplan, another founder of the Jewish Combat Organization, see Yisrael Gutman, *The Jews of Warsaw 1939–1943: Ghetto, Underground, Revolt* (Bloomington: Indiana University Press,1982). (Jerusalem: Hebrew University, Yad Vashem, and Sifriat Hapoalim, 1977), pp. 243–246; idem, *The Revolt of the Besieged* (Hebrew) (Tel Aviv: Moreshet, 1993), pp. 267–270.

the loss of their loved ones, the remaining adults were finally facing the truth, too. On December 5, he wrote:

> Most of the population is set on resistance. It seems to me that people will no longer go to the slaughter like lambs. They want the enemy to pay dearly for their lives. They'll fling themselves at them with knives, staves, coal gas. They'll permit no more blockades. They'll not allow themselves to be seized in the street…[48]

During the break between the deportations from Warsaw, from September 15, 1942 to January 18, 1943, the number of Jews fleeing to the Polish side of the city increased. But very few had this option: primarily it was limited to assimilated Jews, those with close connections with Poles, or property owners who tried to obtain a hiding place in exchange for money or other assets they still possessed. Furthermore, a Pole who gave a Jew a hiding place or helped him in some other way was in danger of being punished by death. Every Jew who crossed over to the "other side" lived in fear not only because of the Germans' unceasing searches for Jews. In fact, the Germans usually did not know how to recognize a Jew by his looks or his Polish accent – but all the Poles did.

When Jews began to infiltrate the Polish side of the city, another phenomenon became common among certain circles of Poles: individuals and organized gangs made a profession of seeking out Jews, looting their property, and turning them in. In addition to the Poles who lurked in waiting near the ghetto walls for escaping Jews, there were also "professional" blackmailers who would follow a Jew, find out where he lived, extort his property and money from him, and through him try to get to other Jewish victims. From time to time, they would hand over those they had thoroughly exploited in order to persuade the Germans that they were being efficient. The existence of this parasitic element in Polish society greatly heightened the danger of hiding both for the Jews and for those Poles who tended to help the persecuted.

48 Ringelblum, *Diary and Notes*, p. 424.

There were fanatic antisemites who informed on Jews and handed them over to the authorities, but there were also individuals among well-known antisemites who extended a helping hand in rescue efforts. Some of the rescuers were motivated by profound humane feelings. The underground was hesitant and late in meting out punishment to the *schmalzowniks* and the informers. Only at the end of 1943, a year and a half after the beginning of the mass murders and many months after the operation of death camps on Polish soil, did the underground that reported to the government-in-exile in London grant its auspices to the rescue mission.

A voluntary body for the rescue of Jews had been founded earlier by a group of enlightened, liberal Catholics within the underground. They engaged in rescue efforts, particularly to save children. The council that was established under the auspices of the general underground and the government-in-exile in London was known as the Council for Aid to Jews (Rada Pomocy Żydom) and was called Żegota. It included representatives of political streams from the Polish center and left, as well as activists of the National Jewish Council and the Bund. The sums of money that were placed at its disposal enabled it to provide meager support to a relatively large number of escaping Jews, most of them in hiding, and opened up a real opportunity for a rescue operation.[49]

Many hid Jews in exchange for payment. However, as Ringelblum noted, no monetary remuneration was too great for the people who loyally and devotedly hid Jews.

Adolf Abraham Berman and his wife Batya Temkin-Berman, who were active in the ghetto underground, moved to the Polish side in the midst of the deportation in early September. Despite the double risk they faced, as Jews and as rescue activists in the underground, they began the rescue work and the help extended to fleeing Jews. Adolf Abraham Berman was the secretary of Żegota and headed the National Jewish Council on the Aryan side. Batya succeeded in contacting Ringelblum from outside the ghetto and

49 Adolf Abraham Berman, *The Days of the Underground* (Hebrew) (Tel Aviv, 1971); Teresa Prekerowa, *Konspiracyjna Rada Pomocy Żydom w Warszawie 1942–1945* (Warsaw: PIW, 1982).

talked to him on the phone. As she relates the conversation with him:

> We urged Ringelblum – we estimated that he, with his [non-Jewish] appearance, could be of benefit on the Aryan side. Besides, it was his duty as an historian to describe the entire period. He, of course, refused to leave his family, and we promised to arrange everything. The first to leave was his 12-year-old son, Uri.[50]

Afterward Ringelblum and his wife also left (under the fictitious name Rydzewski) and moved into different hiding places, which did not live up to his expectations. Ringelblum left the ghetto after the second deportation, between January 12 and 18, 1943, and he continued to be engaged in matters relating to the ghetto even during his activity on the Polish side.[51]

A day or two before the last deportation and the uprising in the Warsaw ghetto, Ringelblum went into the ghetto alone. No one knows what motivated him to do so. According to Temkin-Berman, during his stay on the Polish side, Ringelblum secretly visited the ghetto several times to arrange for the archives to be hidden, and he entered it that last time for the same purpose. According to a different version, he crossed the wall secretly on the eve of Passover in 1942, because he wanted to be among the Jews during the holiday. Both of these versions may be true.[52]

Two days after his arrival in the ghetto, the Great Deportation and the uprising began. Ringelblum was apparently caught near the shops and sent on a transport to the Trawniki labor camp. As a prisoner and worker in the camp, he headed a nucleus of resistance that attempted to store weapons and prepare forged documents and escape from the camp. "Unfortunately," Temkin-Berman writes, "the partisans in this area were from the Armia Krajowa, and they

50 On Ringelblum's last days, see Batya Temkin-Berman, "Pan Rydzewski – Ringelblum's Last Days," *Yalkut Moreshet* (Hebrew), no. 2/1964, p. 13.

51 Turkow, *Azoi iz es geven*, pp. 491–492.

52 Ibid., p. 505.

misled the Jews. No one was waiting for them at the arranged place and they were forced to return to the camp."[53]

When the Jewish underground on the Aryan side learned that Ringelblum was in Trawniki, a complicated release operation was planned. The Pole Teodor Pajewski and the Jewish contact Shoshana (Emilka) Kosower, who were in charge of carrying it out, succeeded in getting him out of the camp. But his transfer by train to Warsaw and the frequent checks on the way presented an even greater danger. The papers and clothing of a railway worker called Rydzewski were prepared for Ringelblum, and finally he arrived safely in Warsaw. As Temkin-Berman testifies, the activists on the Polish side expected that Ringelblum, whose appearance did not give away his Jewishness, would participate in their work, but there were some difficulties in carrying out that plan.

Ringelblum was smuggled out of the camp in June. His family did not believe he was still alive or that they would ever see him again. They were greatly moved by his return, but also very anxious, and they could not bear to part from him. Ringelblum himself complained that the trauma of his months in the camp had left his memory impaired. He felt responsible for the friends who had remained in the camp, and he wanted to make every effort to get them out of there. But probably the most pressing reason for Ringelblum's decision to go into the underground hide out on Grójecka Street was his strong desire to make progress with his writing and to concentrate on efforts to ensure the survival of the written material.

Temkin-Berman writes in retrospect that, "He went down into that accursed hole, to the bunker, and never came out again…" During his stay in the bunker, where more than thirty Jews were hiding in an area of 28 square meters, Ringelblum worked on his writing by the light of a carbide lamp. This may have been his most productive time throughout the war years. In the bunker he composed, in addition to his essay on Polish-Jewish relations during the

53 Temkin-Berman, "Pan Rydzewski," p. 15. On the Armia Krajowa in Lublin and its attitude to the Jewish partisans, see Adam Pulawski, "Postrzeganie żydowskitch oddziałów partyzanckich przez Armię Krajową i Delegaturę Rządu na Kraj," *Pamięć i Sprawiedliwość*, 2(4) 2003, pp. 270–300.

war, the continuation of a series of biographies on leading figures who perished in the ghetto.

Today we possess a detailed document, which for scores of years was in the Ghetto Fighters' House Archives. It is a bundle of letters written by Emanuel and Józia Yehudit Ringelblum from November 25, 1943 to March 3, 1944, a few days before the bunker was discovered and two weeks before its inhabitants and some of its Polish owners were killed.[54] These letters depict a comprehensive and multi-faceted picture of the situation in the bunker, the conditions that prevailed there, the work in which Ringelblum was engaged, and how he encouraged others to write and collect testimonies of Jews in hiding. He himself intended to write the history of the Jewish Combat Organization and of the ghetto uprising.

The letters, in particular the last ones, are pervaded with a sense of imminent disaster. Ringelblum, who was a perennial optimist, had lost his last vestige of hope for survival. In a letter he sent to his friends outside on March 1, he wrote: "I would inform Raphael of the addresses of our warehouses [the place where the archives are hidden]. It would be good already now to appoint Raphael and Aunt Yivo as heirs, in case none of us stay alive after the war."[55]

He was primarily concerned about the historical documentation and wanted to be sure that the information about the horrible suffering and the barbaric murder of the Jews of Europe by the nation that embodied European civilization would be passed on.

On March 7, 1944, after an informant betrayed the location of the bunker at 84 Grójecka Street, Ringelblum, his family, the other Jews living there, and some members of the Polish family that owned the bunker were all taken to the Pawiak prison in Warsaw. Temkin-Berman writes in her article about Ringelblum's last days:

> Every effort was made to save him and we were promised he would not be shot. We received a message that Ringelblum was asking that we send him poison. But one of our contacts

54 See collection of the Ringelblum letters in this book.

55 Ringelblum's letter dated March 1, 1944.

> said that Ringelblum was no longer alive, he had been tortured, they wanted him to give them addresses of other Jews, they sensed they were holding an important person – but he did not give them anything.[56]

There is another record about Ringelblum's last days. In J. Hirshhoyt's memoirs, published in Yiddish in Buenos Aires in 1948, he wrote that a group of inmates in the prison, including "Jews who knew him from the days when he was managing the work in the ghetto," suggested that perhaps he could be saved by having him join a workshop of tradesmen in the prison. Ringelblum asked what would happen to his wife and son. When he realized there was no reply to this question, he turned down the suggestion.[57]

Emanuel Ringelblum and his family, as well as the inhabitants and owners of the bunker were shot to death among the ruins of the Warsaw ghetto. In the March 23 issue of *Biuletyn Informacyjny*, the central weekly of Armia Krajowa, an item of two and a half lines appeared: "On Grójecka Street a hide out was discovered where a *Volksdeutsche* gardener was hiding 37 Jews. They were all shot, including the owner and his wife."[58]

56 Temkin-Berman, "Pan Rydzewski," p. 16.

57 Jacob Shatzky, *Menahem ben Faybish Ringelblum* (Buenos Aires: Tsentral farband fun Poilishe Yidn in Argentine, 1953), pp. 48–49.

58 *Biuletyn Informacyjny*, III, 1944 (Warsaw, 2003), p. 1905.

Writing History as a National Mission: The Jews of Poland and their Historiographic Traditions

David Engel

In late January 1943, Emanuel Ringelblum recorded the history of the endeavor that has come to bear his name – the clandestine archive of the Warsaw ghetto known by the code name *Oyneg Shabes*.[1] At the time Ringelblum stood at a personal crossroads. Some six months earlier, during the mass deportations from the ghetto in the summer of 1942, a portion of the archive had been buried in the cellar of 68 Nowolipki St.; now preparations were underway for concealing the remainder of the documents at the same location.[2] This act effectively obviated a project Ringelblum and his associates had conceived in early 1942 – to assemble from the materials they had collected to that point a broad overview of Jewish life in Warsaw during the thirty months following the outbreak of war.[3] Without immediate access to the materials, the staff of the archive could not write. Ringelblum thus understood that he and his coworkers would not be the ones to relate the story embodied in the documents they had col-

1 Israel Gutman, Joseph Kermish and Israel Shacham, eds., Emanuel Ringelblum, *Ketavim aharonim: yahasei polanim-yehudim, yanu'ar 1943–april 1944* (Jerusalem: Yad Vashem, 1993), pp. 3–22.

2 The second portion of the archive was in fact hidden in the same place about a month later.

3 Ringelblum, *Ketavim aharonim*, p. 6.

lected; that task would be left to those unknown individuals who would one day raise the treasure from its hiding place. Most likely he addressed his history of *Oyneg Shabes* to those future historians, informing them how the collections they had discovered had come into being and how they ought to consider the events and activities he had worked assiduously for years to document.

A principle that guided *Oyneg Shabes* in its work was, according to Ringelblum, the deliberate avoidance of rhetorical flourish in recounting life under Nazi rule. "We strove to describe... what happened in a town, the experience of Jews... in the simplest, most reliable fashion," he explained. "An extra word, a bit of added color, or some literary embellishment was liable to flatten the taste and offend the ear."[4] He even refrained from extolling his own efforts. Only toward the end did he loosen his grip to praise his associates:

> Every individual who took part in the work of *Oyneg Shabes* knew that the burdensome labor, the pain and suffering, the constant danger that attended the drudgery of transporting materials from place to place, were all endured for the sake of a noble ideal, one that society will finally appreciate when liberation arrives. On that day society will bestow [upon the workers of *Oyneg Shabes*] the highest honor in all of Free Europe. *Oyneg Shabes* was a monastic order, a brotherhood that inscribed on its banner [the motto of] self-sacrifice, mutual loyalty, and devotion to the general good.[5]

Ringelblum's pangs of separation from the undertaking he had prized above all else during the previous three years became palpable in these lines. But the text also surprises, for the statement that the archive's staff merited "the highest honor in all of Free Europe" effectively posits a moral equivalence between Ringelblum's documentation work and armed action or entering harm's way in order to save lives or inflict injury upon the enemy. No such scale

4 Ibid., p. 8.

5 Emanuel Ringelblum, *Ksovim fun Geto,* vol. 2; *Notitsn un ophandlungen (1942–1943)* (Warsaw: Yidish Bukh, 1963), p. 102.

of values emerged in any other European resistance movement. To be sure, the large and heralded undergrounds in Poland and France gathered data on the atrocities perpetrated by Germans in their territories and on popular resistance to occupation, but they did so mainly for the benefit of intelligence or propaganda operations, not for preserving the historical record.[6] Though both undergrounds employed professional historians in their documentation divisions,[7] their leaders do not appear ever to have considered putting those scholars' skills to use to achieve what Ringelblum defined as one of *Oyneg Shabes*'s greatest accomplishments – the production of "material... that will serve future generations of historians" by presenting "the whole truth, no matter how bitter," and serve as a faithful record of "the thoughts of different human groups during wartime."[8] European underground movements devoted their resources and energies to activities that would contribute immediately to the war effort. The notion that some of their members might risk their lives for the sake of preserving historical accuracy and that those who did so were no less deserving of praise than those who took weapons in hand – and it was guaranteeing historical *accuracy* that Ringelblum designated as the principal task of *Oyneg Shabes*, not shaping the attitudes of future generations or memorializing the Germans' victims[9] – would have been regarded as idle blather if not dangerous nonsense. Of all the people of occupied Europe, only the

6 On Poland, see Grzegorz Mazur, *Biuro Informacji i Propagandy SZP-ZWZ-AK 1939–1945* (Warsaw: PAX, 1987); on France, François-Georges Dreyfus, *Histoire de la Résistance* (Paris: Fallon, 1996), pp. 122–141.

7 One of the greatest Polish historians, Marceli Handelsman, held a senior post in the Intelligence and Propaganda Department (*Biuro Informacji i Propagandy*) of the Polish underground, in which several future eminent historians of Poland (including Józef Gierowski, Aleksander Gieysztor, Stefan Kieniewicz, and Witold Kula) also served.

8 Ringelblum, *Ketavim aharonim*, p. 10.

9 To be sure, Ringelblum noted that the archive's workers were "thoroughly imbued with a sense of how valuable their work was and how important it was for future generations to preserve [memory of] the tragedy of Polish Jewry" (ibid., p. 7). Still, no intent on his part to select the specific details for preservation is evident. On the contrary, as he put it, "showing as many different sides as possible was the guiding principle of our work" (ibid., p. 10).

Jews of the Polish ghettos[10] appear to have assigned supreme value to activities directed toward the distant future.[11] The documentation project that Ringelblum inaugurated in the Warsaw ghetto thus appears to reflect a unique Jewish cultural attribute whose roots are worth exploring.

To be sure, Ringelblum's words may have expressed nothing more than momentary emotion. Indeed, the heavy heart that beset him at the time should not be taken lightly. In the final entry of his diary, composed in the aftermath of the January 1943 deportation of some 6,000 Jews from the ghetto[12] and the death of his long-time partner in the Warsaw Jewish self-help organization, Yitzhak Gitterman, he sounded an uncharacteristically lachrymose tone. "As I write these words [about Gitterman's death]," he explained, "my hand is trembling. Who knows if the future historian who examines this note [containing a list of the dead] will not add my name – Emanuel Ringelblum."[13] Still, the clandestine archive was not his private affair alone, nor even that of a small circle of ardent enthusiasts. From virtually the moment it was established it became one of the foundation stones of organized conspiratorial activity in the ghetto. It was a public institution in every respect, subject to supervision by the underground political leadership, receiving covert support from the self-help apparatus, in which Ringelblum and sev-

10 Jews in the Italian zone of occupation in France established the *Centre de Documentation Juive Contemporaine* in April 1943. It later defined itself as a "documentary underground" modeled after *Oyneg Shabes*. In truth, however, the *Centre* was founded less out of concern for historical accuracy and more as a way to cope with current needs. Renée Poznanski, "Hakamat haMerkaz leTe'ud yahadut zemanenu beTsarefat: Mitos uMetsi'ut," in Israel Gutman, ed., *MiGenizah leTsiyunei derekh historiyim* (Jerusalem: Yad Vashem, 1996), pp. 161–180.

11 In the event, *Oyneg Shabes* also served immediate needs, chiefly by transmitting information about the actions of the occupier to Jews in the ghettos and to the free world. However, this function appears to have been ancillary to the collection of material for a history of the ghetto; Ringelblum, *Ketavim aharonim*, p. 7.

12 Different sources provide figures ranging from 5,000 to 6,500; Israel Gutman, *Yehudei varshah 1939–1943: Geto, mahteret, mered* (Tel Aviv: Sifriat Poalim, 1976), p. 329.

13 Ringelblum, *Ketavim aharonim*, p. 52.

eral of his associates were active.[14] In other words, not only Ringelblum held historical documentation in high esteem; the bulk of the Jewish resistance movement in Warsaw did so as well. The place the documentation project occupied in the ghetto's scale of values was established long before Ringelblum rhetorically bestowed upon his colleagues the "highest honor in all of Free Europe." Hence the origins of the widespread regard for *Oyneg Shabes* in the ghetto are likely to be found not only in the immediate context of mass extermination but also in a longer tradition that linked the writing of history with public welfare, one that took shape and struck root in the culture of Polish Jews many years before the clandestine archive was founded.

Indeed, Ringelblum himself mentioned that tradition and his own attitude toward it in a short memorial piece for Ignacy Schiper, a senior historian of Polish Jewry who had worked assiduously during the 1920s and 1930s to cultivate the young generation of students of the Polish Jewish past to which Ringelblum belonged.[15] In Ringelblum's view, Schiper (who perished in Majdanek in November 1943) had inaugurated a revolution in Jewish historiography during the first decade of the twentieth century, when he submitted his doctoral dissertation on the economic role of medieval Jewry to the Faculty of Law at the University of Vienna[16] and published a lengthy article on the Jews and the origins of capitalism in the prestigious academic journal, *Zeitschrift für Volkswirtschaft, Sozialpolitik und Verwaltung*.[17] Ringelblum thought that amateurs

14 On the place of *Oyneg Shabes* in the overall resistance and self-help apparatus in the ghetto, see Ruta Sakowska, *Ludzie z dzielnicy zamkniętej* (Warsaw: PWN, 1993), pp. 160–165. The *Centre de Documentation* in France did not receive the same degree of public backing during the war; see Poznanski, "Hakamat haMerkaz," p. 173.

15 Ringelblum, *Ketavim aharonim*, pp. 86–95.

16 The dissertation was published in Polish: Ignacy Schiper, *Studya nad stosunkami gospodarczymi Żydow w Polsce podczaas średniowiecza* (Lwów: Fundusz konkursowy im. Wawelberga, 1911). Ringelblum translated the book into Yiddish in the 1920s. It was published in several editions; Yitzhak Schiper, *Di virtshafksgeshikhte fun di yidn in poyln besn mitelalter* (Warsaw: 1924, 1926).

17 Ignacy Schiper, "Anfänge des Kapitalismus bei den abendländischen Juden im früheren Mittelalter (bis zum anfang des XII. Jahrhunderts)," *Zeitschrift für Volkswirtschaft, Sozialpolitik und Verwaltung*, 15 (1906), pp. 501–564.

like Aleksander Kraushar and Hilary Nusbaum, who had written about Jewish history during the nineteenth century, had been interested only in the Jews' legal status and their relations with the Polish crown. He chided them for representing those relations as friendly and peaceful over the long term and for deriving that representation largely from legendary materials they had failed to subject to scholarly criticism. Similarly, he claimed, the professional historians of Schiper's generation who followed them, led by Majer Bałaban, had overlooked the most important features of Polish Jewish history, even though their work rested upon solid documentary foundations. In his words, although those historians had "produced a picture of [the Jews'] culture and ways of life, of persecutions and [other] significant events in the life of the larger communities, their writings lacked a description of economic realities."[18] Unlike them, he argued, Schiper had illuminated the material dimension of Jewish existence, especially the social tensions he found expressed in communal institutions. Ringelblum quoted approvingly from the introduction to Schiper's 1911 book, *Studya nad stosunkami gospodarczymi żydów w Polsce podczas średniowiecza*, in which the author had taken his predecessors to task for writing only about "the Sabbath and holiday Jew" while ignoring "the weekday, year-round Jew" that formed the subject of his own work.[19] Ringelblum thought Schiper the first Jewish historian to bring historical research to bear upon the solution of contemporary problems of society and government. He praised him for giving prominence to the heroism of the broad Jewish masses, especially the proletariat, and for voicing their affront at being kept from the centers of communal influence

18 Ringelblum, *Ketavim aharonim*, p. 87.

19 Ibid. Ringelblum evidently quoted from his memory; the quotation is not exact. Schiper actually wrote as follows: "Thanks to the great research work carried out by the leading scholars of the Jewish past, from Jost and Graetz through Kayserling, Steinschneider, Harkavy and Dubnow, we have a reasonably reliable picture of the spiritual leaders…However, we still lack a history of the hundreds of thousands of human beings who were sustained not by the spirit but by the labor of their own hands…In a word, we are familiar with the Sabbath Jew and his celebrations. It is now time to become acquainted with his daily life and to shed light on the history of Jewish labor." Schiper, *Studya nad stosunkami*, p. 1.

(and consequently relegated to the margins of historical consciousness). Even though Schiper had eventually abandoned socialism for General Zionism, he wrote, his heart had always been with the common people. Indeed, unlike the other Jewish historians of his generation, who preferred to publish in Polish or German and imitated the style of research and academic writing then popular in western countries,[20] Schiper remained "faithful to the Yiddish language and the popular culture created in that language."[21] Accordingly Ringelblum crowned Schiper "the architect of modern Jewish historiography" and counted himself among his heirs.

From the manner in which Ringelblum described the historiographical tradition he had ostensibly received from his master, it appears that in his view the characteristic that entitled *Oyneg Shabes* to "the highest honor in all of Free Europe" was its ability to fortify the spirit and invigorate the struggle of the ghetto masses in a time of extreme hardship. Indeed, Ringelblum had long assigned the historian's work a similar purpose. In the 1920s, even before completing his studies, he became one of the organizers of the Seminar on Polish Jewish History, which changed its name in the early 1930s to the Historians Circle of the Yiddish Scientific Institute (YIVO) in Warsaw (*historiker-krayz baym YIVO in Varshe*).[22] This group included leading historians of the Jews who received their professional training in independent Poland: Rafael Mahler, Philip Friedman, Isaiah Trunk, Artur Eisenbach, Moshe Kremer, Josef Kermisz, and others. It defined its purpose, in the words of Mahler (who edited its journal, *Bleter far geshikhte*), as "illuminating the dynamics of the Jews' socioeconomic and cultural development, in order to bring scholarship to bear upon the solution of the problems connected with the struggle of the Jewish masses for so-

20 Ringelblum, *Ketavim aharonim*, p. 90.

21 Ibid., p. 91.

22 On the evolution of the seminar and the circle, see Bina Garncarska-Kadary, *BeHipusei derech: Po'alei tsiyon semol bePolin ad milhemet haOlam haSheniyah* (Tel Aviv: Diaspora Research Institute, 1995), pp. 247–248; Cecile Kusnitz, "The Origins of Yiddish Scholarship and the YIVO Institute for Jewish Research," Ph.D. dissertation, Stanford University, 2000, pp. 184–187.

cial and national emancipation in the most efficient way possible."[23] During the 1920s and 1930s Ringelblum himself repeatedly stressed that the working class was both entitled and obliged to demand that historians devote primary attention to its cause, for the proletariat was the sole source of the entire nation's strength and spirit.[24] On that basis many analysts have drawn a direct line between Ringelblum's social, political, and professional activities between the two world wars and the documentation project he established in the Warsaw ghetto.[25] However, even though a significant proportion of those most closely involved with the documentation project were identified with the political left, *Oyneg Shabes* was not an unambiguously class-based enterprise – certainly not in the eyes of such major contributors to its operation as Rabbi Shimon Huberband or the Hebrew teacher Abraham Levin. On the contrary, as an institution claiming communal support it needed to give expression to the widest possible range of social and ideological positions.[26] Presumably, then, the underground Jewish communal bodies that attached importance to the archive and saw fit to direct a portion of their scarce resources to its support were not motivated to do so because its mode of operation matched Ringelblum's particular partisan outlook. Ringelblum's eulogy for Schiper undoubtedly reflected his own personal orientation, but that orientation cannot explain the widespread public backing for *Oyneg Shabes*.

Moreover, Ringelblum's portrayal of Schiper and his place in Jewish historiography is simplistic and at times misleading. It is based primarily upon Schiper's own youthful representation of himself as champion of the disenfranchised classes, one that Ringelblum no

23 [Raphael Mahler], "Fun der redaktzie," *Bleter far Geshikhte* ("Yunger historiker," No. 3), *Historiker-krayz bay der gezelshaft YIVO in Varshe*, Warsaw, 1934, p. 3.

24 Garncarska-Kadary, *BeHipusei derech*, p. 247.

25 Isaiah Trunk, "LeToledot haHistoriyografiyah haYehudit-Polanit," *Gal-Ed*, 2 (1974), p. 264; Raya Cohen, "Emanuel Ringelblum: Between Historiographical Tradition and Unprecedented History," *Gal-Ed*, 15–16 (1997), pp. 112–114; Ruta Sakowska, "Wstęp," *Archiwum Ringelbluma: Konspiracyjne Archiwum Getta Warszawa*, 1: *Listy o Zagladzie* (Warsaw: 1997), p. xii.

26 It was no doubt for this reason that Ringelblum stressed the need to "show as many different sides as possible" when collecting material; see note 9 above.

doubt gladly adopted, as it comported with both his socialist faith and his preferred professional pedigree. True enough, Schiper did demonstrate greater interest than his predecessors and other members of his generation in European Jewish economic history, and he did publish a greater portion of his studies in the Yiddish language. However, his work was not consistently directed toward promoting specifically proletarian class interests. At times, in fact, the opposite was true: his monumental 1937 work on the history of Jewish commerce in Poland, *Dzieje handlu żydowskiego na ziemiach polskich*, was written at the behest of the Central Association of Jewish Merchants in Warsaw in honor of the Association's thirtieth anniversary. Much of it reads like a paean to the Jewish middle class's contribution to Poland's wellbeing, a contribution made despite the obstacles regularly placed in the path of the Jewish bourgeoisie by Polish non-Jewish burghers and their representatives in the political arena.[27] On the other hand, Schiper's purported rival, Majer Bałaban — whose 1942 death in the ghetto prompted Ringelblum to note "the mistaken perspective he adopted toward Jewish studies and the onesidedness of his interests"[28] — was not entirely apathetic to the needs of the weaker strata, neither in his scholarship nor in his public activity. Bałaban's doctoral dissertation on Jewish life in Lwów in the late sixteenth and early seventeenth centuries, submitted at Lemberg University in 1904, concerned itself in large measure with the economic and domestic existence of the common people.[29] In 1931 he published an expanded edition of his monu-

27 Ignacy Schiper, *Dzieje handlu żydowskiego n ziemiach polskich* (Warsaw: Centrala Związku Kupców w Warszawie, 1937), p. v. In the introduction, the author thanked Ringelblum for allowing him prepublication use of a manuscript that included "many invaluable details on the economic life of Warsaw Jewry"; ibid., p. vi. On the Central Association of Jewish Merchants, see Marian Fuks, *Żydzi w Warszawie: Życie codzienne, wydarzenia, ludzie* (Poznań: Daszewica, 1966), pp. 294–295.

28 Ringelblum, *Ketavim aharonim*, p. 98.

29 The dissertation was published in 1906. Majer Balaban, *Żydzi lwowscy na przełomie XVI-go i XVII-go wieku* (Lwów: H. Altenberg, 1906). The section dealing with the Jewish household was published separately a year earlier: Majer Balaban, *Życie prywatne Żydów lwowskich, na przełomie XVI. i XVII. wieku* (Lwów: Kademah, 1905).

mental study of the history of the Jews in Kraków, dedicating all income from sales to the *Nadzieja* society for assistance to tubercular Jewish youth.[30] Bałaban's students at the Institute for Jewish Studies in Warsaw, where he taught history from 1927–39 and was elected to two terms as rector, included several who specialized in economic history, writing theses on such subjects as craft guilds in prepartition Poland and battles over tax collection in the Duchy of Warsaw and the Congress Kingdom.[31] In short, even though differences of emphasis and approach distinguished Bałaban and Schiper, those differences were neither as stark nor as radical as Ringelblum made them out to be. The tradition of militant populist historiography whose standard Ringelblum bore could not by itself have endowed *Oyneg Shabes* with the honor it was accorded in the ghetto, for in the final analysis its roots were quite shallow, and only a relatively small circle of young historians identified with it. The widespread respect that the archive and its workers received must therefore have been rooted in a historiographic tradition different from the one that attracted Ringelblum himself to the undertaking, one that resonated among various social strata and ideological movements beside the working class and revolutionary socialists.

In the event there were two such traditions, and traces of both are evident in the work of *Oyneg Shabes*. Both originated not primarily with Schiper or Bałaban but with the dean of east European Jewish historians, Simon Dubnow. One was born in 1903 following the pogrom in Kishinev, when Dubnow enlisted several of his

30 *Nadzieja* solicited the revised edition of the work, originally published in 1913. Majer Bałaban, *Historia Żydów w Krakowie i na Kazimierzu 1304–1868*, vol. 1: 1304–1655; new enlarged edition (Kraków: "Nadzieja": Towarzystwo ku wspieraniu chorej młodzieży żydowskiej skół średnich i wyższych w Krakowie, 1931), pp. v–vii.

31 Some theses have been preserved in the archives of the Jewish Historical Institute (Żydowski Instytut Historyczny) in Warsaw; microfilms of this collection are in the Information Center of the Inter-University Project for the Study of Illegal Jewish Immigration to Palestine, Tel Aviv University, RG 35, reel 12. See also Abraham Weiss and Pnina Kremer-Weiss, "HaMachon leMada'ei haYahadut beVarshah," *Sefer haShanah/Yorbukh* 1 (1967) pp. 359–380; Israel M. Biderman, *Mayer Balaban: Historian of Polish Jewry* (New York: I.M. Biderman Book Committee, 1976), p. 82.

Odessa colleagues – Ahad Ha'am, Ben Ami, H. N. Bialik, and Y. H. Rawnitzky – in setting up what he later called a "secret bureau for the purpose of gathering every piece of information from the city of slaughter and making [the information] available to our associates abroad for publication in the press and as a means of arousing public protests in Europe and America against the evil regime in Russia."[32] Dubnow and the others considered documentation a central aspect of an all-embracing program of "popular self-help."[33] They did not trust the state authorities to protect the physical safety of Russian Jewry; in fact, they did not believe that the authorities could be counted upon to seek the truth about the pogroms or to bring the perpetrators to justice. Quite the contrary, as Ahad Ha'am explained in a manifesto that both he and Dubnow took part in drafting, the danger that faced Jews in the tsarist empire came not from "the ill-will of certain individuals" but from "the fact that [the Jews] are humiliated and oppressed by the laws of the state themselves."[34] Accordingly they called for organized mass emigration, mainly to North America, and for preparing those Jews who would remain in Russia for self-defense.

Both steps involved action in the political realm. In the first place, both required a climate of tolerance in the countries slated to absorb the migration toward the anticipated tendency of Jewish migrants to settle "in compact masses" in distinct ethnic neighborhoods.[35] Moreover, governments of those countries had to be induced to apply pressure upon the Russian authorities to permit Jews "to defend [them]selves by employing [physical] force on [their] own."[36] The publication of testimonies and documents from the Kishinev pogrom, together with a historical essay on the overall tribulations of Russian Jewry, was meant to advance this campaign

32 Simon Dubnow, "Megilat-setarim shel Ahad Ha'am," *Hatekufah*, *24* (1907), p. 416.

33 Idem, *Michtavim al haYahadut haYeshanah vehaHadashah* (Tel Aviv: Dvir, 1937), p. 105.

34 Idem, "Megilat-setarim," p. 417.

35 Idem, *Michtavim*, p. 108.

36 Idem, "Megilat-setarim," p. 419.

in the international arena.[37] The response of Dubnow and his associates to the pogrom thus wove four strands – flight, physical self-defense, political activism, and documentary compilation – into a unified program of "popular self-help" in which the documentary project supported the remaining components. In this fashion Dubnow charged historians – people skilled in recording events and narrating their course – with an indispensable task in the broad Jewish public struggle for physical safety and material wellbeing. That task, in his view, was no less important than taking up arms against attackers.

In later years Dubnow garnered praise for his own personal example in carrying out the public mission he had assigned Jewish historians.[38] His actions in the aftermath of the Kishinev pogrom served as a model for, among others, the organizers of the Committee to Document and Study the Pogroms in Ukraine, founded in Kiev in 1919 for the purpose of arousing world public opinion against the bloody riots that had claimed upwards of 60,000 Jewish lives in the months following the First World War.[39] The head of the Committee, Eliyahu Tcherikower, later established and directed the Historical Section of YIVO, in which Ringelblum played an active role from its beginning in 1925. Unlike Dubnow, whose plan to publish the Kishinev testimonies was never realized (in part

37 On the structure of the planned book, see Dubnov to Bialik, July 24, 1903, in Simon Rawidowicz, ed., *Sefer Shimon Dubnow* (London-Jerusalem: Ararat, 1953), pp. 332–333.

38 See, for example, Ber Mark, "Shimon Dubnov – Der shefer fun der moderner yidisher historiografie," in Nahman Meisl, ed., *Tsum hundertn geboyrentog fun Shimon Dubnov: Zamlung* (New York: Ikuf, 1961), p. 6. According to Mark, "During the pogrom in Kishinev in 1903, [Dubnow] collected documents that exposed the true face of the tsarist regime and sent them abroad at great risk to himself." In actual fact, Dubnow did not collect any material on his own, nor did he send the material collected by others (in particular Bialik) to western countries. He did plan to publish and disseminate the material worldwide, but the plan was never carried out; see below, note 40. Mark's words attest to the image of the historian-warrior that surrounded Dubnow even when the image was not based upon fact.

39 Zosa Szajkowski, "Di geshikhte fun itstikn bukh," in Elias Tcherikower, *Di ukrainer pogromen in yor 1919* (New York: YIVO Institute, 1965), p. 333.

because of insufficient financial resources),[40] Tcherikower found support among most Jewish public leaders in Poland and elsewhere in eastern and central Europe. The Jewish National Council in Warsaw, headed by Yitzhak Gruenbaum, gave his group many Ukrainian documents in its possession and allotted it a significant monetary stipend. Yitzhak Gitterman also aided the Committee; in his capacity as an official of the American Jewish Joint Distribution Committee in Poland he recorded testimonies of pogrom refugees and even uncovered several important documentary repositories.[41]

Gruenbaum, Gitterman, and the other Jewish communal leaders in Poland and beyond who supported Tcherikower no doubt hoped that his documentary project would serve several interests high on their agenda — interests involving Jewish-Ukrainian relations, organization of migration, refugee absorption, and the position of the Jewish question in international diplomacy.[42] Their support was rewarded in 1927, when the Jew Scholem Schwarzbard went on trial in Paris for assassinating the onetime head of the Ukrainian National Republic, Simon Petliura. Documents obtained from Tcherikower's archive played a decisive role in Schwarzbard's acquittal despite the fact that Schwarzbard had indeed killed the Ukrainian leader, for in the jury's mind they established Petliura's personal responsibility for much of the Ukrainian anti-Jewish violence.[43] The archive also provided the bulk of the material for a com-

40 The complete testimonies were published only in 1991: *Eduyot nifga'ei kishinev 1903 kefi sheNigvu al-yedei H. N. Bialik veHaverav*, edited by Jacob Goren (Tel Aviv: HaKibbutz Hame'uchad, 1991). On the reasons why the work was discontinued in mid-course, see ibid., pp. 39–40.

41 Szajkowski, "Geshikhte," p. 340.

42 See, for example, the correspondence between Gruenbaum and Lucien Wolf, May-June 1921, YIVO Archives, New York, RG 348, file 8.84. See also Yitzhak Gruenbaum, *Milhamot yehudei polaniyah 5673–5700* (Jerusalem: Haverim, 1941), pp. 152–161, 168–170.

43 On the trial, see, *inter alia*, Meir Kotik, *Mishpat Schwarzbard: Retsah nakam al reka haPogromin beUkraina* (Hadera: Niyar, 1972). The role of the Tcherikower archives is reflected in the correspondence between Marvin Lowenthal and the American Jewish Congress concerning the Schwarzbard Defense Committee; American Jewish Historical Society Archives, New York, Stephen Wise Papers, boxes 88, 91. Both Tcherikower and Dubnow were members of the Defense Committee.

pilation of documents about the Ukrainian pogroms that appeared on the eve of the trial. That volume highlighted the tribulations of east European Jewry in general and helped create a favorable climate of public opinion toward Schwarzbard and his deed.[44]

In this fashion the work of the historian revealed itself once again as a supremely significant element in an overall Jewish self-defense strategy. Indeed, on the day following the assassination journalist Avraham Liessin, editor of the prestigious Yiddish-language monthly *Di tsukunft*, wrote that Schwarzbard had "avenged the blood" of the entire Jewish people not only by taking up arms and inflicting injury upon Israel's tormentor, in the fashion of the self-defense groups that had operated in Russia during the 1905 revolution, but also by "put[ting] an end to the murderers' conspiracy of silence" that had enabled Israel's enemies to perpetrate outrage after outrage upon helpless Jews with utter impunity.[45] Liessin's words suggested that anyone who took action against that conspiracy and helped bring the perpetrators of murderous violence to justice – anyone who, as Dubnow put it in a 1922 letter to Tcherikower, worked to ensure that "the Jews' rivers of blood and tears... will not disappear in the sea of the world's misfortunes"[46] – avenged the Jewish people no less than did the one who actually killed the enemy.

Echoes of this notion resound in Ringelblum's essay on *Oyneg Shabes*, and they testify to the influence it exerted upon a significant proportion of the archive's workers and supporters. "There were those who understood," Ringelblum noted, "that the collected material was meant to be distributed throughout the world and to provide information about the acts of brutality being perpetrated against the Jewish population." That realization, he claimed, turned some of the archive's workers from part- to full-time associates.[47]

44 *The Pogroms in the Ukraine under the Ukrainian Government (1917–1920): Historical Survey with Documents and Photographs* (London: J. Bale for the Comité des Délégations Juives, 1927).

45 Avraham Liessin, "Shalom Schwarzbard," *Di Tsukunft* (July 1926), p. 1.

46 Dubnov to Tcherikower, May 19, 1922, quoted in Szajkowski, "Geshikhte," p. 341.

47 Ringelblum, *Ketavim aharonim*, p. 7.

Elsewhere he pointed out that "following the war documents will possess great value for the courts that will put the guilty among the Jews, the Poles, and even the Germans on trial."[48] Still, though, for the most part these functions concerned immediate needs, not the demands of the distant future, which received increasing emphasis in Ringelblum's activity as the hope that any of the archive's directors would survive the war grew ever dimmer. Evidently, then, the defensive tradition, which regarded documentation as a means of resisting an immediate danger or of avenging a recent wrong, was not sufficient to endow *Oyneg Shabes* with its elevated status, especially during the ghetto's final days, when the underground's full energies were directed toward the impending revolt.

In the event, this latter aspect of the archive's work drew upon a second historiographic tradition, also originating with Dubnow, one that had crystallized more than a decade before its defensive counterpart. It originated in two pamphlets that Dubnow published in the early 1890s – one in Russian, entitled "On Studying the History of Russian Jews and the Creation of a Russian Jewish Historical Society,"[49] the other in Hebrew, bearing the name "Let us Search Our Ways: A Summons to Members of the Jewish Intelligentsia Who Will Take It Upon Themselves to Gather Materials for Constructing the History of the Jews in Poland and Russia."[50] In both pamphlets Dubnow contended that neither their biological inheritance nor their religious faith entitled Jews throughout the world to be counted as members of a single nation, only their historical consciousness – "the habit that has become ingrained in us over the course of millennia, the recognition inscribed upon our hearts that we are the oldest of historical peoples, eternal and immortal among the nations."[51] Following the theory of nationality developed by the French writer Ernest Renan in his 1882 essay,

48 Ibid., p. 11.

49 *Ob izuchenii istorii russkikh evreev i ob uchrezhdenii russko-evreiskogo istoricheskogo obshchestva* (Petersburg: A. E. Landau, 1891).

50 *Nahpesah veNahkorah: Kol kore el haNevonim baAm haMitnadvim le'esof homer leVinyan toledot benei yisra'el bePolin veRusia* (Odessa: Abba Duchna, 1892.

51 Ibid., p. 5.

"*Qu'est-ce qu'une nation?*",[52] Dubnow ventured that that historical consciousness would long since have brought Jews a place of honor among the nations of the earth had not Jewish scholars invested their best intellectual energies over the generations in studying and developing Jewish law instead of in documenting their people's past. That neglect, Dubnow lamented, had relegated the Jewish people in the eyes of other nations to the status of "Negroes..., desert savages lacking any history at all, gypsies who live entirely in the present, with no past and no future."[53]

Dubnow viewed this situation with deep anxiety. Citing Cicero that "not to know history is to remain forever an infant," he warned that until Jews increased knowledge of their own history, their status among the nations would remain comparable to that of an infant among adults, bereft of rights and ever dependent upon the beneficence of others.[54] Indeed, he claimed, in the east European political climate of the late nineteenth century, in which the principle that sovereignty inhered in nations, and nations alone were the legitimate constitutors of states, was gaining growing currency, the appearance of Jews as a barbaric mass devoid of history stood to condemn them to constant discrimination, oppression, and persecution. Only by working assiduously to erase the false impression that had resulted from ignoring the documents that confirmed their existence as a "historical people," he suggested, would Jews stand any chance of deflecting the coming catastrophe and of joining together with other peoples of the region in establishing

52 Dubnow quoted Renan's definition of nation as "soul, a spiritual principle," *Ob izuchenii istorii*, pp. 6–7. Cf. also S. M. Dubnov, *Kniga zhizni: Vospominaniia i razmyshleniia* (Moscow-St. Petersburg: Evreiskii Universitet v Moskve, 1998), p. 160. There is no small irony in Dubnow's appeal to Renan, not only because the latter did not regard the Jews as a nation and even hoped for their disappearance from the stage of history, but also because of his postulate that academic study of the past is liable to undermine the myths upon which the historical consciousness that unites nations is founded. For more on Renan's influence on Dubnow, in particular on the relationship between Renan's *Histoire des origines du Christianisme* and Dubnow's studies on hasidism, see Robert Seltzer, "Simon Dubnow, A Critical Biography of his Early Years," Ph.D. dissertation, Columbia University, 1970, pp. 144–150.

53 Dubnow, *Nahpesah veNahkorah*, p. 8

54 Dubnow, *Ob izuchenii istorii*, p. 1.

a regime of true civic and national equality. Accordingly, he proclaimed, "erecting the edifice of history is a *national affair*, meaning that all members of the nation capable of expressing themselves in writing are obligated to take part in it." "Let us set to work," he declared; "let us gather our scattered [documents] from all corners of their dispersion, let us set them in order and reveal them publicly, and then let us erect the foundations of the shrine of history."[55]

Dubnow's call to gather documentary material for the purpose of writing a history of the Jews in Russia and Poland was suffused with the language of redemption. He regarded history writing as the bedrock upon which the security of the Jewish people among the nations of eastern Europe would rest in the coming decades. The historiographical undertaking he urged was thus not meant to serve only immediate needs. It was no less important to him that the right of Jews as individuals and of the Jewish people as a collective to civic and national equality, together with all of the other citizens and nations that comprised the states of the region, be clear to future historians as well. Hence he placed particular emphasis upon the need to go about the work of collection and writing without bias or preconceived notions. Jews must not be afraid to expose their shortcomings and blemishes, he admonished; the Jewish people's longevity and continuity were sufficient to prove the value of its cultural patrimony, and "with such a royal legacy we shall always be able to afford telling the truth" about the past.[56] He believed that one of the primary tasks of Jewish historians was to work according to methods that would inspire trust in their findings and conclusions for generations to come.

The influence of this second tradition, which assigned value to historical writing as a means for solidifying the political status of the Jewish people over the long term, was evident in a number of documentation projects that began during the First World War. On January 1, 1915, for example, the Warsaw Jewish newspaper *Haynt* published a call to east European Jews to "document, record, and gather" materials concerning the spreading conflagration in

55 Dubnow, *Nahpesah veNahkorah*, p. 24.
56 Dubnow, *Ob izuchenii istorii*, p. 90.

their region, with a mind "to preserve for the near and distant future every mark that the march of history leaves upon our people." The authors of the call, led by the writer Y. L. Peretz (who in 1891 had himself employed, without reference to Dubnow, the image of Jews as children because of their purported lack of interest in history[57]), advised that the war would "produce a revolution in the lives of people and nations," in which "national histories... will be weighed upon a giant balance" in order to determine their place in the new world order taking shape on the horizon. If Jews failed to preserve a record of the role they had played in the war and of the suffering it had caused them, they warned, "our account will be empty," and "our [political] rights and our right to justice will be expunged for a long time to come." Hence, the authors advised, "we must become the historians of our participation" in the war, so that those who undertook to represent the case of the Jewish people in the future "would not lack for material from which to extract the truth."[58]

Dubnow himself also took advantage of the opportunity that presented itself briefly following the fall of the tsarist regime to return to the Kishinev pogrom. Even though the matter was no longer urgent, Dubnow devoted considerable energy to publishing a collection of documents about the pogrom that he had discovered in newly-opened Imperial Russian archives, so that "future historians will be able to offer a complete picture of these events and to elucidate their causes objectively." In the introduction to the volume he explained that, in arranging the documents for publication, he had "begun with the notion that in such a complex case each document carries particular importance, and it is preferable to publish... several versions [of a document] in order to shed light upon the events in as complete a fashion and from as many aspects as possible."[59] Dubnow believed that such a multifaceted,

57 Y. L. Peretz, "*Vegn geshikhte*," in idem, *Ale verk*, New York, 12, 1920, pp. 34–36.

58 The call was signed by Y. L. Peretz, Jacob Dineson, and S. An-ski (Rappaport).

59 S. M. Dubnow and G. Ia. Krasnyi-Admoni, eds., *Materialy dlia istorii antievreiskikh pogromov v Rossii*, vol. 1: *Dubossarskoe i Kishinevskoe dela 1903 goda* (Petrograd: 1919), p. v.

objective approach would prove conclusively that the Kishinev pogrom originated chiefly in the desire of the authorities to warn the Jews of Russia against any political activity, especially involvement in the revolutionary movement, so that future historians could come to no conclusion other than that "the old regime fell... among other reasons thanks to the sacrifices offered by Jews upon the altar of Russia's *true* liberation."[60] Publishing the documents thus seemed to him an invaluable weapon Jews might employ in their struggle for civic and national rights in the new Russian state.

Both Dubnovian traditions became doubly important not only to Ringelblum and his associates but to the entire Polish Jewish historiographical enterprise between the two world wars. Their importance reflected to a large extent the esteem in which the writing of history was held in the political culture of the Second Polish Republic. Like their Jewish counterparts, Polish historians of the era assigned themselves and their profession a central role in shaping their community's national consciousness and in promoting its collective political demands. Many of them even became active in the political life of independent Poland and occupied influential public positions.[61] Their attitude was reflected, among other places, in the words of Michał Bobrzyński, dean of contemporary Polish historians, written in 1920: "Academic research today must elicit from our history... those things that are capable of serving as a foundation for our new state...; the new synthesis of our history must be centered about... the question, How did we raise ourselves up from extinction, and by virtue of what moral and physical resources did we manage to establish the state?"[62] Public discourse in the Second Republic was filled with learned exchanges concerning

60 Ibid., p. xxxii. Emphasis in source. The words were written by Gregori Krasnyi-Admoni, Dubnow's co-editor.

61 See, *inter alia*, Stefan Kieniewicz, *Historyk a świadomość narodowa* (Warsaw: Czytelnik, 1982), pp. 162–168; Anita Shelton, *The Democratic Idea in Polish History and Historiography: Franciszek Bujak (1875–1953)* (New York, Boulder, CO: East European Monographs, 1989), pp. 58–59, 90–91.

62 Quoted in Andrzej Grabski, *Zarys historii historiografii polskiej* (Poznań: Wydawnictwo Poznańskie, 2000), p. 167.

the relative contribution of various elements to the state's creation, as if the value of every sector of society and cultural attribute was indeed being weighed upon the "giant balance" of which Peretz and his colleagues had spoken in 1915.

Jews were among the elements whose contribution to the establishment of the state was discussed with keen interest. To their consternation, however, few Polish historians gave them and their continuous centuries-long presence upon Polish soil a positive assessment. Most accepted without question the judgment of such senior scholars as Franciszek Bujak and Stanisław Kutrzeba[63] to the effect that Jews comprised "an element from abroad," lacking any true historical connection to Poland – one that had consistently undermined the country's Polish character,[64] impeded the economic development of the Polish population, and prevented its national aspirations from being fulfilled.[65] Another prominent historian, Roman Rybarski, who served during the 1930s as chairman of the right-wing National Democratic faction in the Polish Sejm, crudely summarized the principal conclusion of most Polish historians with regard to the Jews in 1937, when he declared that "the role played by Jews in our economic history... has been consistently harmful" (*bezwzględnie ujemna*).[66] Such assessments were not confined to the academy but served to justify repeated efforts by successive Polish governments and political leaders to relegate the country's Jews to second-class citizenship and to banish them from their sources of livelihood in preparation for their mass emigration.[67]

63 The two were also leading figures in the political arena; the former in the Peasant Party, the latter in the Christian-Democratic Party (Chadecja).

64 Stanisław Kutrzeba, *La question juive en Pologne: Essai historique* (Kraków: Imprimerie de l'université, 1919), p. 2.

65 Franciszek Bujak, *The Jewish Question in Poland* (Paris: Imprimerie Levé, 1919), pp. 3, 9, 45.

66 Roman Rybarski, *Program gospodarczy* (Warsaw: 1937), p. 113. Rybarski wrote to refute the claim – which he ascribed mainly to Werner Sombart – that "the Jews were the initiators of modern economic development" and that "the Jews are inexorably linked to our economy." In his view it was the Jews themselves who introduced this claim into public discourse, although "a simple chronological review of the facts" would prove its utter falsehood; ibid., pp. 112–113.

67 Bujak raised this idea as early as 1919; Bujak, *The Jewish Question*, pp. 47–48.

No wonder, then, that historians of the Jews active in Poland between the two world wars, of all ideological orientations, hitched themselves to the Jewish national mission of repelling attacks upon their continued existence in the Polish national state. Indeed, one of the principal themes in Jewish historical writing of the period, which the generation of Bałaban and Schiper shared with that of Ringelblum and his contemporaries, was the firm root Jews had struck in Polish soil and the common fate that linked the Jewish and Polish peoples. Historians of the Jews wrote much about how the two peoples had suffered together in times of crisis and about the cultural benefits they had derived from their ongoing interaction. They also stressed the continuing identification of Polish Jews with a specifically *Polish* Jewish community, even after the Polish state disappeared from the political map at the end of the eighteenth century. They were aware that their choice of subjects was influenced decisively by the political context in which they lived. However, they found no fault with that influence. On the contrary, as early as 1926 Ringelblum declared the purpose of the Historians Circle he headed to be "not only to become familiar with the Jewish past but to lay the groundwork for the struggle of Polish Jewry for national and social liberation."[68] He and his fellow Polish Jewish historians regarded their concern with contemporary affairs as a reflection of their commitment to the Dubnovian imperative. As Eliyahu Tcherikower explained in the introduction to the *Festschrift* YIVO presented Dubnow on the occasion of his seventy-fifth birthday, "Dubnow's historicist approach, which is fundamentally oriented toward the present and draws connections between the past and affairs of the day, stands near to the hearts of the present gen-

On the eve of the Second World War the encouragement of emigration was a cornerstone of the Polish government's policy vis-à-vis the Jews. See Emanuel Meltzer, *Ma'avak medini beMalkodet: Yehudei Polin 1935–1939* (Tel Aviv: Diaspora Research Institute, 1982), pp. 313–319.

68 Quoted in Samuel Kassow, "Politics and History: Emanuel Ringelblum and the Oneg Shabes Archives," in Raya Cohen, ed., *European Jews and Jewish Europeans between the Two World Wars* (Tel Aviv: Diaspora Research Institute, 2004), pp. 53–54.

eration of scholars, which is deeply involved in the national and social problems of modern Jewish life."[69]

Interwar Polish Jewish historians hoped no doubt that through meticulous archival research and historical synthesis according to the best practices of the modern academy they would persuade their Polish colleagues of the benefit Jews had brought Poland in the past and could continue to bring in the future. Their effort, however, fell largely upon deaf ears. In 1937 the Polish Historical Association, headed by none other than Franciszek Bujak, published a special double volume of its flagship journal, *Kwartalnik Historyczny*, in honor of the Association's fiftieth anniversary. The volume purported to present a comprehensive picture of Polish historiography in all areas of specialization and interest. Yet in its more than 500 pages Jewish historians were mentioned only once, in a single paragraph from a 35-page article on economic and social history. The author of the article suggested that readers interested in the history of the Jews in Polish cities turn first to surveys by Bujak and Kutrzeba. He also praised two other Polish scholars who had written on the subject. Only toward the end did he mention that "there is a whole series of works on the history of the Jews... written by Jews: [Mojżesz] Schorr, Schiper, Bałaban, Friedman, etc."[70] The hint was clear: Jews who studied their own past could be safely ignored, for they wrote from a parochial perspective that did not meet proper standards of professional objectivity.

Castigation of the ostensibly negative role of Jews in Poland's political and economic life continued to be heard even following the German and Soviet invasions of the country in September 1939. The generally friendly greeting Jews extended to the Soviet occupation forces strengthened the image of the Jews as a foreign, treacherous element in the eyes of many Poles. Accusations were heard about Jewish involvement in black marketeering and price gouging in the German zone of occupation and even about Jewish collaboration with the Nazi authorities. In certain Polish circles it became

69 "Shimon Dubnow tsu zayn 75-yorikn yoyvl," in Elias Tcherikower, ed., *Historishe shriften*, vol. 2 (Vilna: YIVO, 1937), p. xiii.

70 Stefan Inglot, "Rozwój historii społecznej i gospodarczej," *Kwartalnik Historyczny*, 51, nos. 1–2 (1937), p. 401.

commonplace to minimize the gravity of the Jews' situation and to portray them as passive and craven toward the enemy. [71] In February 1940 the Polish underground emissary Jan Karski reported that the "attitude [of the Poles] toward the Jews is overwhelmingly severe, often without pity," adding that the Polish public failed to understand that "both peoples are being unjustly persecuted by the same enemy."[72] Such talk could not help but deepen Jews' anxiety not only over their immediate fate under the German yoke but over their status and security in the Polish state that would be re-established once the country was liberated. Indeed, Jews displayed a well-grounded concern that if the false impression that had been spreading throughout the Polish community from the beginning of the war was not corrected, the end of Nazi rule would witness a renewed round of violence and persecution at the hands of their Polish neighbors. Such persecution would be rationalized, moreover, by reference to histories written by Polish scholars, who would not have access to sources that revealed a true picture of the Jews' situation. Hence Polish Jews came to value complete, reliable documentation, compiled as objectively and reflecting as many different points of view as possible, as an indispensable tool for correcting falsehood.

This was the context in which *Oyneg Shabes* was founded, well before the Jews of Poland could have anticipated impending doom. One of the project's principal tasks in its early stages was without doubt to lay a firm foundation for continued Jewish existence in Poland once occupation came to an end, just as Dubnow and Peretz had assigned a similar purpose to the documentary projects they encouraged.[73] Thus when Ringelblum decided in May 1940 that "it would be useful to endow this important work [of collecting docu-

71 David Engel, *In the Shadow of Auschwitz: The Polish Government-in-Exile and the Jews 1939–1942* (Chapel Hill: University of North Carolina Press, 1987), pp. 60–61, 168–169.

72 David Engel, "An Early Account of Polish Jewry under Nazi and Soviet Occupation Presented to the Polish Government-in-Exile, February 1940," *Jewish Social Studies*, 45 (1983), p. 10.

73 Ringelblum made sure to disseminate information his organization collected among the Polish underground. See Kassow, "Emanuel Ringelblum," p. 78.

ments on the current situation] with a public character,"[74] he managed without difficulty to recruit broad public support and even to persuade a growing circle of volunteers to risk their lives for the "noble ideal" whose banner he carried. The tradition of collecting documents that began with Dubnow at the end of the nineteenth century, combined with the tradition of self-defense dating from the Kishinev pogrom, nourished the strong link between history and resistance, writing and redemption, evident in the written legacy of so many Holocaust victims. The declaration on behalf of his colleagues by *Oyneg Shabes* worker Israel Lichtenstein, who supervised the burial of the two sections of the archive in 1942 and 1943, that "we are the redeeming sacrifice of the Jewish people,"[75] and the observation by Dolek Liebeskind, commander of a Jewish armed underground organization in the Kraków ghetto, that "we are fighting for three lines in history,"[76] sprang in the final analysis from the same cultural soil and represented two aspects of a single idea. It appears that that soil also gave rise to Emanuel Ringelblum's resolute faith that his partners in the "monastic order" he had founded would be greeted upon liberation with "the highest honor in all of Free Europe."

74 Ringelblum, *Ketavim aharonim*, p. 4.

75 Quoted in Joseph Kermish, ed., *To Live with Honor and Die with Honor!: Selected Documents from the Warsaw Ghetto Underground Archives O.S.* (Jerusalem: Yad Vashem, 1986), p. 56.

76 Quoted in Yael Peled (Margolin), *Krakov haYehudit: Amidah, mahteret, ma'avak* (Tel Aviv: Bet Lochamei Hageta'ot, 1993), p. 163.

Not Only *Oyneg Shabes*
Emanuel Ringelblum in the Circles of Social Action

Lea Prais

In his memoirs, Nathan Eck, one of the leading activists of the "public sector" and a refugee from Łódź who lived in Warsaw, pointed out that during the war, Emanuel Ringelblum was most concerned with "work of the present." He wrote:

> Ringelblum thought his public work during the war was of prime importance, but as he came to realize that it was ineffectual and had no chances of success, he began to find consolation in his notes. It was clear that his preoccupation with his historical work was for him a refuge from the present.[1]

It turns out, however, that historians have their own agenda. As a result, we find that in most of the scholarly discussions on Dr. Emanuel Ringelblum's work, the spotlight is naturally turned to his historical activity, and, in particular, to *Oyneg Shabes*, the vast documentation and research project that he initiated and established. His daily activity in the public sector is relegated to the sidelines.

In this article, I should like, therefore, to focus on Ringelblum's social work and on the public sector that he headed. They should be regarded, despite their singular nature, as an inseparable part of

1 Nathan Eck, *The Lost Ones on the Way to Death* (Hebrew) (Jerusalem: Yad Vashem, 1959), p. 29.

the "Jewish self-help organization" in Warsaw after the occupation. This was a small group of dedicated public activists, out of the thousands that were active under the aegis of this sector. In addition, I will point to the link between the social work carried out under the umbrella of the sector and the archival documentation project that was meant to reflect the life and extinction of the Jewish community in Poland during World War II.

The public sector took its first steps in early April 1940. At that time the first signs of the Nazi policy vis-à-vis the Jews of Poland began to impact their lives strongly. More and more Jews became poor and ill, were orphaned, lost their homes, and were wandering from place to place as refugees. In addition, at this time the Joint (JDC) experienced a financial crisis. The well-known Jewish aid organizations were unable to provide significant help to the needy Jews whose number was constantly growing.

Ringelblum read the situation correctly. Moreover, basing his actions on the socialist ideology he advocated, he tried to enlist the constructive forces within the public at large, as well as from the needy population, in order to engage in extensive public activity. This would give some real validity to the concept of "Jewish self-help."

Ringelblum, together with Yitzhak Gitterman, had engaged in public work on behalf of the Joint in Zbąszyń prior to the war, at the end of 1938. The principle that guided Ringelblum and his co-workers in their social activity was to encourage self-help, "rather than the stale spirit of philanthropy," as Ringelblum later wrote to his friend Raphael Mahler.[2] These operative patterns, which had been formulated in the 1920s and 1930s, intensified with the outbreak of the war.

The activities of the bodies that operated under the umbrella of the public sector rose from below, from the broad layers of the population, who enlisted in public work out of a sense of need and urgency created by the reality of the war. Some were volunteers;

2 Israel Gutman, Joseph Kermish and Israel Shacham, eds., *Emanuel Ringelblum, Last Writings: Polish-Jewish Relations, January 1943–April 1944* (Hebrew) (Jerusalem: Yad Vashem, 1994), p. 305.

others received a salary; and only a few were professional public activists. Those, as Ringelblum noted, found positions in the institutions of the Judenrat. The democratic dimension was often expressed in the way these people were selected, but mainly in the sense of trust that the general public, in particular the needy, demonstrated toward them.

At a meeting held on April 4, 1940, attended by Yitzhak Gitterman, Michael Weichert, Abraham Stolzman, Menahem Linder, and Emanuel Ringelblum, heads of the Jewish self-help organization, the basic lines of the sector's activity were laid down. On that occasion Ringelblum stated that the centrality of the House Committees was a fundamental condition of public work.[3] But the public-social activity of the House Committees did not begin with the occupation. According to David Ben-Shalom, who studied the subject, in 1937, a group of Jewish women in Warsaw, headed by Felicia Sznajberg, had established "women's circles." These were house committees composed of women for the sake of the needy, following the increase in their number in Jewish society.

When the war broke out, the House Committees in Warsaw became an instrument used by the authorities for civil defense needs in the face of the wave of bombardments of the city. After the occupation these committees took on new functions, primarily related to the variety of problems affecting the house and its tenants.[4] Therefore, in establishing the public sector within the Jewish Self-Help, Ringelblum was not starting from scratch. The active social infrastructure of the Jewish public, which was spread throughout the city, served as a point of departure for him. However, following the change that had already occurred in the situation of the Jews in the early days of the occupation, Ringelblum understood that all the Jewish public bodies in Warsaw should be activated within one broad, organized framework. This would enhance the social

3 "Protokol fun der tzweiter sitzung fun der reorganizir-komisia dem 4tn April 1940, 8 a zeiger frie," YVA, M.10/AR.2.7.

4 David Ben-Shalom, *Jewish Self-Help as a Framework for the Activity of the House Committees in the Warsaw Ghetto* (Hebrew), M.A. thesis, The Hebrew University of Jerusalem, 1995.

solidarity within the Jewish population and prepare them for the serious changes that were anticipated.

In order to encompass the majority of the Jewish public in Warsaw, which, prior to the establishment of the ghetto, was dispersed throughout the city, the sector aspired to expand its ranks, to set up committees in buildings where none existed, and to transfer them under its auspices. Quite a lot of effort was invested in persuading the committees to join the new unified framework and to pay a sum of money regularly to go to the needy and to the joint organization. Moreover, according to the bye laws that were written, the committees undertook, in time of need, to work beyond the confines of their own house. They were supposed to extend aid to other houses whose tenants had difficulties in establishing their own representative body, or to relief institutions founded for the sake of the weak elements in the community, such as orphanages, soup kitchens, nearby "refugee stations," and the like.

The attempt by Ringelblum and heads of the sector to deepen the sense of solidarity and mutual commitment often fell on deaf ears. Most of the House Committees were concerned with their own problems and their own destitute tenants and naturally tended to confine themselves to the affairs of their own house.[5]

One of the exceptional committee heads who enlisted in general public work was Eliyahu Kahan, head of the House Committee at 23 Nalweki Street.[6] According to Ringelblum, Kahan was one of the people who remained loyal to the ideals of self-help even during the most terrible moments experienced by Jewish Warsaw. Among all of them, he was, as Ringelblum put it, "the first and perhaps the best and the finest." But except for a few reports on his public activity that remained in the *Oyneg Shabes* archives, very little is known about him. In his notes Ringelblum writes that, before the war, Kahan was a successful merchant with no history of public service. He felt the urge to engage in this activity only after the outbreak of the war. Through the House Committee he established, Kahan

5 Eck, *The Lost Ones on the Way to Death, p. 23;* House Committee Report, 23 Nalewki Street, YVA, M.10/AR.1.67.

6 Ibid.

provided aid to the first refugees who had lost their homes during the bombardments of the city and were sleeping in the stairwells or entrances to houses.[7]

Only a few months after the occupation, Kahan, who was described in the report of the House Committee he headed as "the living conscience of the tenants' committee," had foreseen that the situation of Warsaw Jewry was likely to deteriorate. As a result, he took steps to build an orderly, permanent setup for extending public assistance, to replace the spontaneous aid campaigns that randomly cropped up: "spontaneous campaigns and public moods are effective only in the short term…public aid requires a regular tax. This tax will not lose its voluntary nature," he argued before his skeptical co-workers on the House Committee. Kahan and his assistants waged a difficult struggle to realize their plan, and its success, it must be admitted, was only partial.[8]

Over time Kahan worked tirelessly to establish House Committees throughout Warsaw. Within them, he set up aid committees, and, from the wealthier among them, he founded the "patronats." Since they were so vital, Kahan expanded their activity and organized them into a central committee (CKP), headed by him, as a sub-committee within the public sector.[9] On the bloody night of April 17–18, 1942, when fifty-two men were shot to death in the ghetto, Kahan was among the murder victims.[10]

Who were the members of the patronats? Most of them were publicly aware men of means and access, from the House Committees, who organized in the framework of Ringelblum's plan to expand the circle of public activists. The second wave of refugees that inundated the Jewish collective in Warsaw, in the winter of 1941, had an appalling effect on the economic structure of the ghetto, which was shaky in any case. The difficulties that the Judenrat faced in trying to cope with the flow of tens of thousands of Jews who had been abruptly deported and usually left without any means,

7 Ringelblum, *Last Writings*, p. 34.
8 House Committee Report, 23 Nalewki Street.
9 Report of the meeting of the presidium of the central committee of the patronats, YVA, M.10/AR.2.33.
10 Ringelblum, *Last Writings*, p. 34.

made the voluntary institutions in the ghetto indispensable. The patronats were the mainstays of these institutions, particularly in providing initial support to the homeless refugees, who crowded into refugee houses, and to the abandoned children whose number was growing daily. Had it not been for the immediate aid extended by the patronats in the form of food, medicines, and sanitary facilities, the rate of illness and mortality in the ghetto, particularly among the needy, would have been considerably higher than it was in any case.[11]

What did the patronats do? The patronat of the children's home at 18 Mylna Street, for example, was composed of eighteen members (although only three of them were active). They raised money from various sources, including the House Committees, and organized charity performances. The profits were then transferred to the patronat fund for the purchase of food for the children in the home. The average sum that the patronat contributed to the home was somewhat more than 20 percent of its overall monthly expenses.[12] In other institutions – for example, the shelters for refugees – the direct aid of the patronats for the purchase of food and clothing was their only source of income.

The activity of the patronats, however, was not concentrated only on fundraising; they also engaged in daily grassroots work with the needy population. One example is that of the patronat workers at the quarantine at 109 Leszno Street. This institution was one of the tragic focal points of the Jews of the ghetto. It was a holding camp for those Jews who were about to enter the ghetto officially – mostly refugees – as well as for those who returned from forced-labor camps, or were isolated because of the suspicion that they might be infected with typhus.[13] Since the quarantine was outside the area of the closed quarter, far from the public eye, and because of the building's horrific sanitary conditions, the work of

11 On the activity of the patronats in the Warsaw ghetto, see YVA, M.10/AR.1-1104, M.10/AR.1.116; impressions from a visit to the children's home at 29 Ogrodowa Street, on February 28, 1942, ibid., M.10/AR.2.111; Gazeta Żydówska, 18.3.41.

12 Report of the patronat to the CENTOS children, 18 Mylna Street, YVA, M.10/AR.2.95.

13 The quarantine at 109 Leszno Street, ibid., M.10/AR.1.143.

the voluntary patronat workers was a remarkable humanitarian contribution. Each day they left the ghetto with a close escort, and went to a closed building in which hundreds of starving, freezing, ill, and despairing people were interned. As part of their work, the patronat workers received the arriving transport, guarded the belongings that the refugees brought with them to make sure they were not stolen by others in the building, distributed food, took care of medical treatment, and helped those who had completed the isolation process to locate their baggage and find housing. In addition, they served as a channel of communication between the quarantined inhabitants of the ghetto and their relatives for the transfer of food and essential items.

In the introduction to the diary that one of these workers left behind, she wrote:

> We worked voluntarily. Hungry ourselves, we distributed bread to others. As a result of the return from the death (forced-labor) camp at Pomiechowek, those ill with typhus were isolated. Out of nine members of the Patronat who worked at that time, five fell ill, including 27-year-old Isaac Granevicz, our friend, who was the most devoted of us all. He died, leaving a wife and child.[14]

This activity was not the only manifestation of solidarity and social commitment. Women in the ghetto were similarly motivated to take action. The vacuum left in the individual relief work in the dwellings, a considerable proportion of whose tenants became impoverished and also were in need of support, brought to the fore of public service people who formerly had been far removed from any activity for the general good. Women especially filled this vacuum, and, in the framework of women's committees annexed to the house committee, set up public kitchens and relief projects for needy children and orphans.[15]

14 [Diary of a patronat worker]: Quarantine/Leszno 109–111; ibid., M.10/AR.1.143.

15 Adolf Abraham Berman, *In the Place that Fate Assigned me: With the Jews of Warsaw 1939–1942* (Hebrew) (Tel Aviv: Bet Lochamei Hageta'ot and Hakib-

One of their important enterprises was the establishment of an institute to give first aid to the street children, one of the most horrible social phenomena in the ghetto. During February 1942, 1,633 children, the remnants of families who had starved to death and were collected in the ghetto streets by the police, passed through this institution. A report on the women's activities notes that these were homeless children, wrapped in rags, exhausted from hunger and cold. Some of them were incapable of walking because of the sores on their feet; some were brought in such poor condition that soup had to be poured into their mouths through their clenched teeth. Mrs. Strzemeska, one of the leaders of the public sector for women in the ghetto, emphasized that "If we do not remove them from the quagmire of the street, the children will die twice, both morally and physically."[16]

The women actually created the broadest, most solid social infrastructure in the ghetto. Although these frameworks, which encompassed thousands of women, began as a spontaneous initiative, over time they became an organized, formal body that was part of the system run by the public sector in conjunction with the women's sector of the Jewish self-help organization.[17] As we noted, this activity, too, was not the result of an idea dictated from above, but rather a local ad hoc initiative.

Shulamit Mukarski, a refugee from Łódź and a public activist there, was the driving force. She worked tirelessly to introduce branches of the network of women's committees into the house committees, in the apartment houses in the ghetto, and to make sure that women were on the committees of the homes for abandoned children and the shelters for refugees. Mukarski, who over time became a member of the presidium of the central commit-

butz Hame'uchad, 1977), p. 83; Report of House Committee, 23 Nalewki; Ringelblum, *Last Writings*, p. 35.

16 Protocol of a meeting of the public sector for women, 24 February 1942, 5 March 1942, YVA, M.10/AR.2.59.

17 "Tetikayt baricht fun der sektsye far gezelshaftlekher arbet bay der Yiddisher gezelshaft far aleynhilf farn monat februar 1941 1941 yor," YVA, M.10/AR.1.80.

tee of the patronats, alongside Eliyahu Kahan,[18] carried out her public service in Warsaw in the framework of the public sector. At the time of the "great deportation," during the search conducted in the brush shop, Shulamit Mukarski was caught and sent to Treblinka.[19]

The *landsmanschaft*, a society of people from the same city, was another public body run by the sector. Like the house committees, the patronats and the matronats, the *landsmanschaften* were established as an independent initiative. In this case, refugees from the same town or city who fled or were deported to Warsaw banded together, especially as a result of the urgent need to extend help to others from the same locale who were in desperate straits.[20]

However, in Warsaw this type of organization was unique in that it was a new framework and a direct product of the refugee situation imposed on Polish Jewry in the wake of the occupation. For the refugees the representatives of the *landsmanschaft* constituted a reliable, authentic institution and a first-class source of aid, even though they had very meager financial resources at their disposal. Inside the overcrowded and alienated ghetto, the refugees found an intimate, warm shelter in the public kitchens set up by the *landsmanschaften* or an attentive ear to their problems from the committee members.

As the scope of Jewish refugees streaming into the city grew, and the social problems worsened as a result, it became clear that these organizations were very important as a mediating factor between the aid institutions and the needy. However, they also operated independently and directly with the needy. These societies opened public kitchens, organized campaigns to collect funds and essential items, helped find work places for former residents of

18 Report of the meeting of the presidium of the central committee of the patronats.

19 Ringelblum, *Last Writings*, p. 35; Shulamit Makarski (née Brot) was born in Łódź in 1889. She married Yehuda Leib Mukarski and was murdered in 1943, The Central Database of Shoah Victim's Names, YVA, nos. 686680, 738107.

20 Jonas Turkow, *Azoy iz es geven* (Buenos Aires: Tsentral farband fun Poilishe Yidn in Argentine, 1948); *Gazeta Żydówska*, 7.2.1941.

their city, provided religious services, as well as encouragement and advice to those exiled from their homes.

Shulamit Mukraski, who had begun her public service in Warsaw in the Łódź *landsmanschaft*, was one of these representatives. Another representative from the hundreds of others was Bernard Kampelmacher, a refugee from Grodzisk. He had been deported to Warsaw with other residents of his city in the second wave of the deportations in the winter of 1941. In his native city, he had been a school principal and a public activist, but, when he arrived in Warsaw, his world was shattered. He found some consolation in his activity in the *landsmanschaft*, and he invested all of his energy in helping people in Warsaw from his city, some of whom were starving. His first mission was to set up a public kitchen. In a handbill addressed to the former residents of Grodzisk in the ghetto, he wrote:

> We call on all the ex-residents of our city to cooperate, so that there will not be even a single person who does not add one brick to the activities in support of relatives, friends and acquaintances, and so that after the war he will be able to say to himself, with a clear conscience, that in time of need he helped his brethren.[21]

However, like most of the other former residents of Grodzisk, Kappelmacher did not live to see the day of liberation. His intensive work among the starving, sick refugees evidently determined his fate. "In the midst of his work in his *landsmanschaft*," Ringelblum wrote, he contracted typhus and never rose out of his sickbed."[22]

The public sector organized the *landsmanschaften*, and their representatives served on the Central Refugees Committee (Centralna Komisja Uchodźców – CKU) that was later established and became the central institution representing the thousands of refu-

21 Landsmanschaft – Grodzisk and the Vicinity in Warsaw, 58 Żelazna Street, YVA, M.10/AR.1.320; the *landsmanschaft* of the Jews of Sochaczew came out with a similar public call; see "*Sochaczewer yiden*!" YVA, M.10/AR.1.329

22 Ringelblum, *Last Writings*, p. 9.

gees living in Warsaw. Hirsch Wasser, a refugee from Łódź and a member of Left Poalei Zion, was the first secretary of the CKU. He claimed that at first the Jewish refugees were not represented by the apparatuses of the communal administration that determined the fate of the destitute Jews in Warsaw. According to what he described, the refugees in Warsaw were forced to struggle in order to gain recognition and appropriate representation in the institutions handling their affairs. Only then did they have a sense of participation and real involvement in determining their fate. "Nothing that affects us will be done without us," Wasser stated.

His words, written when the ghetto was about to be closed, reflect the problems resulting from the refugees' status and their modes of response in face of the new situation in which they found themselves. They wanted to be subjects, not objects, playing an active role, as an equal partner, in the social actions that concerned them. It was the public sector that established the organizational infrastructure for the realization of their aims.[23]

However, the protocols of meetings left by these bodies indicate that, as time went by, particularly after the ghetto was closed, as a result of the flow of thousands of refugees into its gates and the worsening economic crisis, the appalling ordeal of the Jews became uncontrollable. The activists of the public sector often found themselves helpless in face of this situation. Although between 8,000 and 10,000 activists were on the House Committees alone, there was a growing shortage of voluntary manpower, and this situation grew more severe as time went by. A large proportion of the hostels for refugees and the homeless, which very quickly became health hazards and houses of death, were left without any help and no chance of a basic change in their condition. Over time the inmates of the refugee hostels became people who were present and yet absent, until even persons of public sensitivity and good will demonstrated a crass indifference toward them. This was both because of the fear of being infected by disease and because their suffering, neglect, and helplessness were simply unbearable. At the same time, the re-

23 Joseph Kermish, "The Diary Notes of Hirsch Wasser," *Yad Vashem Studies*, 15 (1983), pp. 170,196.

sources of the patronats were dwindling. Some of them were dismantled, and the sector had a hard time finding replacements.[24]

The central committee of the patronats was also concerned about the difficulty in enlisting more women in activity for the sake of the growing number of destitute Jews. In addition, the *landsmanschaften* and the Central Refugee Committee had no source of finances. When it came to aid, over time they were taken over by the house committees, who naturally gave priority to the needs of the veteran tenants in their houses, who also gradually became recipients of relief.[25] Moreover, numerous complaints were voiced by the ghetto population at large about the nature of the self-help institution's public activity. As a rule, as more time passed and the number of the needy in the ghetto increased, it became abundantly clear that the public bodies were incapable of providing significant aid and reducing the dimensions of sickness and death.

In his memoirs, Adolf Abraham Berman wrote that it was absolutely necessary to admit openly that the social self-help was not able to alter the situation of the masses of refugees. And Ludwik Hirszfeld, a renowned scientist who closely followed the deterioration of the tenants in the shelters in the ghetto, did not hesitate to state in his memoirs that, for humanitarian reasons, it would have been better to bring about their immediate death.[26] In an essay written after the deportation about *Oyneg Shabes*, Ringelblum also wrote that, "Social aid has a right to exist only if it has large sums of money at its disposal and when it has the power to really help the needy. Social work with limited means is a labor in vain."[27]

It is not without reason, then, that Nathan Eck noted that, over time, cracks of disappointment and despair appeared in the resolve and sense of purpose that characterized Ringelblum's social-public activity. Thus, he began devoting himself more and more to his historical work. But in this area, too, his social work made a substantial

24 Protocol of meeting of Central Refugees Committee held on September 10, 1942, September 14, 1942, YVA, M.10/AR.1.1104.

25 Joseph Kermish, ed., *To Live with Honor, To Die with Honor: Selected Documents from the Warsaw Ghetto* (Jerusalem: Yad Vashem, 1986), p. 17.

26 Ludwik Hirszfeld, *Historia Jednego Życia* (Warsaw: Pax, 1957), p. 340.

27 Ringelblum, *Last Writings*, pp. 18–19.

contribution, since at first the work of collecting historical material was focused on taking testimonies from many representatives and refugees who came to Warsaw about what was happening in the Jewish communities in the Polish provinces after the occupation.

In May 1940, the heads of *Oyneg Shabes* decided to endow the documentation project with a public character and to expand its activity. For this purpose people with social and political skills were enlisted in the project. One of these was Hirsch Wasser, who came to Warsaw from Łódź and was active on the Central Refugee Committee. Ringelblum noted that Wasser's involvement and his close contacts with representatives of the refugees made it possible for hundreds of monographs to be written on the fate of the Jews in the provincial towns and cities. These, in Ringelblum's view, were the most important treasures in *Oyneg Shabes*.[28]

To write these notes, Wasser and Eliyahu Gutkowski, the second secretary of the archives and a refugee from Łódź, too, chose the documenters from among the *landsmanschaft* activists. They also appointed suitable people to collect material from former residents of other cities. One of them was Bernard Kampelmacher, who, along with his activity in the *landsmanschaft*, worked, in the framework of *Oyneg Shabes*, at collecting documents and writing a monograph on his town of Grodzisk. Ringelblum wrote about him that he found a balm for his soul.

Another documenter was Mordechai Schwartzbard, a refugee from Łódź, who ran one of the public kitchens set up by refugees from that city in the Warsaw ghetto. He collected notes and letters that were in the possession of people from Łódź, who numbered more than 30,000 in the ghetto, and he also wrote a personal diary.[29] His description of Rumkowski's meeting with the former residents of his city in Warsaw is probably the most accurate and reliable.

Rabbi Shimon Huberband was another of the important se-

28 Ibid., pp. 4–5.

29 Hirsch Wasser, "The Ghetto Archives — Dr. Emanuel Ringelblum's Project" (Hebrew), in *Symposium in Honor of Dr. Emanuel Ringelblum* (Jerusalem: Yad Vashem, 1963), p. 21; Mordechai Schwarzbard, "Notitzn fun geto," *Bleter far Geshikhte*, 8 (3–4) (1955), pp. 106–145.

nior documenters on the *Oyneg Shabes* team. Along with his work of collection and historical writing, he engaged in public activity among the rabbis in Warsaw, the majority of whom were refugees who had fled or were deported with their communities.[30]

Moreover, the refugees in the ghetto unwittingly became the major bearers of information about the mass murders being perpetrated outside of Warsaw, not only as eyewitnesses but also through the letters they received from friends and relatives. Some of these were given over to the *Oyneg Shabes* archives.

Hirsch Wasser and his wife Bluma, also a member of the clandestine archives team, who maintained constant contact with the recently arrived refugees, brought to the ghetto one of the most appalling testimonies to reach Warsaw Jewry. That was the testimony of Szlamek Feiner, who, after being forced to work as a gravedigger in Chełmno, had fled from there and had come to Warsaw. In order to avoid exposing his true identity, he was called Jacob Grojanowski.[31]

In addition, then, to the personal support that the *landsmanschaft* representatives gave to the refugees who had fled, they also engaged in the work of documentation and collection of testimonies. In fact, it is impossible to draw a sharp division between the historical work of Ringelblum and his team and their social activity; these two blended together into one whole.

As a social historian Ringelblum emphasized documenting the daily lives of the entire public during the war. The outgrowth of his intent to present a multi-dimensional, pluralistic, and reliable picture of the events meant that the lives of various sectors and groups were described from a variety of perspectives. The archives team — some of whom were key activists in the public sector — managed to establish a direct relationship of trust with the marginal population of the ghetto. As these people are generally pushed to the wings of the historiographic stage, the collection gave them a rare voice. The unique colors that the archivists used to paint in words the reality around them is what made *Oyneg Shabes* such an extraordinary treasure.

30 "Reshime fun di loinen fun di mitarbeter in geselshaftlekhn sektor," YVA, M.10/AR.2.56.

31 Ruta Sakowska, "Two Forms of Resistance in the Warsaw Ghetto — Two Functions of the Ringelblum Archives," *Yad Vashem Studies* 21 (1991), p. 198–199.

Emanuel Ringelblum: The Man and His Writings
From the Great Deportation to the Ghetto Uprising[1]

Havi Dreifuss (Ben-Sasson)

Dr. Emanuel Ringelblum's life in general and his activity in the Warsaw ghetto in particular have been a focus of scholarly interest since the end of the Holocaust – and for very good reason. His work on behalf of the Zbąszyń deportees, his part in establishing the house committees, his activities in the social self-help organization, and his initiative in starting the *Oyneg Shabes* project to document life in the ghetto are important components in our knowledge of Jewish life during World War II. For this reason many scholars have researched and written about Ringelblum's activity from the outbreak of the war until July 1942, when the majority of Warsaw Jewry was deported to Treblinka.[2] But Emanuel Ringelblum remained

1 This lecture, which was prepared for a conference held at Yad Vashem to mark the sixtieth anniversary of Emanuel Ringelblum's murder, could not have been written and presented without the help of my dear sisters, Moriya Brot and Hilla Ben-Pazi. In addition, I should like to thank Prof. Israel Gutman for his comments and insights.

2 To the bibliography in Israel Gutman, Joseph Kermish and Israel Shacham, eds., Emanuel Ringelblum, *Last Writings: Polish-Jewish Relations, January 1943–April 1944* (Hebrew) (Jerusalem: Yad Vashem and Ghetto Fighters House, 1993), pp. 367–369, the following should be added: the articles collected in Israel Gutman, ed., *From Archives to Historical Milestones* (Hebrew) (Jerusalem: Yad Vashem, 1996), pp. 13–18; Israel Gutman, "Emanuel Ringelblum's Last Request, March 1, 1944," *Yad Vashem Studies*, 31 (2003), pp. 7–9; as well as Samuel Kassow, "Polish-Jewish Relations in the Writings of Emanuel Ringelblum," in Joshua D. Zimmerman, ed., *Contested Memories: Poles and*

in the ghetto even after the deportation, until February 1943, and also entered it on the eve of the uprising in April of that year. What did he do during those last months, and why did we stop taking an interest in Ringelblum and his life after the deportation?

In actual fact, a similar process occurs in relation to the overall Jewish public. Our perception of Jewish society as active and fervent usually applies until July 1942, despite the large amount of existing documentation.[3] Although tens of thousands of Jews continued to live, albeit temporarily, within the ghetto boundaries even after this date, research on Warsaw Jewry after the great deportation shifts from the masses of the people to sub-groups within the Jewish public. It tends to focus on the death of the deportees to Treblinka, on the one hand, and the organization of the youth movements for the armed uprising, on the other.

Unquestionably, knowledge about the defensive measures taken in the ghetto is immensely important, as is an understanding of the fate of the Jews sent to Treblinka. Nonetheless, research on the lives of the Jews of the Warsaw ghetto in the last nine months of its existence should not be neglected, nor should we ignore Ringelblum's activity during this period.

In this article I shall attempt to depict the reality of life in the Warsaw ghetto from the time of the great deportation (July 1942)

Jews during the Holocaust and its Aftermath (New Jersey and London: Rutgers University Press, 2002), pp. 142–157; ibid., "Vilna and Warsaw, Two Ghetto Diaries: Herman Kruk and Emanuel Ringelblum," in Robert Moses Shapiro, ed., *Holocaust Chronicles: Individualizing the Holocaust through Diaries and Other Contemporaneous Personal Accounts* (New York: Ktav Publishing House, 1999), pp. 171–215; Samuel Kassow, "Politics and History: Emanuel Ringelblum and the Oneg Shabes Archive," in Raya Cohen, ed., *European Jews and Jewish Europeans between the Two World Wars*, Michael, 16 (2004), pp. 51–80.

3 Ringelblum, his co-workers on the *Oyneg Shabes* archives and the archives of the Jewish National Council, which largely constitutes its continuation, continued to follow the various strata of Jewish society also in the last nine months of the ghetto's existence. See Israel Gutman, Joseph Kermish and Israel Shacham, eds., Emanuel Ringelblum, *Diary and Notes from the Period of the War: The Warsaw Ghetto September 1939–December 1942* (Hebrew) (Jerusalem: Yad Vashem, 1992), pp. 393–444; ibid., *Last Writings*; Batya Temkin-Berman, "On Our Archives on the Aryan Side" (Hebrew), *Yedioth bet Lochamei hageta'ot*, 2–3 (14–15) (1956), pp. 31–35.

until the ghetto uprising (April 1943), as well as to follow Ringelblum's fate as a man, a public activist, and a historian.[4]

Although so many Jews lived throughout the years of the ghetto's existence under dreadful conditions, this did not prepare them for the greatest catastrophe of the deportation. Throughout the summer of 1942, the majority of the ghetto's Jews were sent to Treblinka and murdered there. In the course of about two months, from the eve of *Tishah B'Av* (July 22, 1942) until the eve of Yom Kippur (September 21), more than 265,000 Jews were deported from the ghetto – where 350,000 had lived prior to that period. In addition, several thousand Jews fled to the Aryan side; about 11,000 were sent to forced-labor camps; and another 10,000 were killed or died inside the ghetto.

The documentation work of Ringelblum and his co-workers on the *Oyneg Shabes* archives was confronted by a new reality: on July 29, 1942, a tragic meeting of the archives' workers took place. Those attending discussed the arrangements of ownership and the ways in which the documents could be transmitted in case all those involved in the documentation work were to perish.[5] A few days later, on August 3, 1942, Israel Lichtenstein, Nachum Grzywacz, and David Graber buried the documents that the *Oyneg Shabes* workers had collected until then in the basement of a house at 68 Nowolipki Street. As Ringelblum wrote: "There was a break of several months in our work. It is impossible to carry out systematic collection work when at every moment there is a constant danger of being caught and sent to Treblinka."[6] He stopped writing his own daily notes, and the overall work on the archives was discontinued for a time. Yet

4 This article does not replace the need for a study of the life of the Jewish public in Warsaw during this period. In the following I will relate only to those aspects that are relevant to Ringelblum's life. For a partial study on this subject, see Havi Ben-Sasson, "'At the Present Time, Jewish Warsaw Is Like a Cemetery': Life in the Warsaw Ghetto during the Great Deportation," in Moshe Zimmermann, ed., *Three Generations of Historians on German and Jews under the Nazi Regime: Festschrift in Honor of Otto Dov Kulka* (Jerusalem: The Hebrew University Magnes Press, 2006), pp. 353–383.

5 Antony Polonsky, ed., Abraham Lewin, *A Cup of Tears: A Diary of the Warsaw Ghetto* (Oxford: Blackwell, 1988), p. 141 (July 29, 1942).

6 Ringelblum, *Last Writings*, p. 21.

even during those horrific days, there were some who carried on with the work of writing and collecting material.[7]

In the first days of the deportation, there was a shortage of food in the ghetto: "The [food] stores were closed from the first day when the destruction of the ghetto began…Smuggling was discontinued and everyone began to feel the shortage of food…within hours the prices rose and concomitantly everyone's mood fell."[8]

A few days later, the lack of food in the ghetto reached immense dimensions, and a considerable number of the ghetto residents were on the verge of death from starvation.[9] The promise of the Germans that, from July 29, 1942, those reporting voluntarily for deportation would receive 3 kilograms of bread and 1 kilogram of jam fell on fertile soil – and particularly on empty stomachs. Thousands reported to the *Umschlagplatz*: Treblinka was still a rumor, while the danger of death by starvation was real.

Emanuel Ringelblum was among the thousands who crowded into the square. He did not volunteer to be deported, but, as a member of the self-help organization, he was among those distributing the bread and jam to the volunteers. He tried to take advantage of his being there to remove Jewish intellectuals from the square: "I will never forget how Mieczysław Szmerling – the commandant of the *Umschlagplatz* on behalf of the Jewish police – attacked me with a whip in his hand because I intervened for the pianist Halina Dikstejn, the artist Regina Mundlak and the economist Dr. J.

7 Lewin, *A Cup of Tears*, pp. 135.242, as well as the following partial list: "a statistical report on the mortality rate in the Warsaw Ghetto," YVA, M.10/AR.2.195; "the demographic structure of the Jewish population in July 1942," ibid., M.10/AR.2.285; Israel Lichtenstein, "Un es iz geshen," ibid., M.10/AR.1-1190; Menahem Kon, "daily notes on the situation in the ghetto," ibid., M.10/AR.2.208; Yehiel Gorny, "the destruction of Warsaw," ibid., M.10/AR.2.198.

8 Logadia Schmidt's diary, YVA, 033.1521, p. 4; see, also, Kaplan, *Scroll of Agony: The Warsaw Diary of Chaim A. Kaplan* (Bloomington and Indianapolis: Indiana University Press, 1999), p. 338 (July 28, 1942).

9 Thus, for example, in the first three days of the deportation, the mortality rate in the ghetto was 200 people a day. During those days and a considerable part of August, most of those who perished died a "natural death," as it was called in the ghetto. See "the statistical report on the mortality rate in the Warsaw ghetto," YVA, M.10/AR.2.195.

Lipowski."[10] But despite Ringelblum's efforts, most of the rescue attempts failed.

In the first week of the deportation, Ringelblum was still able to console himself with the illusion that, even if he were unable to save others, his public position and that of his wife, who ran the CENTOS storeroom, would protect them and their son from deportation. But on July 31, 1942, the number of SS forces and auxiliary units carrying out the deportation increased greatly. As a result, people with papers, who until then had been protected, including many who were employed in the public institutions, were also deported.

In early August 1942, the wife and two children of Shakhne Sagan, Ringelblum's friend and one of the heads of Left Poalei Zion and a public activist, were caught. When Sagan heard that, he rushed to join them, and all the efforts to save him were in vain.[11] For Ringelblum, Sagan's deportation was not only the loss of a close friend, but it also shook his sense of personal security. The deportation brought home to him the fact that his position did not provide any protection for him and his family. Owing to the information he possessed about the murder of Jews throughout Poland, he knew that the real meaning of the "resettlement" – *Umsiedlung*, as the Germans called it – was death. This understanding and the deportation of those with papers apparently prompted him to move his wife Yehudit (Józia) and their twelve-year-old son Uri to a hide out apartment on Nowolipki Street. There they spent the larger part of the long weeks of the deportation.[12]

During this period Ringelblum concentrated his efforts on saving his family and apparently also stayed with them in the hiding place – despite the criticism of some of his friends.[13] But it seems

10 Ringelblum, *Last Writings*, p. 33. See, also, ibid., p. 110; idem, *Diary and Notes*, p. 429.

11 Ibid., *Last Writings,* p. 81.

12 Idem, *Diary and Notes*, p. 439.

13 Yitzhak Zuckerman, *A Surplus of Memory: Chronicle of the Warsaw Ghetto Uprising* (Berkeley: University of California Press, 1993), p. 195; Israel Lichtenstein, "Un es iz geshen," YVA, M.10/AR.1-1190. On the meeting with Ringelblum during the deportation, see also Menahem Kon, "daily notes on the situation in the ghetto," ibid. (August 6, 1942), M.10/AR.2-208.

that even then Ringelblum did not totally abandon his public activity and continued to try to help Jewish intellectuals and those who shared his political and social beliefs to evade the German blockades. Thus, for example, the writer and lecturer Genia Silkes tells how she was saved by Ringelblum from the "Cauldron" *aktion* (Pol. *kocioł*, Yid: *kesl*) that closed the days of the deportation:

> At that moment, when we remained totally alone, when [all] the possibilities of rescue had vanished, the glowing face of our comrade Ringelblum appeared from afar. It is not hard to describe how we felt. He saw us and came towards us, warning us that from this place the first victims would fall…The situation was desperate but Ringelblum's presence encouraged us and somewhat alleviated the horror…Emanuel helped us find a way out […]He moved us to a hiding place…through holes, ruins, backyards and alleys […]He urged us to be careful and parted from us. Now, he can go back…He brought us to the goal. He saved us from the selection.[14]

Although this rescue by Ringelblum was a success, the days of the deportation made it clear to him, as well as to other public activists, that they were incapable of protecting their friends or even themselves and that most of the organizations active in the ghetto were helpless. At this stage most of the social, cultural, educational, and religious organizations that had operated in the ghetto since its establishment, despite the enormous difficulties, were dismantled, and most of their members were sent to Treblinka. Those organizations that had previously survived and, at times, had even been bolstered during the ghetto period also disappeared with the deportation.

That is what happened to the house committees, that vital social system in which Ringelblum had so much faith. In the summer of 1942, most of the tenants were deported from their homes, and

14 Genia Silkes, "Two Meetings with Dr. Ringelblum," YVA, Jerusalem.1209/44.1. I am grateful to Ms. Leah Preiss for referring me to this important collection and in particular to this source.

the activity in the courtyards became meaningless. Moreover, the Jews who were permitted to remain in the ghetto (albeit temporarily) were uprooted from their homes, and this had a destructive effect on the texture of the life that had existed in the ghetto prior to the deportation. The sense of cohesiveness and the life of mutual responsibility that had characterized many houses and other social frameworks – and which had been an important part of the way Jewish society coped with the reality of life in the ghetto – were severely undermined.

In this article I am unable to describe the horror of the days of the deportation: the uncertainty of the masses of Jews, the existential ordeal of families and individuals, and the widespread German brutality that became a daily routine that went on day after day for nearly two whole months. But during the summer of 1942, the Warsaw community changed disastrously: about 90 percent of the men and women who had lived in the ghetto in the past were brutally murdered. Among the children and the elderly this figure was 99 percent. The disappearance of the elderly and the children from the streets of the ghetto had a decisive effect on the way the Jews perceived their past and their future both from a public and a personal standpoint: on the public level, the murder of the children symbolized the loss of the future of the Jews. On the personal level, the extermination of the elderly proved that an older Jew had no chance of surviving the period of the Nazi occupation. Moreover, the very fact that the chances of an individual's survival largely depended on his/her age and gender (the relative female majority prior to the deportation was replaced by a male majority) – traits that are not given to human control or to change – manifested for many their inability of influencing their fate.[15]

15 Adolf Abraham Berman, *The Days of the Underground* (Hebrew) (Tel Aviv: Hamenorah, 1970), p. 57; Peretz Opoczynski, the history of the Warsaw ghetto (December 10, 1942) YVA, M.10/AR.2.289; Eugenia Szajn-Lewin, *In the Warsaw Ghetto: July 1942–April 1943* (Hebrew) (Tel Aviv: Ghetto Fighters House, 1990); Yehoshua Perle, "4580 [remarks by a worker in the shops]," YVA, M.10/AR.2.245; Yitzhak Katznelson, *Last Writings* (Hebrew) (Tel Aviv: Bet Lochamei Hageta'ot and Hakibbutz Hame'uchad, 1988), p. 51.

> In the deserted ghetto, night after night, a hoarse bark is heard...the last dog. This last dog in the ghetto, in his orphaned bark, sends a shudder through one's bones. When a man tosses on his bed at night and in his exhausted mind, his sleep wanders, this bark resonates like the scream of thousands of ruins. The wail of an orphaned dog against the background of a large city in ruins. And what casts a greater terror? When the dog stops his wailing for a moment, the ceaseless whistle of trains is heard, and that is no less terrifying. These are not trains that bring greetings from far-off places, from open fields, but from sites of massacre and murder and from slaughter houses. The trains themselves seem to be wailing in their loneliness like the last dog in the ghetto.[16]

At the end of the deportation, only 35,000 Jews who were able to prove they were employed in German factories (*"shops"*) inside the ghetto or outside it (*platzuvkas*, pl: *placówka*) were allowed to remain within the boundaries of the ghetto. In addition, there were another 15–20,000 "wild" Jews, illegal Jews who had hidden and evaded the deportation.

During the days of the deportation, Emanuel Ringelblum lost people very dear to him. For example, in mid-August, Shimon Huberband, his co-worker on the archives, was taken. Ringelblum wrote about him: "A noble soul; it is hard to find men of his ilk in these times."[17] And in early September, his brother Leon, his sister-in-law Sela, and their three-month-old son were murdered.[18]

Even after the deportation ended, those left in the ghetto could no longer delude themselves as to their future: "We know that we are all doomed to die. We just do not know the date of our execution."[19] Those with economic resources and connections on the Pol-

16 Opoczyński, The History of the Warsaw Ghetto (October 9, 1942).

17 Ringelblum, *Last Writings*, p. 26.

18 Lewin, *A Cup of Tears*, p. 180 (September 15, 1942).

19 Writings of Stefan Ernest, Archives of the Jewish Historical Institute, 302.195, p. 195. See also, Ringelblum, *Last Writings*, pp. 424, 437.

ish side tried to leave the ghetto, while those without any means had no choice but to remain.[20]

In view of the violence and the loss, Ringelblum's wife also wanted to leave the ghetto as soon as possible. Fortunately for them her husband had the necessary resources and connections to move his family, and, first of all, his son, Uri. Adolf Abraham and Batya Temkin-Berman, public activists who had moved to the Aryan side in early September, helped find a devout Christian family who agreed to take Uri into their home. There was some delay in his departure from the ghetto for an unforeseen reason, about which Ringelblum later wrote:

> There were children who resolutely objected to being moved to the Aryan side, they did not want to go to the 'other side,' and preferred to die with their parents. It took me a long time to convince my son that it was important for our people to save as many of our children as possible.[21]

In the end Uri gave in to his parents' appeals, and soon afterward his mother left the ghetto, too. After a brief stay in a temporary hiding place, Józia Yehudit Ringelblum explicitly asked to move to the bunker at 81 Grójecka Street, where she was joined shortly by her son.[22]

Emanuel Ringelblum remained in the ghetto and invested all of his energy in his renewed public activity. But the ghetto after the deportation was totally different than it had been before, and not only in its human composition. The "small ghetto" and the southern part of the "large ghetto" were returned to the Aryan side of the city, and three islands were created in the remaining area: the

20 See, for example, Lewin, *A Cup of Tears*, p. 188 (October 5, 1942).

21 Ringelblum, *Last Writings*, p. 239. Jonas Turkow asserts that there was a prior attempt to get the boy out of the ghetto during the great deportation. According to him, although Uri Ringelblum had a "good appearance," he was returned to the ghetto because the Poles were afraid to hide circumcised children. This description is not corroborated in any other sources. Jonas Turkow, *Once There was a Jewish Warsaw* (Hebrew) (Tel Aviv: Tarbut veHinukh, 1970), pp. 144–145.

22 Batya Temkin-Berman, "Pan Rydzewski – Ringelblum's Last Days," *Yalkut Moreshet*, No. 2/1964 (Hebrew), p. 13.

central ghetto, the area of the *shops*, and the brushmakers' *shop*. Jews were forbidden to stay in any other parts, and the penalty was immediate death.[23]

The horrific life in the ghetto gave rise to phenomena that had previously not been seen on the Jewish street: drunkenness, sexual permissiveness, and theft became everyday occurrences. Many people adhered to the sentiment "eat and drink for tomorrow we die," and, as a result, no one had any regard for anyone else's private property. In the ghetto the value of human life, or, to be more precise, the value of a Jewish life was cheapened. Shmuel Winter, an *Oyneg Shabes* worker, wrote in his diary that the general feeling was that: "Each man devours his fellow alive"; and the existential distress from the days of the deportation was replaced by severe psychological depression.[24]

23 It is interesting to note that during that period there were two general phenomena in the shops: on the one hand, the incidents of sabotage by the underground or private people increased in number, while on the other hand, the Jews of the ghetto understood that their very existence depended on the profitability of the shop: "A Damocles sword of annihilation constantly hangs over the necks of the Warsaw Jews. Their fate depends on the shops. As long as the shops have orders, the Jews have a right to live...if the shops no longer exist, their right to live will be lost too." Ringelblum, *Diary and Notes*, p. 409. During this period the armed underground stepped up its attacks against collaborators with the Germans and called on the Jews not to give any credence to promises made by the Germans. Dawid Efros testimony, YVA, M49E 2816, pp. 3–4; Aryeh Neiberg, *The Last Ones: At the End of the Warsaw Ghetto Uprising* (Hebrew) (Merchavia: Sifriat Hapoalim, 1958), p. 50; Ringelblum, *Diary and Notes*, pp. 410–413, 422, 425, 437; "The Writings of a Jewish Policeman (Roda ?)," Archives of the Jewish Historical Institute, 302.129, pp. 188–189; Opoczyński, "The History of the Warsaw Ghetto (October 9, 1942) (November 7, 1942)"; Lewin, *A Cup of Tears* , p. 192 (October 20, 1942), p. 193–194 (October 30, 1942).

24 Shmuel Winter, "From the Diary of Shmuel Winter," in Nahman Blumental and Joseph Kermish, eds., *Resistance and Revolt in the Warsaw Ghetto* (Hebrew) (Jerusalem: Yad Vashem, 1964), p. 193. See also Zivia Lubetkin, *In the Days of Destruction and Revolt* (Ghetto Fighters' House: Hakibbutz Hameuchad, *1981)*, p. 164; Israel Gutman, *The Revolt of the Besieged: Mordechai Anielewicz and the War of the Warsaw Ghetto* (Hebrew) (Merchavia: Sifriat Hapoalim, 1963), p. 263; Ringelblum, *Diary and Notes*, p. 415; The Writings of a Jewish Policeman (Roda ?), Archives of the Jewish Historical Institute, 302.129, p. 206; Genia Silkes, "In the Warsaw Ghetto during April 1943," *Yedioth Yitzhak Katznelson Bet Lochamei Hageta'ot for the Heritage of the Holocaust and the Revolt*, no. (9–

In the following days the German terror – physical and mental – in the streets of the ghetto did not stop. Hundreds of Jews caught in the street were shot to death, and others were executed at their places of work. In early November 1942, Brandt, the head of the "Jewish section" of the Gestapo, ordered the community to open a home for the abandoned children, cynically stating that, "every people has to take care of its children." He also took the opportunity to call on the Jews still left in the ghetto to open theaters and cafés in the *shops*. This news aroused immense anxiety among the Jews, and Ringelblum wrote that: "the public is fearful of good news because [even] before the deportation in Warsaw such good news were spread."[25]

In retrospect, it seems these orders actually expanded the scope of Jewish activity in the *shops*, and several of them set up stations for the care of children and established funds for mutual aid in case of illness. Within a short time a kind of local patriotism began to develop in the *shops* and the *platzuvkas*, and they set up social frameworks to replace those lost during the deportation. Ringelblum and his co-workers in the public sector, primarily Yitzhak Gitterman, the Joint director, hastened to take advantage of these initiatives created in the *shops* in order to carry out welfare activities, and they began rehabilitating the mutual-aid system. Public activists in the *shops* were mobilized, and in each a "self-help committee" (*Komitet Samopomocy*) was established. The committees were asked to look after the needy workers in the shop. For this purpose special cultural evenings were organized, with the revenue going to those in need.

The by-laws written by Ringelblum for the umbrella organization that united the committees stated that the rich *shops* had to support the poorer ones. This was a remarkable continuation of the

10) 2–3 (April 1955), pp. 11–12; Szajn, *In the Warsaw Ghetto: July 1942–April 1943*, p. 65; Opoczynski, The History of the Warsaw Ghetto (September 20, 1942) (December 10, 1942); Lewin, *A Cup of Tears*, p. 227 (December 28, 1942); "An Anonymous Diary," Archives of the Jewish Historical Institute, 302.229, pp. 8, 11.

25 Ringelblum, *Diary and Notes*, p. 414; Opoczynski, "The History of the Warsaw Ghetto (November 2, 1942)"; Lewin, *A Cup of Tears*, p. 195 (October 31, 1942), pp. 197 (November 3, 1942); "The Writings of a Jewish Policeman (Roda ?)," Archives of the Jewish Historical Institute, 302.129, p. 193.

widespread activity that had previously existed in the ghetto, particularly with respect to the principle of mutual responsibility on which it was based. The aid committees were also asked to enlist in helping the "wild" Jews, who constituted about a third of the ghetto's inhabitants, since they were illegal residents who did not receive any food allowance. This relief activity, however, was not without friction. For example, some residents opposed the use of public money to support anyone who, during the deportation, had served as a policeman.[26]

During that same period, the *Oyneg Shabes* archives also renewed its regular work: writings from the days of the deportation were collected; testimonies were taken from survivors of Treblinka; and information about the murder of Jews throughout Europe was documented. In November 1942, the archives published the first issue of *Wiadomości* ("information," in Polish). It was followed by five other issues; these provided information on events in the occupied countries and left no room for any illusions. One by one these publications, as well as the underground newspapers, revealed what was taking place in Treblinka and warned that the fate of the Jews remaining in the ghetto would be no different. The extermination of the Jews in various communities was made public, and instances of resistance to deportations within the Jewish population were described in detail.[27]

In addition to Ringelblum's work in the archives and on behalf of the *shops'* relief activities, he was assigned other public tasks by the Coordination Council, the underground public leadership of the ghetto. These also included raising funds for the committee's use.[28] Although Ringelblum and the other members of the Finance Committee did not succeed in raising the required resources, as part of this endeavor he was exposed to the underground actions in

26 Ringelblum, *Diary and Notes*, pp. 411, 413, 431; idem, *Last Writings*, p. 65; "An Anonymous Diary," Archives of the Jewish Historical Institute, 302.229, p. 19.

27 Israel Shacham, ed., *The Jewish Underground Press in Warsaw*, 6 (March 1942–July 1944) (Hebrew) (Jerusalem: Yad Vashem, 1997), pp. 530–533, 553–566, 576–602.

28 Zuckerman, *A Surplus of Memory*, p. 273; Winter, "From the Diary of Shmuel Winter," p. 193.

the ghetto. He visited the headquarters of the Jewish Military Union (Żydówski Związek Wojskowy — ŻZW), but he supported and was sympathetic toward the Jewish Combat Organization (Żydówska Organizacja Bojowa - ŻOB) from the time of its establishment.[29]

Apparently, Ringelblum's attempts to draw close to the former organization and to follow its activities were not welcomed. But when the young members of the underground needed to transmit information quickly from one part of the ghetto to another, they did not shrink from turning to Ringelblum. He acceded to their requests and carried out these tasks willingly and seriously.[30]

Ringelblum's actions were not limited to the ghetto. At the end of the deportation, when Adolf Abraham and Batya Temkin-Berman, members of the Jewish National Council (Żydówski Komitet Narodowy — ŻKN) on the Aryan side, learned that Ringelblum was alive, they renewed their contact with him. Using the telephone in the offices of Hallman's shop, where Ringelblum was officially employed, Dr. Edward Rydzewski, i.e., Ringelblum, carried on clandestine conversations with the Aryan side. Sometimes he also went with the Jews of the *palatzuvkas* to workplaces outside the ghetto and, despite the danger, met there with members of the Council.[31]

Despite his numerous activities inside and outside the ghetto, his personal sense of commitment to his family never flagged. With the help of the Bermans, he was able to stay in touch with his son and wife, who persistently urged him to join them in their hiding place on Grójecka Street. The Bermans also hoped that Ringelblum would move the center of his activity to the Aryan side and join in the public activity of the Council. For many weeks Ringelblum remained undecided about whether to continue his activity inside the ghetto or outside. Apparently, the January *aktion* caused him finally to decide to leave the ghetto.

On January 18, 1943, the Germans entered the ghetto for the purpose of deporting more than 8,000 "wild" Jews. Within four days, more than 5,000 Jews were caught, and another 1,700 were

29 Ringelblum, *Last Writings*, pp. 45–52, 252–256.

30 Jacob Putermilch, *In Fire and in Snow* (Hebrew) (Tel Aviv: Bet Lochamei Hageta'ot and Hakibbutz Hame'uchad, 1981), pp. 42–43.

31 Temkin-Berman, "Pan Rydzewski," pp. 12–13.

shot in the ghetto streets. During the days of the January deportation, the first public armed resistance took place in the ghetto. This later became known as the "January revolt," or the "small revolt."[32]

On the first day of the *aktion*, Yitzhak Gitterman, the Joint director and Ringelblum's co-worker in the relief activity of the *shops*, was shot to death. This shocked Ringelblum:

> Yitzhak Gitterman was a victim of the second deportation from Warsaw. When he visited me, he was working on a list of those who had perished and he added various names to it. Now he also appears alongside the additional names he wrote down in his handwriting. As I write these words, my hand trembles. Who knows if the historian who will in the future look at the note will not add my name too — Emanuel Ringelblum. In any case, we are already used to death. It no longer makes any impression on us.[33]

Shortly after Gitterman's death, the second half of the *Oyneg Shabes* archives was hidden, and a few days later Emanuel Ringelblum left the ghetto. Despite the Bermans' opposition, Ringelblum moved to the dangerous hide out at 81 Grójecka Street, where he was united with his wife and son, who were waiting for him there. According to Batya Temkin-Berman, he also made it a condition of his activity on the Council that he would not be asked to part from them again.[34]

32 For details, see Israel Gutman, *The Jews of Warsaw 1939–1943: Ghetto, Underground, Revolt* (Brighton, Sussex: Harvester Press, 1982), pp. 307–323; Barbara Engelking and Jaceb Leociak, *Getto warszawskie: po nieistniejącym mieście* (Warsaw: Wydawnictwo IFiS PAN, 2001), pp. 720–722.

33 Ringelblum, *Last Writings*, p. 52.

34 Temkin-Berman, "Pan Rydzewski," p. 13. According to Orna Jagur, who was with Ringelblum in the hideout: "Dr. Ringenblum was only physically present in 'Krysia'. His thoughts were far away from there. He did not take part in the everyday life of the bunker. He showed no excitement or involvement in moments of danger or relief. He did not take part in discussions or quarrels. His intensive work and the presence of his family were, evidently, his escape from the gray monotony of the passive existence in the bunker, which was to become the last stage of his life… Dr. Ringenblum kept his intellectual activity and his human dignity up to the tragic end"; Orna Jagur, *The Hiding Place* (Łódź: Oficyna Bibliofilów, 1997), p. 45.

For the Jews of the Warsaw ghetto the cessation of the deportation after only several thousand Jews were sent out on transports was not only a German failure but also a Jewish victory. The members of the fighting undergrounds believed that the armed resistance was the main reason that the deportation had been stopped. Consequently, they began reorganizing the groups of fighters and stepping up fundraising efforts in order to re-arm them.[35] Some of the inhabitants of the ghetto were in favor of active resistance in the ghetto, while others disapproved of it.[36]

But in the eyes of many of the inhabitants of the ghetto, the refusal of the Jews to report as ordered was the main reason that the deportation was delayed. As a result, they concentrated on building hiding places inside the ghetto. For example, this is what Shmuel Winter wrote when the small deportation ended, on January 22, 1943:

> Today it is six months since the beginning of our destruction [the time of the great deportation]. If we [then] had shown resistance or at least as much resistance as we did in the last *aktion*, it would not have been so easy for the Nazis to annihilate such a large Jewish community. If at least the Jews had not gone willingly, but had tenaciously hidden as they did in the recent days, then the *aktion* would inevitably have lasted for months. To our sorrow, a quarter of a million Jews had to lose their lives before the rest understood the true situation and drew the correct conclusions.[37]

35 Lubetkin, *In the Days of Destruction*, p. 165; Ringelblum, *Last Writings*, p. 51.

36 See, for example, Winter, "From the Diary of Shmuel Winter," p. 192: "It seems that the entire idea of resistance was badly presented: propaganda should have been conducted, so that the masses would actively resist and not go like sheep to the slaughter, instead of a few idealists shooting and then the whole group going to its death." For a favorable description of the rebellion, see Yehiel Gorni, "Aktion Number 2," YVA, M.10/AR.2.288.

37 Winter, "From the Diary of Shmuel Winter," p. 193. See, also, Hirsch Berlinski, "Events in the Ghetto from January 17–21, 1943," in Nahman Blumental and Joseph Kermish, eds., *Resistance and Revolt in the Warsaw Ghetto* (Hebrew) (Jerusalem: Yad Vashem, 1964), p. 183: "All those who hid, are here. The others in the Umschlagplatz...their papers did them no good...The Treblinka ma-

Unquestionably, the January rebellion deterred the Germans from carrying out widespread searches in basements and attics. Nonetheless, the documents collected by means of the infrastructure laid by Ringelblum in his archival work show that, for the masses of the Jews, it was not only the fighting that halted the deportation in January but also — and perhaps primarily — the fact that so many hid.[38]

The failure of the January deportation and the annihilation of Jewish collaborators within the ghetto by the undergrounds added to the defeat of the German army in Stalingrad and the advance of the Russian army.[39] It also largely dispeled the ever-present consciousness of death that had prevailed in the ghetto since the deportation. For the first time in a long while, there was the belief that the delayed implementation of the deportations, even for a few months, would in the end save the remaining inhabitants of the ghetto. For many the hiding places were an important weapon in their struggle against the Germans, and thus they held the greatest hope for the future.

Following the events of January, the ghetto residents reacted in two different ways. During the days when members of the underground movements were busy acquiring weapons and organizing the resistance movement, the masses invested all their energy and strength in creating satisfactory hiding places inside the ghetto. In contrast to the temporary hide outs of the deportation days, this time the Jews began to build well-equipped bunkers that could hold dozens or even hundreds of people for many months. Hundreds of kilograms of dried foodstuffs were hoarded; some of the bunkers were connected to the municipal water, electricity, and sewage network; and some tried to make sure that medical personnel were

chine swallows everything." Berlinski's memoirs were also published earlier, in Hirsch Berlinski, "Memoirs," *Yalkut Moreshet*, I (1963).

38 Nevertheless, we cannot overlook the fact that the main factor that deterred the Germans from widespread searches in basements and attics was the fighting resistance.

39 The inhabitants of the ghetto learned about the approach of the front not only from the news that arrived from afar but also from the growing number of Soviet bombardments of Warsaw.

present in their hiding places. For some bunkers, weapons were also purchased, and tunnels were dug to go through to the Aryan side as part of the mind set of resistance that had permeated from the underground movements to the ghetto inhabitants at large. In the weeks prior to the outbreak of the revolt, a real underground city was built in the ghetto. Nearly every one of the 40,000 Jews remaining was assured of a hiding place in one of the bunkers.[40]

Around that time Ringelblum moved to the Aryan side of the city. He exchanged his activity in the *shops* and the archives for service on the Jewish National Council. Very quickly he became a leading force on the Council.[41] Apparently one of the areas Ringelblum was involved in was an ambitious plan to save Jewish intellectuals who were still in the ghetto. For this purpose he returned to the ghetto on several occasions, bringing with him money and information about hiding places on the Aryan side. Ringelblum took advantage of each brief stay of two or three days to promote the interests of the *Oyneg Shabes* archives, which continued to exist inside the ghetto even in his absence. Although he had initiated the archive and created the framework of its activity, it was able to function without him.

In mid-April 1943, Ringelblum entered the ghetto area for the last time. Later some people claimed that the reason was because he wanted to celebrate the Passover holiday, which fell a few days later, with his friends. But that seems strange: in 1940, Ringelblum celebrated Passover with Sagan and Gitterman, his friends who had already been murdered by 1943; in 1941, he was preoccupied with the distressing hunger that prevailed in the ghetto; the 1942

40 Shoshana Baharir, Testimony, YVA, O.3.5469, p. 11; Report by an eyewitness (September 15, 1943) YVA, O.33.160; Icchok Sznajman, Testimony, YVA, M.49E 16; Aryeh Neiberg *The Last Ones: At the End of the Warsaw Ghetto Uprising*, p. 68; Vladka Meed (Fejgele Peltel Miedzyrzecki), *On Both Sides of the Wall: Memories from the Warsaw Ghetto* (Ghetto Fighters' House and Hakibbutz Hameuchad Publishing House, 1972), p. 171; Ringelblum, *Diary and Notes*, pp. 424, 438–441; idem, *Last Writings*, p. 255; the Writings of an Anonymous Woman, Archives of the Jewish Historical Institute, 302.21, p. 18; Dr. Polisiuk, "The Last Siege (27.5.43–19.4.43)," in Nahman Blumental and Joseph Kermish, eds., *Resistance and Revolt in the Warsaw Ghetto*, p. 310.

41 Temkin-Berman, "Pan Rydzewski," pp. 13–14.

holiday he spent with many friends, dedicating a public kitchen. By the time of Passover in 1943, about 97 percent of his friends, so he wrote, had perished.[42] The friends with whom he had spent holidays were gone; those few who still remained in the ghetto were concentrated in the brushmakers' shop. But Ringelblum went to the central ghetto. Apparently this time he was carrying out a public mission.[43] His wife and son were waiting for him on the Aryan side. If everything had gone right, he would have had time to go back to them after a day or two in the ghetto, before the holiday. But the last deportation of Warsaw's Jews and the uprising that broke out in its wake disrupted his plans.

On April 19, 1943, large German forces encircled the ghetto. Members of the underground and residents of the ghetto spread the news quickly, and the Jewish public went into hiding. In the following days, there was fighting in the ghetto streets between the German forces and the fighters of the ŻOB and the ŻZW. Simultaneously, an additional front, an essentially civilian one, waged its own battle. The Germans tried to catch the Jews in order to deport them from the ghetto, but the Jewish population was entrenched in the bunkers:

> Among thousands of men and women, the elderly and the children, a desire to resist was born, which abolished the natural anxiety, the fear of death and suffering. Masses of the people understood that by refusing to succumb, they were fighting the enemy in a special way, and making it hard for him to carry out his act of destruction and devastation.[44]

42 Ringelblum, *Diary and Notes*, pp. 117, 266; idem, *Last Writings*, pp. 66, 79.

43 Ibid., pp. 93, 141; Turkow, *Once There was a Jewish Warsaw*, p. 185; Temkin-Berman, "Pan Rydzewski," p. 13.

44 Hirsch Wasser, "Figures of Fighters," in Melekh Neusztadt, *The Destruction and Revolt of Warsaw Jewry: Testimonies and Commemorations* (Hebrew) (Tel Aviv: The Executive Council of the General Labor Federation, 1946), p. 210. On the fighting between the German units and members of the ŻOB and the ŻZW during the uprising, see Gutman, *The Jews of Warsaw*, pp. 364–401; Engelking and Leociak, *Warszawskie*, pp. 733–757. Unfortunately, no similar study exists dealing with the central role of the civilian population during the Warsaw ghetto uprising. In the limited scope of this article, I can only comment that,

Most of the inhabitants of the ghetto crowded into the bunkers, but, on the second day of the uprising, these had already been disconnected from the electricity, gas, and water systems. Out of fear of informers, everyone quickly understood that it was best if all those who knew about the bunker's existence remained inside it, and many more people than had been planned for were cramped into most of the hiding places. As a result, not only was the ventilation system incapable of bearing the load, but since so many people who had not prepared food for themselves in advance entered the bunkers, soon there was a shortage. Their distress endangered all the others in the bunker, and in some places the Jews began to apply the system that had been in effect in the House Committees and had continued in the *shops*. The rich were called upon to contribute from their food for the hungry; the food was cooked in an organized manner and distributed to the needy.

It is interesting that, although there was no contact between the bunkers, many of them chose this way of coping with the problem of hunger. The relief system created in the bunkers did not draw its strength from an umbrella organization, but rather from the principles that had been instilled in the Jewish public during the war years. The long-standing social action of people like Ringelblum helped to create a consciousness of mutual help among the Jews, which continued to exist even in their absence.[45]

from an analysis of Stroop's reports regarding the course of the uprising – and the unfounded numbers contained in them – it is clear that the Germans devoted enormous resources to the deportation of the Jews but were unable to actually carry it out. See Joseph Kermish, ed., *The Warsaw Ghetto Uprising in the Eyes of the Enemy: The Reports of the Commandant of the Warsaw Ghetto, General Juergen Stroop* (Hebrew) (Jerusalem: Yad Vashem, 1965), pp. 121–194.

45 Neiberg, *The Last Ones: At the End of the Warsaw Ghetto Uprising*, p. 73; the Writings of an Anonymous Woman (Stefa), Archives of the Jewish Historical Institute, 302.180, pp. 9–10, 11–14, 15, 23, 33–36, 38; Dr. Polisiuk, "The Last Siege (27.5.43–19.4.43)," p. 310. Mordechai Anielewicz, commander of the ŻOB, also related to the harrowing conditions in the bunkers, in his famous letter dated April 23, 1943: "It is impossible to describe the conditions under which the Jews of the ghetto are now living. Only a few will be able to hold out. The remainder will die sooner or later. Their fate is decided. In almost all the hiding places in which thousands are concealing themselves it is not possible to light a candle for the lack of air"; Yitzhak Arad, Yisrael Gutman, and Abra-

On April 23, 1943, the Germans began to systematically destroy and burn the ghetto buildings. The raging fire succeeded where German soldiers had failed: the supports of the buildings in the central ghetto were made of wood, and when they were set on fire the buildings collapsed at once, turning the bunkers into death traps. Huge mounds of concrete blocked the exits from the bunkers, and some of those trapped within them, so the Jews testify, were cooked alive. In the brushmakers' shop and in the area of the *shops*, the supports were made of iron, so they collapsed only partially, and the inhabitants of the bunkers there suffered a different fate: the bunkers remained, but the conditions were inhuman. Due to the fires the temperatures in the hiding places rose to an intolerable level; the water in the pipes boiled and burst; the stores of food that were not burned were spoiled by the heat; the dry air made it difficult to breathe; and the smoke that penetrated the bunker was blinding. At the same time the smoke-filled air was a warning to the people inside of the inferno raging above their heads and a sign that they ought to abandon their hiding place. Nonetheless, despite the conditions, "life in the boiling cauldron of the ghetto did not cease. Despite the many calls by the Germans to surrender, no one in the ghetto even considered doing so. The Germans had to capture every shelter, every bunker by armed force."[46]

ham Margaliot, eds., *Documents on the Holocaust: Selected Sources on the Destruction of the Jews in Germany and Austria, Poland and the Soviet Union and Austria* (Lincoln, NE, London, and Jerusalem: University of Nebraska Press and Yad Vashem, 1999), p. 315.

46 Hirsch Wasser, "Figures of Fighters"; see also Shmuel Zurman, testimony, YVA, 03.5985, pp. 16–20; Shoshana Baharir, testimony, ibid., 03.5469, pp. 12–14; Devorah Reichart, testimony, ibid., 03.5750, p. 17; Simha (Kazik) Rotem, *Memoirs of a Warsaw Ghetto Fighter: The Past within Me* (New Haven: Yale University Press, 1994), pp. 37–38; Gutman, *Revolt of the Besieged*, p. 362; Lubetkin, *In the Days of Destruction*, pp. 201–203; Neiberg, *The Last Ones: At the End of the Warsaw Ghetto Uprising*, pp. 88–89; Marek Edelman, *The Ghetto Fights* (New York: American Representation of the General Jewish Workers' Union of Poland, 1946), p. 37–38; Tadeusz Stabholz, *The Seven Circles of Hell* (Hebrew) (Tel Aviv: Ministry of Defense, 1992), p. 12; Writings of an Anonymous Man, Archives of the Jewish Historical Institute, 302.229, pp. 3–4; Anonymous, "The Burning Ghetto," in Blumental and Kermish, eds., *Resistance and Revolt in the Warsaw Ghetto*, pp. 319, 321; Silkes, "In the Warsaw Ghetto in April 1943," pp. 12–13.

During those days when the ghetto was burning, the inferno reached its peak, and, finally, the fire and the harrowing ordeal it created succeeded where the Germans had failed. The inhuman conditions tipped the scales. The Jews were forced to leave the bunkers. The survivors who came out of the bunkers saw an unrecognizable world; others, who remained in the bunker, were burned alive.

However, the Jewish entrenchment in the bunkers despite the extremely harsh conditions, forced the Germans to go from house to house. In the words of Jürgen Stroop:

> It isn't the number [of the Jewish fighters] that count here. The important thing is that the group's very existence influenced the entire Ghetto population community, causing a chain reaction. The Miła street leaders may never have known how effectively it aroused thousands of previously submissive Jews.[47]

It was the combination of Jewish fighters and Jews dug into bunkers that gave the Warsaw ghetto uprising its strength and turned it into a mass rebellion.

During the revolt Ringelblum was in Bauer's shop on Nalewki Street. From afar he watched the underground organizations fighting the Nazis; apparently he stayed in a bunker with other Jews. At the end of April, the workers of the shop were deported to Trawniki, and Ringelblum was sent with them. In the days prior to their deportation, he must have been in hiding. Since he had no food, we can only hope that the principles of mutual aid that he and others had imbued in Jewish society over such a long period were applied in the bunker where he was hiding.[48]

All contact with Ringelblum was broken off during the uprising, and only weeks later did his friends on the Jewish National Council learn that he was in the Trawniki camp.[49] In June 1943,

47 Kazimierz Moczarski, *Conversations with an Executioner* (Englewood Cliffs: Prentice-Hall, 1981) p. 177.

48 Ringelblum, *Last Writings*, pp. 141, 257.

49 Apparently, there too Ringelblum continued to engage in public activity as well as his documentation work. Although the article he wrote on the camp

Ringelblum was smuggled out of the camp thanks to the brave action taken by Shoshana (Emilka) Kosower and Theodor Pajewski. He returned to his hiding place, to his wife and son, and continued writing and engaging in public activity, until the hide out was discovered.[50]

In March 1944, the Jews held in the Pawiak prison learned that Dr. Ringelblum and his family had been arrested. These Jews began to plan how to arrange for him to be transferred to them, to the group of tradesmen working there, in order to save his life. Julian Hirszhaut, a Jewish journalist who knew Ringelblum personally, was sent to make contact with him and let him in on the plan:

> My meeting with Ringelblum only lasted a few minutes, but those few are deeply engraved in my memory.
> [When I explained the plan to Ringelblum], he pointed to his son and asked: "And what about him?…And what will happen to my wife?..."What could I answer him?...From my silence, Ringelblum understood the truth and added at once, "I prefer to go the way of *Kiddush Ha-Shem* [the Sanctification of God's Name] together with them…."
> [Later he asked] "Is death so hard to bear?"And in a few seconds, went on in a voice broken by despair "What is the little

was lost, in his other writings he referred to the activities of the ŻOB members that was continued in the camp, as well as cultural and public events. He wrote: "Remember that our workers were faithful to the ideals of our culture as long as they still drew a breath. The flag of culture and of struggle with barbarism was clenched in their hands until their death"; Ringelblum, *Last Writings*, p. 326; see, also, pp. 94, 111, 153.

50 Shoshana (Emilka) Kosower, testimony, YVA, 033.50; see, also, Batya Temkin-Berman, *Diary in the Underground* (Hebrew) (Tel Aviv, 1955), pp. 37–39. The *Biuletyn Informacyjny*, March 30, 1944, printed verdicts passed by a special underground court, including a death sentence imposed on Leo Lakiński for collaborating with the occupier and handing over Polish citizens of Jewish descent. According to Prekerowa, eighteen-year-old Lakiński, who had lost his mind, was almost certainly the one who informed the Germans about the bunker at Grójecka Street where Ringelblum and other Jews were hiding. Lakiński was also responsible for handing over to the Germans several members of the Krajowa army, and he was killed by the Polish underground. Teresa Prekerowa, *Konspiracyna Rada Pomocy Żydom w Warszawie, 1942–1945* (Warsaw: Państwowy Instytut Wydawniczy, 1982), p. 286.

> boy guilty of?" – he again pointed at his son – "it breaks my heart to think of him."
> I did not know what to answer him. And a wave of sorrow also swept over my heart.[51]

Ringelblum was not only a historian or an important public activist. He was also, and primarily, a man. He was appalled by the murder of the masses, was pained by the death of his close friends, and was fearful for the fate of his loved ones – his wife and, particularly, his son.

At the beginning of the war, Ringelblum had already decided to embark on activity based on his ideological view as a member of Left Poalei Zion. His historical writing was intended to reflect the voices of the silent masses – those who in their diversity shape the character of the people. His public activity was based on the principle of mutual responsibility and the participation of the public at large in the aid projects. Consequently, the public work carried out in the ghetto even after the great deportation – with all its limitations – still adhered to these principles that Ringelblum had laid down.

Moreover, the documents that Ringelblum and his co-workers collected in the last nine months of the ghetto's existence also largely moved the focus of the research back on the masses of the Jewish people. Along with the death of hundreds of thousands in Treblinka, the documents also expose the disaster of the lives of those who remained, albeit temporarily, in the ghetto. The uprising in the ghetto is depicted not only as the armed struggle of the undergrounds but also as the struggle of the masses of inhabitants who were entrenched in bunkers.

At the same time, the self-help activity during the ghetto uprising was not directly dependent on Ringelblum. The depiction of the Jewish society in the last months of the ghetto's existence as an active, fervent society is based mainly on the work of all the members of the archive team. Even at those times when Ringel-

51 Julian Hirszhaut, *Finstere nacht in Pawiak* (Yiddish) (Buenos Aires: Tsentral farband fun Poilishe Yidn in Argentine, 1948), pp. 198–199.

blum stopped writing and discontinued his public work – either because of his other activities, due to his personal state, or because he had physically left the ghetto – the archives did not discontinue its widespread activity nor did the self-help work cease.

Ringelblum, it seems, was able, by the force of his personality and deeds, to impart his mission and his ideas to a broad public. The elements to be included in the writing, the idea of mutual responsibility, and the participation of the public at large in the aid projects that Ringelblum set out struck root and continued to exist even in the worst of times – and even in Ringelblum's absence.

Nothing is more impressive than deeds that continue to live even after a man is gone.

The Legacy of Emanuel Ringelblum and the Historical Awareness of the Holocaust

Feliks Tych

In December 2003, the Polish historical magazine *Karta*, in cooperation with the Jewish Historical Institute (ŻIH), published a small anthology of texts (about fifty pages) from the Ringelblum Archive that were thought to be of interest to the general Polish public. This publication was the first of its kind, notwithstanding the earlier initiatives of ŻIH itself,[1] and the anthology received much attention in the Polish media.

The short introductory text written by the editor of *Karta* included an important statement: "We have known about the Ringelblum Archive for a long time, yet we did not know much more than the fact that on the terrain of the former ghetto documents had been dug up from the time of the Second World War".

Remarkably, this sentence was penned by the Polish historian Zbigniew Gluza, who had been working on the history of World War II for at least twenty years. One can only assume that he knew what he was saying. To a large extent, however, his statement is relevant not only with regard to Polish readers; it is possible to extend it to include also a substantial proportion of Jewish readers.

Certainly Poland is a specific case. For forty years following the war, with few exceptions, works on the Holocaust primarily reached only a limited circulation of mainly Jewish readers. In the

1 Ruta Sakowska, ed., *Archiwum Ringelbluma: Getto warszawskie, lipiec 1942–styczeń 1943* (Warsaw: PWN, 1980).

Polish educational curriculum, the Holocaust as a subject practically did not exist until the mid-1990s. Materials from the Ringelblum Archive were also rarely cited in the Polish historiography of World War II. None of Ringelblum's pre-war works – neither his book *The Jews of Warsaw from the Earliest Times to the Last Expulsion in 1527* (published in 1932), nor his second book, *Jews in the Kościuszko Uprising* (published in Yiddish in 1937, and in Polish in 1938)—were reprinted after the war. In the period that ŻIH could have organized the means for such a project – i.e., in 1947–1966 – it did not understand the importance of these early topics, and later, after 1967, ŻIH was struggling to survive through the most difficult years of its existence.

What led to the comparatively modest presence of Ringelblum, his legacy, and, foremost, of his *Oyneg Shabes* Archives in Polish and other historiographies – perhaps aside from the Israeli?

The historiography of the Holocaust developed – not only in Poland – according to a certain logic. Jewish historians were first mainly concerned with the calculation of Jewish losses in order to comprehend the size of the catastrophe. Research conducted not only by Jewish historians focused on the circumstances of the crime: the decision-making processes and motivations of the perpetrators, the mechanism, places and techniques of genocide. Only later did historians begin to pay more attention to the Jewish resistance movement and, generally, to the Jewish condition during those years. Systematic research on the attitudes of local non-Jewish societies – an essential element to understanding the Holocaust in its essence – began even later, mainly in the 1990s. This and, perhaps to a larger extent, the language barrier explain why the main corpus of the Ringelblum Archive is still dormant in the archives waiting for historians and the broader public. Lurking behind these research problems, however, and influencing the results of the research and the broader historical perspective, is in essence historical truth itself. The essential element is whether the research takes into account Jewish sources as well.

And here we approach the real dimension of Ringelblum's work and the legacy of the *Oyneg Shabes* group. In fact, it is the most important corpus of sources in the world documenting the Holocaust by the victims themselves, as the Jews themselves perceived it then and there, in real time, at the moment when they were experiencing all the horrors.

Although, without these documents, there is no truth about the Holocaust, they are still little known around the world. They are rarely cited by historians, other than Israelis and those working in Poland. Two major factors stand in the way: first, meager knowledge of the historians themselves about what this unique collection actually contains; and, second, the aforementioned language barrier. The vast majority of these documents were written in Yiddish or in Polish, and merely a fragment have been issued in widely accessible languages: the only substantial published collection of documents from the Ringelblum Archive in English is still Kermish's one-volume anthology published by Yad Vashem in 1986.[2]

As we know, the systematic publication of the entirety of this extraordinary documentation has begun in two countries: in Israel, with the publication in Hebrew of the underground ghetto press from the Ringelblum Archive (Yad Vashem, 1979–1997), Ringelblum's two-volume Hebrew wartime diary and last writings (Yad Vashem and Ghetto Fighters' House, 1992–1994), and Kermish's anthology in English; and in Poland, with the publication by the Jewish Historical Institute (1997–2002) in the original languages of the documents (Polish, Yiddish, and Hebrew – as facsimiles of the original and a Polish translation) of three successive, thematically conceived volumes. These comprise the beginning of the planned publication of all the texts in the Ringelblum Archive.[3] The fourth volume, Gela Seksztajn's papers and works, is ready for publication.

2 Joseph Kermish, ed., *To Live with Honor and Die with Honor: Selected Documents from the Warsaw Ghetto Underground Archives "O.S." (Oyneg Shabes)* (Jerusalem: Yad Vashem, 1986).

3 The published volumes are Ruta Sakowska, ed., *Listy o Zagładzie* ("Letters About the Holocaust") (1997); idem, *Dzieci – tajne nauczanie w getcie warszawskim* ("Children – Secret Schooling in the Warsaw Ghetto") (2000); and Andrzej Żbikowski, ed., *Relacje z Kresów* ("Testimonies from the Borderlands") (2000).

The problem, however, is that the six volumes of the ghetto press that were published by Yad Vashem, as well as the three volumes of ŻIH, are in languages that are not widely known – Hebrew and Polish. For instance, the volumes that ŻIH issued attracted no interest from either Yad Vashem or the U.S. Holocaust Memorial Museum in Washington, and the first foreign language into which they were translated was French.[4]

In English, besides Kermish's anthology, only Ringelblum's *Notes from the Warsaw Ghetto* (abridged) and his study *Polish-Jewish Relations during the Second World War* is accessible. The situation is similar for German-language publications. German historians, who have written extensively about the Holocaust, rarely cite Ringelblum or material from his archive. In a certain sense, the fact that in Walter Laqueur's *The Holocaust Encyclopedia*[5] only five lines were dedicated to Ringelblum and not much more to the *Oyneg Shabes* group reflects the general situation, except for Israel and Poland.

Now that the U.S. Holocaust Memorial Museum (USHMM) in Washington and the Jewish Historical Institute have jointly published in English the first full catalogue of the Ringelblum Archive, worldwide interest in this unique corpus of documents will substantially increase and will influence Holocaust historiography.[6] It will widen the arsenal of knowledge about the Holocaust above all from the point of view of the victims and their state of mind. It will reflect the then and there, and not a record of the events fifty years later – as in the case of the Spielberg project, or the avalanche of memoirs written during the last two decades by survivors toward the end of their lives.

The recently published catalogue is based only on the information contained in the main part of the Ringelblum Collec-

4 Archives clandestines du getto de Varsovie: vol. I, Lettres de l'anéantissement (Paris, 2007), vol. II, Les enfants et l'enseignement (Paris, 2007).

5 Walter Laqueur, ed., *The Holocaust Encyclopedia* (New Haven: Yale University Press, 2001).

6 Robert M. Shapiro and Tadeusz Epsztein, eds., *Introduction by Samuel Kassow, The Warsaw Ghetto Oneg Shabes – Ringelblum Archive, Catalogue and Guide* (Indiana University Press, 2009).

tion, which is in the possession of the ŻIH. As we know, however, some other parts of the Ringelblum Collection are to be found in the YIVO Archives in New York and at the research center of the Ghetto Fighters House Archives (part of Adolf Abraham Berman's papers). Some new documents from the Ringelblum Archive were also recently discovered in the ŻIH. Thus, a common effort of all the above-mentioned institutions is necessary in order to produce a supplement to the USHMM and ŻIH catalogue that will reflect these new findings.

The need to translate these documents into widely read languages, the so-called "congress-languages," and, above all, into English, remains urgent, because the time spent by millions of Jews in the ghettos created by the Germans – which is the main subject of the *Oyneg Shabes* Archives – is still insufficiently illuminated by the historiography. The physical and spiritual conditions of life in the ghettos were without precedent in the entire history of the Jews. Regardless of how long each ghetto inhabitant had to live, we are still talking about *life* and not about dying – although death was already close.

The human condition of the Jews from the beginning of the German occupation to the "Final Solution" is still a less explored field of research than the act of murder itself. Too little research has been done on the economic situation and the social stratification in the ghettos. The same can be said about the Judenräte. In addition, too little research has been conducted about the Jews' religious life behind the walls. The publication of the Ringelblum collection could significantly help change this very complex situation. The greatest contributions of Ringelblum and his group for posterity lie in the documentation of this period.

We have this documentation. We have had it for over the past half century. However, as long as we do not publish this material in widely accessible languages, primarily in English, it will remain dormant, as it has been for almost sixty years.

Nachman Blumental, one of the founding fathers of the Jewish Historical Institute in Warsaw, wrote in a Polish-Jewish newspaper shortly after the discovery of the first, main part of the Ringelblum Archive: "There is not one area of human life that the Ringelblum

Archive did not take into consideration."[7] He was absolutely stupefied by the richness and comprehensiveness of the material.

In a situation in which those who survived the Holocaust were constantly disheartened by the ease with which the Germans succeeded in sending to death 2,800,000 Polish Jews, Blumental perceived in the Ringelblum Archive irrefutable testimony of the spiritual resistance that existed in the ghetto. This was a powerful antidote to the widely disseminated notion of Jewish passivity, to the stereotype of Jews "going like sheep to the slaughter."

> The unearthing of the collections, through the miracle of a surviving archive, buried four years ago – during the prime of German imperialism, which stood at that time at the height of its strength – by a small group of idealists sentenced to death, is to a certain extent a symbol of the age-old struggle between good and evil as well as the ultimate victory of good over evil. Therefore let this fact be for us an incentive, and the luminous shape of Dr. Ringelblum will serve for us as an example of a fighter dedicated to the cause, believing irrefutably in the indestructible power of our nation and in the ultimate victory of academic truth.[6]

A separate problem is the familiarity with this documentation in Poland, the country with which it is concerned. Ringelblum's two most important single works from the war years were published in Polish in the 1980s, when censorship in Poland had eased somewhat: *Chronicle of the Warsaw Ghetto: September 1939–January 1943* (1983 and 1988) and *Polish-Jewish Relations During the Second World War* (1988), both prepared for publication by Artur Eisenbach. Earlier, in 1980, an edition of the *Chronicle*, which had been abridged as a result of censorship, had been published (*The Warsaw Ghetto, July 1942-January 1943*). It was possible to put out Ringeblum's works in Yiddish substantially earlier precisely because they were written in a language known only to the small Jew-

7 Nachman Blumental, "Czym jest dla nas archiwum dra Ringelbluma," *Opinia* no. 7 (20), November 8, 1946.

ish community. These works *Ksovim fun Geto* (Yiddish) consist of volume 1, *Togbukh fun Varshever Geto* ("Journal from the Warsaw Ghetto") *1939–1942*; volume 2, *Notitsn un Ophandlungen* ("Notes and Essays") *1942–1943*, prepared by Artur Eisenbach, Tatiana Berenstein, Ber Mark, and Adam Rutkowski.[8]

The publishing house Czytelnik intended to make available for Polish readers fragments of Ringelblum's *Chronicle of the Warsaw Ghetto,* which Adam Rutkowski cautiously selected in consideration of what would be possible within the constraints of censorship at the time. The book was already in proofs, but it was literally removed from the printing press in 1968, a very difficult year for Polish Jews.

Besides the above-mentioned volumes, fifty important groups of documents from the Ringelblum Archive were published in two journals of the Jewish Historical Institute: *Bleter far Geshikhte* (Yiddish) and the Bulletin of the Jewish Historical Institute – BŻIH (Polish).

In the public debate in Poland, in 2000–2002, about Jedwabne, only a few participants (Andrzej Żbikowski, Dariusz Libionka) cited documents from the Ringelblum Archive. Except for them in this debate no one in Poland referred to Ringelblum's general view on Polish-Jewish relations during World War II. After all, it was one of the most important books that he wrote.

This situation has its origins in several factors, different in nature. The first and most important concerns the general condition of Polish historiography from the end of World War II to the mid-1990s. Until not long ago, the history of Poland in both the educational curriculum as well as at the university level was written almost exclusively from the point of view of the history of ethnic Poles. With a certain degree of simplification, it is possible to say that the history of Polish Jews and the history of Poles were each pursued separately. Moreover, until the 1980s, those in Poland who were working and writing on the history of Jews were almost exclusively Jews themselves. Non-Jewish historians, such as Teresa Prekerowa or Władysław Bartoszewski, are the exceptions. In this

8 The volumes were published by ŻIH; the first in 1961, and the second in 1963.

respect, the first five postwar decades are a rather sad landscape. During the last few years this situation has completely changed – for the better.

Why did so few Polish historians refer to Ringelblum in their presentations of the events of 1939–1943 in Poland? The cause is rooted in the fact that, until the last years of the twentieth century, the Polish historiography of World War II concentrated almost exclusively on Polish martyrology, on the Polish-German and Polish-Soviet axes, as well as the Polish-Western allies axis. The catastrophe of Polish Jewry, which *in toto* claimed a larger toll among Polish citizens than all the other segments of Polish society combined, was a subject that attracted hardly perceptible attention in the Polish historiography. This was also true with regard to the Polish media in the broader sense of the word, including school textbooks, popular articles on historical themes in the press, TV, and other media, historical and regional museums, and so on. This very circumstance marginalized the work of Ringelblum in a certain sense. It was left to the almost exclusive sphere of interest of the Jewish Historical Institute, an institution established in 1947, by Jews and for Jews, with no intention of influencing the rest of Polish society.

To a certain degree, ŻIH – the only institution of its kind in the entire sphere of Soviet influence – was tolerated by the communist authorities only on condition of the specific ghettoization of its activities; i.e., the circulation of its publications only within Jewish circles. Officially, everyone was able to purchase these publications, but, other than Jews, few actually bought them. However, apart from the elements of political and ideological constraint, it was difficult not to observe also an element of voluntary self-ghettoization by the historians working at ŻIH. Those who did not want to tolerate the political constraints of Polish and Jewish communists emigrated. Others continued in the isolated and besieged fortress that was ŻIH from 1948 until the 1980s. Undoubtedly, if he had survived, Ringelblum also would have emigrated, although it is not entirely certain whether he would have done so if he knew that it would not be possible to take his archive abroad.

The recipients of ŻIH publications were Jews in Poland and in other countries, mainly in South America, where Yiddish was then still widely known. Lists of subscribers and recipients in the ŻIH archives, however, indicate that they were rarely ethnic Poles.

At a time when the communist government, fighting for its legitimacy, summarily glorified the attitudes of broad layers of Polish society, it was not possible for one of Ringelblum's most important works, *Polish-Jewish Relations*, to be accepted by the majority of Polish historians. Regarding the true scope of collaboration during the war, there was either silence, or it was portrayed as a phenomenon that concerned only a small number of people from the margins of society. This was the only area about which, with few exceptions, both orthodox-communist historians and nationalist historians agreed. This theme was not comfortable for anyone — which is true not only in Poland.

The situation already began to change in the 1980s, but a qualitatively new stage was not reached until recent years. The young generation of Poles simply wants to know history as it truly happened. This tendency, therefore, is gradually beginning to establish roots among a wider and wider segment of young Polish historians.

Over the last decade the ŻIH in Warsaw has made a concerted effort to draw the attention of a broader public in Poland and abroad to Ringelblum's heritage. In 2008, it published, together with the Polish research center "Karta," a basic (220 pages) anthology of the Ringelblum papers.[9] Earlier the institute initiated a series of large exhibits devoted to Emanuel Ringelblum and the Warsaw ghetto. The first exposition was held from September 2000 to January 2001 at the Jewish Museum in Frankfurt. A year later a slightly different exhibit was displayed in the seat of the Bavarian State Chancellery in Munich and in Berlin. After the success of the first expositions, which attracted thousands of visitors, including dozens of schoolchildren, the authorities of the Rheinland-Westfalen State asked the ŻIH to prepare a traveling exposition tailored to the needs of their educational system. Subsequently, the exposition was shown in more than sixty cities.

9 *The Ringelblum Archive: Annihilation – Day by Day* (Warsaw: ŻIH and Karta, 2008).

Ringelblum exhibits were also presented by the ŻIH in 2001/2, in New York, at the Museum of Jewish Heritage, in San Francisco, and in other U.S. cities. There were exhibits in several cities in Spain and, in 2006, at the Memorial de la Shoah in Paris.

Whereas the ŻIH has done much to raise the awareness of Emanuel Ringelblum's legacy, the main challenge – the publication of most of the works of the *Oyneg Shabes* group – is still in its initial stage. Let us hope that in years to come the situation will change for the better. In a certain sense, the ŻIH is still a victim of the 1968 exodus.

Polish-Jewish Relations in Emanuel Ringelblum's Writings

Samuel Kassow

From his student days at Warsaw University until the tragic end of his life in 1944, Emanuel Ringelblum placed the problem of Polish-Jewish relations at the center of his scholarly interests.

Ringelblum tried to counter two starkly different perceptions of Polish-Jewish relations. The first was the image of Poland as a land distinguished by age-old traditions of liberalism and tolerance; and the second was the opposite perception that Polish-Jewish relations were rooted in a history of unbridgeable antagonism and mutual alienation. The truth, according to Ringelblum, was more complicated. Polish-Jewish relations reflected a constant interplay of rivalry and cooperation, religious alienation and close personal ties, economic tension and mutual collaboration.

Ringelblum sincerely believed that one reason for Polish-Jewish tension was a lack of mutual knowledge, which historians could help overcome. By means of historical explanation, historians could undercut deeply held prejudices and thereby build mutual understanding between Jews and Poles. As early as 1926, Ringelblum stressed that historians could act as bridges between the two peoples.[1] Reaching out to Polish society was a goal that Ringelblum continued to pursue for the rest of his life.

1 Emanuel Ringelblum, "Dray yor seminar," *Yunger Historiker* (Yiddish), no. 1 (1926).

With the beginning of World War II, amidst a brief interlude of Polish-Jewish cooperation, Ringelblum set out to chronicle the history of the occupation in the hope that he would be serving not only future scholarship but also future understanding between the two peoples. Once the mass murder started, however, he confronted a starkly different reality. Nonetheless, in late 1942, the "*Oyneg Shabes*" Archives issued a bulletin in the Polish language, *Wiadomości*, which was aimed as much at Poles as at Jews.[2]

For Ringelblum and other young Jewish historians in Poland — who had no hope of being appointed to any academic post — history was less a career than a mission. In the mid-1920s, Ringelblum wrote that Jewish historians had to provide ammunition for the dogged battle that Jews were waging for equal rights and national dignity.[3] After more than a century, with Jews once again under Polish sovereignty, historians on both sides reached back to the pre-partition past to define a proper relationship between the two peoples. Countering the charge that Jews were alien parasites and exploiters, Jewish historians, in Ringelblum's words, had to defend Jewish honor and make it clear that Jews lived in Poland by right and not on sufferance.[4]

Ringelblum quickly discovered that, in the highly charged atmosphere of 1930s Poland, even scholarly work on early Polish Jewish history could be political dynamite. Thanks to the help of

2 *Wiadomości* also tried to remind Poles that their turn might be next; see, for example, the sixth issue of *Wiadomości* (January 9–15, 1943): "Today nobody has the illusion that the German murder will end with the Jews." See also Israel Shaham, ed., *The Jewish Underground Press in Warsaw, Volume 6: March 1942–July 1944* (Hebrew) (Jerusalem: Yad Vashem, 1997), p. 594.

3 Ringelblum, "Dray yor seminar"; see also "An Interesanter Onheyb," *Literarishe Bleter* (Yiddish), no. 27 (1931).

4 In his introduction to Isaiah Trunk's history of the Jews of Plock, published in 1939, Ringelblum wrote that "this book appears in a time when the rights of the Jewish population of Poland are under attack; at a time when the Polish Jews, who have lived in the land for centuries, are being cast by reactionaries as aliens who have just arrived here. [This book] shows that Jewish history in Poland began many centuries ago, at the very beginning of economic life in Poland. The economy had been undeveloped and needed the competent skills of merchants and artisans." Isaiah Trunk, *Geshtaltn un gesheenishn* (Yiddish) (Tel Aviv: Y.L. Peretz, 1983), p. 55.

Professor Marceli Handelsman and the Warsaw Society of Friends of History, his first book, on the history of Warsaw's Jews up to 1527, was published in 1932. (He even received a small grant from the Warsaw city government.)[5] However, the book led to bitter attacks on Ringelblum in a stormy meeting of the society in 1933.[6] The prestigious *Kwartalnik Historyczny* published a savage review — with clearly antisemitic overtones — by a prominent legal historian, Professor Jozef Siemieński.[7] Nevertheless, Ringelblum made a valiant effort to bring Polish and Jewish historians together.

Thanks to Handelsman's readiness to help, Ringelblum organized a section on Jewish history at the 1933 International Conference of Historians, which was held in Warsaw. However, the steady deterioration in Polish-Jewish relations in the 1930s also affected the world of scholarship. In its 1937 issue, especially devoted to the modern historiography of Poland, *Kwartalnik Historyczny* pointedly ignored Jewish history and Jewish historians.[8]

5 Emanuel Ringelblum, *Żydzi w Warszawie od czasów najdawniejszych do ostatniego wygnania w r. 1527* (Warsaw: Towarzystwo Milosników Historji, 1932). As Yitzhak (Ignacy) Schipper bitterly noted, Poles were ready to help publish this book while the Warsaw Jewish Community Council (*kehillah*) showed absolutely no interest whatsoever; see Yitzhak Schipper, "Di eltste Geshikhte fun Varshever Yidn," *Haint* (Yiddish), September 9, 1932.

6 Emanuel Ringelblum, *Ksovim fun Geto* (Yiddish), vol. 2 (Tel Aviv: Y. L. Peretz, 1985), pp. 174–175. One source of contention was Ringelblum's assertion of a late fifteenth-century pogrom allegedly instigated by Juan Capistrano. According to Ringelblum, "the antisemitic historians resented the fact that I wrote about pogroms organized by the Polish clergy, about the 'gifts' paid by Jews to the Polish kings for letting Jews reside, about usury practiced by Christians, etc."

7 *Kwartalnik Historyczny*, 47 (1933). One cannot help but note the parallel fate that linked the Polish nationalist scholar Siemieński and the young Jewish historian. Like Ringelblum, Siemieński devoted much of his life to the preservation of archives — in this case, Polish archives — as an indispensable resource for the safeguarding of national memory and identity. He was murdered in Auschwitz in 1941, just three years before the Gestapo killed Ringelblum, his family and thirty-five other Jews on the Aryan side of Warsaw (along with two Poles who had hid them).

8 See, for example, the article by Stefan Inglot on social and economic history, "Rozwój historii społecznej i gospodarczej," *Kwartalnik Historyczny* 51 (1937), p. 401. Professor Stefan Inglot devoted one short paragraph to Jews, in which he singled out the work of Bogdan Wasiutynski, Franciszek Bujak, Jan Ptaśnik,

In this first book on Warsaw Jewry, Ringelblum repeatedly emphasized the interconnectedness of Polish and Jewish history. No "Chinese wall" separated Poles and Jews, and Jews borrowed liberally from Poles: names, food, clothing, and even linguistic expressions.[9] Certainly this keen sense of Jewish-Christian interconnectedness was a major reason for Ringelblum's interest in the history of medicine and the social and cultural role of Jewish physicians. In early modern Poland, Ringelblum argued, physicians were the Jews most likely to straddle two worlds. It was the physician who, with his access to non-Jewish education, often served as a conduit of secular culture into the Jewish community.[10]

This Jewish-Polish interconnectedness had to be impressed upon Poles as well as on Jews. Ringelblum complained that most Polish historians usually ignored the Jews in their work. In his book on the participation of the Jews in the Kościuszko Uprising of 1794, Ringelblum outlined another task for the Polish Jewish historian: to revise the Polish view of Jews as an "undifferentiated other."[11] The Jewish historian could show Poles that Jews were a varied and complex community and demystify a group that was intimately and intricately bound up with the life of the country.

Implicit in Ringelblum's historical work was also the conviction that the Jewish question was a barometer of Poland's political maturity and stability. In an important work on failed attempts to productivize the Jewish population in the eighteenth century, Ringelblum tried to argue that the effort to solve the problem of

and Stanisław Kutrzeba. Not one of these historians could read Hebrew or Yiddish! At the end of the paragraph, Inglot added that "there is also a whole variety of works on local and general Jewish history written by Jews: Schorr, Schipper, Bałaban, Friedman and others." In a letter to Eliyahu Cherikover at the beginning of 1939, Meyer Bałaban hinted that the *Kwartalnik Historyczny* had broken a promise to publish one of his articles. It should be noted that the *Przégląd Historyczny* maintained a slightly more forthcoming attitude to Jewish scholarship. See YIVO Archives, Cherikover Collection.

9 Ringelblum, *Żydzi w Warszawie*, p. 129.

10 See "Apikorses un frumkayt tsvishn yidishe doktoyrim," in Emanuel Ringelblum, *Kapitlen Geshikhte* (Yiddish) (Buenos Aires: Tsentral farband fun Poilishe Yidn in Argentine, 1953), p. 221.

11 Emanuel Ringelblum, *Żydzi w Powstaniu Kościuszkowskim* (Warsaw: Księgarnia Popularna, 1938), p. 34.

Jewish destitution and poverty in that period was stymied by Poland's dysfunctional political system and the negative effects of serfdom.[12] The same theme reappeared in his wartime writings. Only far-reaching structural reforms of the Polish state and society (including the end of capitalism) would guarantee a long-lasting solution of the Jewish question.

Just as Ringelblum wanted to demystify Jews in the eyes of Poles, he also wanted Jews to rethink their relationship to the non-Jewish world. Ringelblum had little patience with the idea that antisemitism was inevitable and eternal. In book reviews he attacked Yehezkiel Kaufman and Philip Friedman for exaggerating the intractable nature of antisemitism.[13] He praised a group of amateur historians in Pružany for writing a local history that saw Poles and Jews as part of an integrated socio-economic system.[14]

If young Jewish historians found themselves outside the academic guild, they could compensate by crafting a vision of history as a collective praxis bringing together scholars and ordinary Jews. In the *Yunger Historiker Krayz* (Young Historians Circle), organized by Ringelblum in 1923, and later in YIVO, *Zamlen* (the collection of documents and folklore) would ensure that future generations would not have to rely on Gentile sources and hostile official documents in order to study topics pertaining to the Jews; it signaled the determination of a stateless people to protect their identity and their national dignity. (Indeed, the secret *Oyneg Shabes* Archives that Ringelblum organized in the Warsaw ghetto was a direct continuation of this YIVO imperative of engaged scholarship. Whatever happened to the Jews, at least the future generations would not have to depend on German sources.)

12 Emanuel Ringelblum, *Projekty i próby przewarstwowienia Żydów w epoce stanisławowskiej* (Warsaw: Instytut Badań Spraw Narodowościowych, 1934).

13 Emanuel Ringelblum, "Bleter far geshikhte," *Arbeter Tsaytung* (Yiddish), no. 35 (1934); on Friedman, see Emanuel Ringelblum, "A solide geshikhte arbet," *Literarishe Bleter* (Yiddish), no. 39 (1929).

14 "We feel that the writers see proud working Jews. They don't feel that they're guests in Pružany. Rather they regard themselves as long established veterans who have put down deep roots in the local area thanks to their work and toil." See "An interesanter onheyb," *Literarishe Bleter*, no. 27 (1931).

Ringelblum took a broad view of history. Of all the YIVO historians, it was Ringelbum who was the most enthusiastic advocate of *Landkentnish*, (educational tourism) as well as amateur history.[15] Collecting chronicles, photographing synagogues and cemeteries would buttress a new, healthy, secular Jewish nationalism and give Jews a deeper sense of their ties to Poland. *Landkentnish* drew strength from a growing popular fascination with Polish Jewish history, as evidenced in novels such as Scholem Asch's *Kiddush hashem* and Joseph Opatoshu's *In poylishe velder*, which both became best sellers. Historians Meyer Bałaban and Yitzhak Schipper wrote history columns regularly in the daily press.

Like many other younger Jewish historians in Poland, Ringelblum was a dedicated member of Left Poalei Zion. This was not a large party, and, during the 1930s, it steadily lost both influence and members.[16] All the more telling, therefore, was the devotion of those who remained committed. And Ringelblum stayed to the very end.[17]

The party transmitted a powerful legacy. One factor was the engagement with Jewish history. In interwar Poland many young Jewish historians were members of Left Poalei Zion, including Ringelblum, Artur Eisenbach, Raphael Mahler, and Bela Mandelsberg. The movement also imparted a love of Yiddish, a devotion to

15 "*Landkentnish*," Ringelblum wrote, "really means not only learning [*derkenen*] a city's past, its monuments and buildings; it also means getting to know the people [*folk*] with its centuries-old folklore and creative traditions." For an important precis of the significance of *Landkentnish* for Ringelblum, see Emanuel Ringelblum, "Fun der reaktsiye," *Landkentnish* (Yiddish), no. 1 (1933); see also David G. Roskies, "Landkentnish: Yiddish Belles Lettres in the Warsaw Ghetto," in Robert M. Shapiro, ed., *Holocaust Chronicles: Individualizing the Holocaust through Diaries and other Contemporaneous Personal Accounts* (Hoboken: Ktav, 1999), p. 11.

16 The definitive study on Left Poalei Zion in Poland is Bina Garncarska-Kadri, *In Search of a Path: Left Poalei Zion in Poland until World War II* (Hebrew) (Tel Aviv: Mifalim Universitaim lehotza'ah la'or, 1995); see also Samuel Kassow, "The Left Poalei Tsiyon in Interwar Poland," in Zvi Gitelman, ed., *The Emergence of Modern Jewish Politics: Bundism and Zionism in Eastern Europe* (Pittsburgh: University of Pittsburgh Press, 2003), pp. 71–85, 99.

17 See, for example, his essay on Shakhne Sagan in Ringelblum, *Ksovim fun Geto*, vol. 2, pp. 103–122.

the Jewish masses, and a deep sense of moral pathos — which had both positive and negative effects on Ringelblum as a historian.

Unlike the Bund, Left Poalei Zion saw the Jews as a worldwide people, affected by cultural and social models developing in territorial bases such as Palestine and Birobidzhan. One task of the politically engaged historian was to facilitate this process of cross-fertilization.[18]

It is highly revealing that, when the party split for a time in the mid-1930s, Ringelblum stayed with the Buchsbaum-Zagan faction, which opposed Yitshak Lev's call for closer ties to the World Zionist Organization and to pioneering Zionist youth movements.[19] Ringelblum, like his mentor Zagan, did not want the party to turn its back on the Jewish masses of Poland in favor of Palestinocentric and Hebreocentric elitism. By 1937, however, the party had indeed changed its position and joined the World Zionist Organization. Yet Ringelblum's stance during the split was quite telling. It showed the depth of his Yiddishism and his identification with Polish Jewry.

One should preface a discussion of the impact of his radical politics on his view of Polish-Jewish relations by saying that Ringelblum took his scholarly integrity seriously. He believed that the best way historians could defend the Jewish people was to write fairly and objectively.[20] We certainly see this quest for objectivity in the *Oyneg Shabes* Archives. In a pre-war book review of Philip Friedman's *History of the Jews of Łódź*, Ringelblum admitted that Jewish historians had to "navigate" — in his words — a narrow course between the Scylla of apologetics and the Charybdis of nationalist megalomania.[21] He defined the latter as a propensity to react to

18 See, for example, Uriel (Raphael Mahler), "Di kultur badaytung far di yidishe masn in dem kamf farn territorialn arbeter tsenter," *Arbeter Tsaytung* (Yiddish), no. 50 (1935); Nathan Buchsbaum, "A PPSesher broshur gegn bund un bundizm," *Arbeter Tsaytung*, no. 4 (1938).

19 There is a good discussion on the split in Garncarska-Kadri, *In Search of a Path*, pp. 385–394.

20 See, for example, his essay on the *Oyneg Shabes* Archive in Ringelblum, *Ksovim fun Geto*, vol. 2, pp. 82–84.

21 A copy of this review can be found in the YVA (YVA), M.10.AR2/408.

antisemitism by exalting the alleged spiritual superiority, moral power, and political unity of the Jewish people.[22]

In the same review, Ringelblum made a rather startling statement about nineteenth-century Jewish history, on which he had written relatively little. Yes, he admitted, nineteenth-century history had many more available sources. But the closer a historian came to the present, the greater the danger of succumbing to ideological pressure and stepping over the thin line that separated scholarship from propaganda. In his own party, for example, he had bitterly resisted calls from ultra-leftists in the early 1930s to boycott YIVO.[23]

Still, the late Nachman Blumental went too far when he praised Ringelblum for completely transcending party biases.[24] Indeed, as the war progressed and as Ringelblum struggled to find shreds of hope and optimism, the party's tradition and ideology became even more important to him, as we can see in letters written to Adolf Abraham Berman in January 1944.[25]

A close reading of Ringelblum's wartime writings reveals certain political biases. His pre-war antipathy to the "Jewish bourgeoisie" emerged as a constant theme in his ghetto diary, and he was not completely fair in his treatment of Adam Czerniaków, the head of the Warsaw Judenrat. He bitterly resented the alleged favoritism shown by Czerniaków to prominent converts in the ghetto. Ringelblum had little sympathy for the counterargument made by Czerniaków and Judenrat member Abraham Gepner that to boycott converts like Professor Ludwik Hirszfeld and Police Chief Jozef Szeryński would be a demonstration of disloyalty to Poland at a time of national emergency. Gepner, in turn, reacted angrily to

22 Nevertheless, Ringelblum was also accused of a tendency to engage in national apologetics, for example, Jacob Shatzky, "Menakhem Ben Faivish Ringelblum," in Ringelblum, *Kapitlen Geshikhte*, pp. xxxi-xxxii.

23 Emanuel Ringelblum, "Der YIVO un di yidishe arbetershaft," *Arbeter Tsaytung* (Yiddish), August 1931.

24 Nachman Blumental, "Der historiker-tsu der ferter yortsayt," *Arbeter Tsaytung*, no. 3 (1948).

25 Six weeks before he died, Ringelblum again reiterated his devotion to the party; letter of Emanuel Ringelblum to Adolf Abraham Berman, January 24, 1944, Adolf Abraham Berman Collection, Ghetto Fighters' House Archives.

Ringelblum's attacks on the Judenrat's attitude to converts and accused him of a lack of Polish patriotism.[26]

One can also see the imprint of his political culture in his discussion of the Poles. Ringelblum used the conceptual framework of "generic fascism" – the last-ditch defense of a dying capitalist system – to explain both Nazi and Polish antisemitism. In both cases he emphasized the instrumental nature of antisemitism, how it was manipulated from above to serve the interests of a dying capitalist system.[27] As late as May 1942, he wrote that when the German people learned of the mass murder of the Jews, they would pressure Hitler to stop it.[28] Ringelblum used the same conceptual framework of generic fascism to explain the upsurge of Polish antisemitism in the 1930s. He was too quick to see it as a doctrine cynically imposed from the top down so as to defend vested interests.[29]

Ringelblum's analysis of the overall political situation in pre-war Poland was also flawed, as he overestimated the potential benefits of agrarian reform. In addition, he erred in his assertion that ordinary workers had a better record than other Poles in saving Jews. This is not borne out by the more recent research.[30] To be sure, these flaws in Ringelblum's analysis were far outweighed by his determination, from the very onset of the war, to lay the groundwork for a serious and thorough study of Polish-Jewish relations.

Ringelblum's pre-war writings on Polish Jewish history often stressed that the true story of Polish-Jewish relations often lurked behind the visible evidence of legal decrees and official documents. Practice and theory were often quite different. Assimilationist Jewish historians like Kraushar and Nussbaum had taken an overly rosy view of Polish liberalism and tolerance, because they failed to look at the reality behind formal charters.[31] On the other hand,

26 Ringelblum, *Ksovim fun Geto*, vol. 1, p. 232.

27 *Ibid.*,, vol. 2, p. 241.

28 Ibid., vol. 1, p. 373.

29 Ibid., vol. 2, p. 241.

30 Ibid., p. 349; Feliks Tych, *Długi cień zagłady* (Warsaw: Żydówski Instytut Historyczny, 1999), p. 50.

31 He expressed this view as early as 1924; see "Di yidishe arbetershaft un di geshikhtsvisnshaft," *Di Fraye Yugnt* (Yiddish), no.1 (1924).

antisemitic decrees, like bans on Jewish urban settlement, often foundered on hard economic realities and the self-interest of the *szlachta* (nobility).[32]

Ringelblum saw Polish-Jewish economic relations between 1939 and 1941 as a continuation of this long-standing conflict between, to use his own words, "gray theory" and the "tree of life"(*ets hayim*). Economics trumped antisemitism. The combination of economic self-interest, Jewish resilience, and Polish-Jewish cooperation (in smuggling) sabotaged the Nazi determination to strangle Polish Jewry through ghettos, starvation rations, and punitive economic decrees.[33]

Many documents of the *Oyneg Shabes* Archives described how the establishment of ghettos helped isolate Jews from Poles and tore asunder the web of daily contact. However, the archive also offered ample testimony to the fact that, when it came to trade, even ghetto walls failed to break Polish-Jewish relationships. One particularly interesting reportage by Peretz Opoczynski, "Goyim in Geto" ("Gentiles in the ghetto"), described how Jews regarded the Poles who sneaked into the Warsaw ghetto in order to trade. Even though the Jews knew that these Poles took advantage of their desperate situation to make handsome profits, they still appreciated their presence in the ghetto. They saw this as a form of moral support, a sign that they were not entirely isolated and forsaken. Opoczynski stressed that the Poles took a personal risk by stealing into the ghetto, and this was a major boost to Jewish morale. When Polish women smugglers would give money to Jewish children for their prayers "to the Jewish God," Jews saw this as a small link, however tenuous, to the past.[34]

32 This was a major theme of his unpublished second volume of the *History of the Jews of Warsaw*, which covered the period from 1527 to 1795.

33 "The Jews," Ringelblum wrote, "were able to overcome all the economic barriers… and continued their pre-war production for the needs of the Aryan market. They had overcome the [pre-war boycott of the Polish antisemites]... and also the current invaders who wanted the Jews to starve en masse in the ghetto. Economic life knows no differences of nationality and race." See Ringelblum, *Ksovim fun Geto*, vol. 2, p. 279.

34 Peretz Opoczynski, "Goyim in Geto," Ringelblum Archive, Part I, no. 323: "The bridge that linked Jew and gentile," Opoczynski wrote, "was made of bad

Unfortunately, much of what seemed important in 1940–1941, such as smuggling, had become tragically irrelevant by late 1942. From the very beginning of the war, Ringelblum understood how vital it was to encourage writing "from inside the event," writing that would not be skewed by the distorting lens of retrospective recollection and selective memory. To collect material, to record impressions, and to write them down immediately were the watchwords of *Oyneg Shabes*.[35]

Memory was tricky, Ringelblum insisted, especially in the ghetto. Under the pressure of unprecedented events, Jewish society changed at lightning speed. Ringelblum realized, even before he was aware of the "Final Solution," how quickly trauma could efface memories of all that had preceded it, how unimportant the "everyday" would seem when viewed through the prism of greater suffering. All the more vital, therefore, was the need to capture the "everyday" Jewish society under German occupation, to meld thousands of individual testimonies into a collective portrait.

One can see that these same principles held true in the study of Polish-Jewish relations. In 1939 or mid-1941, Ringelblum obviously did not foresee the onset of physical annihilation. He was hoping — at least in part — to create a viable past for the postwar era. But he knew that one should not wait to collect material — and he was right. By November 1942, for example, the study of the Jewish role in the siege of Warsaw or the September campaign had taken a back seat to more pressing and tragic questions. Polish sympathy to expelled refugees in 1940, or expressions of warmth and friendship when Jewish friends and neighbors entered the ghetto in November 1940, had now been overshadowed by the indifference and even hostility that became so painfully evident in 1942. Had the war ended in mid-1941, the picture of Polish-Jewish relations conveyed by the *Oyneg Shabes* Archives would have been one of complex am-

material — speculation — but it served a good purpose — to save many Jews from starvation...these Polish smugglers [worried about their own pockets] but still served a national purpose: to maintain the ties between loyal citizens of Poland and stretch out a brotherly hand to the persecuted. Thereby they sow the seeds of morality in a time of major moral degeneration."

35 Ringelblum, *Ksovim fun Geto*, vol. 2, p. 87.

biguity, but certainly not of unbridgeable national hatred or bitter resentment. Indeed, one important member of the *Oyneg Shabes* Archives, Abraham Lewin, wrote as late as June 7, 1942, that the war had exerted a favorable influence on Polish-Jewish relations.[36]

In his essay on the *Oyneg Shabes* Archives, probably written in early 1943, Ringelblum called the collection of monographs on provincial towns "the most important treasure" of the archive.[37] One reason for this assertion was that Ringelblum knew their value for the future study of Polish-Jewish relations. He understood that there was a different texture to Polish-Jewish contact in small towns than in big cities. Now that the German expulsions had ended the Jewish presence in many small towns, it was important to collect as many eyewitness accounts as possible.[38] These monographs, which mostly deal with the 1939–41 period, reflect the complexity of Polish-Jewish relations before the great rupture of 1942, before the onset of mass annihilation. There are several accounts of rabid Polish antisemitism, but also many essays that recorded Polish sympathy and kindness.

These *shtetl* monographs were but one example of Ringelblum's determination to use the archive in order to build a better future, to put postwar Polish-Jewish relations on a firmer foundation. For these reasons Ringelblum understood how important it was to doc-

36 Lewin supported the view that "the majority of Poles have been gripped by philo-semitic feelings... I see Polish-Jewish relations in a bright light. I think that this war will wash this earth of ours clean of much filth and savagery... There will be no refuge here for antisemitism, at least not for public aggressive antisemitism. They will be ashamed to deal in it. I believe that the Polish people too has been purified by the terrible fire that has swept the face of the earth. Let us not forget that the Poles are in second place in the table of tragic losses among the nations, just behind the Jews..."; see Abraham Lewin, *A Cup of Tears* (Oxford: Blackwell, 1988), p. 124.

37 Ringelblum, *Ksovim fun Geto*, vol. 2, p. 88.

38 Ringelblum wrote in this essay that "there is a widespread opinion [among Jews] that antisemitism has increased sharply during the time of the war and that most Poles are happy about the misfortunes that have beset the Jews in the cities and small towns of Poland. But the attentive reader of our materials will find hundreds of documents, which show the opposite. In more than one report from a *shtetl* he will read about how warmly the Polish population treated Jewish refugees. You will find hundreds of examples of peasants hiding and feeding Jewish refugees from nearby *shtetlekh*"; ibid., p. 86.

ument the September 1939 campaign, which he compared to the famous Polish-Jewish rapprochement during the 1863 uprising.

Before the beginning of the mass murder, therefore, Ringelblum approached the problem of Polish-Jewish relations from much the same perspective that had informed his pre-war scholarship. The Jews had a future in Poland, he believed, and historians could help bridge the differences between the two peoples.[39]

Amid a welter of contradictory observations, one particularly disturbing pattern stood out from the very beginning of the German occupation: the disparity between the "personal" and the "civic" behavior of the Polish population. Many Poles showed great kindness to individual Jews and to starving Jewish children. On the other hand, even shared suffering at the hands of the common enemy did not soften their tendency to regard "Jews" in the abstract as an alien, even hostile body, quite outside the sphere of Polish moral responsibility. In other words, Polish kindness to Jews all too often rested on individual rather than on "civic" or "political" considerations.

From the very beginning of the war, Ringelblum understood that ugly accusations of Jewish collaboration with the Soviets provided many Poles with a ready-made excuse to see the Jews as a disloyal, alien element. Until 1941, Ringelblum tended to approach this explosive issue carefully; his writings reflected the intellectual caution of a historian who understood how much this question would weigh on future relations between the two peoples. No doubt he thought that when the war would end, charges and counter-charges would fill the air, and historians could help provide some perspective on this and other sensitive issues. After all, similar controversies had raged over Jewish-Polish relations in Vilna and Lwów in 1919.

39 In early 1942, Ringelblum composed guidelines for the study of Polish-Jewish relations; see Ringelblum Archive, Part I, no. 492. These guidelines include dozens of different questions and reflect Ringelblum's determination to avoid hastiness and oversimplification in the study of Polish-Jewish relations. The last set of questions concerns Polish reactions to the news of Chelmno and Vilna. Mass murder had already begun, but Ringelblum was only beginning to guess at its true scope.

Thus, in the beginning, Ringelblum was quite ready to record Polish complaints that Jews had acted disloyally to Poland. No doubt he had also read several Jewish accounts given to the *Oyneg Shabes* Archives that seemed to corroborate some of these Polish claims.[40] In April 1940, for example, Ringelblum mentioned Jewish testimonies from Białystok and Zamość that described how Jews had jeered Polish officers and former civil servants.

When the mass extermination of the Jewish population began, however, a marked change came about in Ringelblum's approach to the problem. This was no longer a quarrel that could be understood by reasoned and patient analysis. This was no longer 1940, when mass expulsions of Poles from the Warthegau and brutal German/Soviet repression of the Polish intelligentsia gave many Poles ample reason to think that their fate was as bad as the Jews'. Instead, an enraged Ringelblum saw the scepter of the *Żydokomuna* (a pejorative Polish term that loosely translates as Yid-Communist Conspiracy) as a convenient alibi that Poles used to rationalize and excuse their passivity and indifference to the mass murder of their Jewish neighbors. He now dismissed the Polish complaints of Jewish collaboration with the Soviets as exaggerations and as "groundless nonsense."[41] The *Żydokomuna* had become one of the most reliable staples of German propaganda, and most Poles had fallen for the bait.

After the onset of the mass murder, Ringelblum faced a painful inner conflict between his determination to remain an objective historian and his grief at the mass extermination of his people. He had hoped historians like himself could build bridges between Poles and Jews; but how many Jews would be left? Ringelblum's introduction to his last work, on Polish-Jewish relations during World War

40 An extreme example of this kind of testimony was the account of a twenty-two-year-old Jewish refugee who had fled to Vilna in 1939, and who had returned to Warsaw in late 1941. It was the kind of testimony that could have been furnished by any rabid Polish antisemite: "Under the Bolshevik occupation Polish antisemitism increased markedly. In large part the Jews themselves are responsible for this. They used every occasion to jeer the Poles and to yell, 'Your Poland is gone.' Jewish Communists denounced Poles, Jews disarmed Polish soldiers and spit in their face ..."; Ringelblum Archive, Part I, no. 932.

41 Ringelblum, *Ksovim fun Geto*, vol. 2, p. 261.

II, reflected his inner turmoil and his sense of enormous personal responsibility:

> When a *sofer* [Jewish] scribe sets out to copy the Torah, he must, according to religious law, take a ritual bath in order to purify himself of all uncleanness and impurity. This scribe takes up his pen with a trembling heart, because the smallest mistake in transcription means the destruction of the whole work… I am indebted to the Poles for having saved my life twice during this war…
>
> It is my wish to write objectively, *sine ira et studio*, on the problem of Polish-Jewish relations during the present war. In times so tragic for my people, however, it is no easy task to rise above passion and maintain cool objectivity.[42]

For anyone seriously interested in the study of Polish-Jewish relations during the war, Emanuel Ringelblum's masterly essay, "Polish-Jewish Relations during the Second World War," remains an indispensable source. Written in an underground bunker on the Aryan side of Warsaw, Ringelblum's work, even when read many years later, still radiates considerable moral authority.

Rarely has a historian set out to write a study under more intense circumstances. When Ringelblum began this book in late 1943, he had just made a dramatic escape from the Trawniki labor camp, smuggled out by two intrepid couriers, one Polish and the other Jewish. He was packed into a crowded hideout together with his wife and son and thirty-five other Jews. He was forced to become exactly as he had described other Jews in hiding: a helpless child, totally dependent on his Polish protectors for everything. While thirty-eight people passed their time in enforced idleness, often arguing, sometimes even screaming, while they lived through the paralyzing fright of possible capture, Ringelblum sat in a corner of the bunker day after day, writing page after page. "The noose was

42 I have used the English translation of Joseph Kermish and Shmuel Krakowski, eds., Emanuel Ringelblum, *Polish Jewish Relations during the Second World War* (Evanston: Northwestern University Press, 1992), pp. 1–2.

tightening around [the] necks of Warsaw's remaining Jews…we lived in constant fear of denunciation," phrases taken from Ringelblum's book also aptly described his own situation.

The Ringelblum essay was a unique synthesis of the immediacy of contemporaneous testimony with the analytic perspective of retrospective historical analysis. The book reflected the tension between the imperative of historical objectivity and the shock of the enormous crimes that he witnessed not as a bystander but as a direct victim. Detached historians could make necessary distinctions between perpetrators and bystanders, between Polish and German antisemitism, between active complicity and indifference. For a member of a victimized people to do so required a major effort of intellectual discipline.

Ringelblum recognized that the Polish people could not have averted the Holocaust or have saved most of their Jewish neighbors. He paid tribute to their national pride and their highly developed sense of national honor. He took great care to note the terrible risks that Poles took to hide Jews. All the more telling, therefore, are his accusations of indifference and moral abandonment by the Home Army and by large sections of the population.

Żegota (Council for Aid to Jews) aside, Polish help to Jews was largely a private matter, conducted by heroic individuals who assumed terrible risks, which he in no way minimized. But the record of Polish behavior on the civic level failed the important standards of solidarity and basic human decency. In resisting the Germans, the Poles showed great courage. Confronted with the mass murder of their fellow citizens, however, they failed the test. On the one hand, the Poles' lack of moral support greatly complicated the Jews' ability to resist. Perversely, the Poles then used this alleged lack of resistance to taunt the Jews for lacking pride and honor. But even in the relatively simple matter of suppressing the blackmailers and informants who plagued Jews on the Aryan side, the underground state could not be bothered.

The Poles could not have stopped the Holocaust. But Ringelblum asks whether it was inevitable that the Jews, looking their last on this world as they rode in the death trains speeding from different parts of the country to Treblinka or other places of slaughter, should have to see indifference or even gladness on the faces of their neighbors?[43]

His final verdict was harsh:

> Polish Fascism and its ally, antisemitism, have conquered the majority of the Polish people. It is they whom we blame for the fact that Poland has not taken an equal place alongside the Western European countries in rescuing Jews.

But, to the very end, Ringelblum remembered that, as a historian, he bore important responsibilities to future generations. Written in Polish, this last book was aimed as much at Poles as at the handful of Jewish survivors who would emerge after the war. It represented the last action Ringelblum could undertake in the fight for a better Poland.

43 Ibid., p. 7.

Moral Issues in Emanuel Ringelblum's Writings from World War II

Barbara Engelking

The writing of history, establishing an order in remembering the past, as well as attaching meaning to history are all part of the biblical canon. Whereas Emanuel Ringelblum describes events and cares about memory, he avoids reading meaning into the Holocaust. Did he think that this task traditionally belongs to rabbis, who, throughout history, have read the messages from God to the Jews? Or perhaps he thought that there was no sense to be found?

We can distinguish four stages of narration in the writings that Emanuel Ringelblum has left us, complementing the four collections of texts from the war period. The first stage is the text of the *Chronicle* (*Kronika*), until July 1942; the second is notes from the time of the deportation and immediately afterward; the third is texts that were written in a shelter, i.e., *Polish-Jewish Relations* (*Stosunki polsko-żydowskie*) and *Portraits* (*Sylwetki*); and the fourth is letters from a bunker, by nature the most personal genre. Reflection on those texts allows us an insight into the evolution of Ringelblum's consciousness, his reactions to what was happening around him, as both a historian and as a participant in those events, and also – the topic of this article – his moral views. Throughout the analysis of these texts, I will attempt to show whether and how his ethical code, his hierarchy of values, and his attitude toward people changed.

Barbara Engelking

Witness of History: Chronicle (Kronika)

As a historian Ringelblum tries to be as impartial as possible; thus, he relates events without commenting on them. Yet in spite of the attempted objectivity, the author's outlook on life, his moral attitude, and his hierarchy of values influence the selection of facts and the way he presents them.

One of the traditions that strongly influenced and molded Ringelblum was the Polish socialist tradition. This had emerged during the partition period and offered an attractive ethical proposal – a model of a leftist intellectual activist. Since the 1880s, educational, social, and political activists had worked out a universal model of an engaged civic attitude and had also formulated social tasks for intellectuals. To simplify, we can say that such a point of view is characterized by a belief in the progress of society and civilization, by a conviction that through work reality can be changed, and by nonconformist ethics and civic courage. The criteria of a person's value are social service and work, as understood as engaging in the common good. This particular ethical heroism was also a feature of Emanuel Ringelblum's personality. From the perspective of a Jewish intellectual who has a strong sense of the separateness and peculiarity of the history of Polish Jewry, the universalism of socialist ideology was attractive both as a proposed vision of humanism and as a dimension of the ethical aspects of social activity.

Ringelblum, an active social and political worker, with definitely leftist views, sees and describes the world in categories of historical materialism. He looks at historical processes from a perspective of class divisions and conflicts, and sometimes he is tempted by the simplicity of Marxist interpretation. He looks at people through the social class to which they belong; for example, when describing Abraham Gepner, he states: "this noble and respectable man, who impresses many with his civic courage, his proud attitude, **is however** (concerning tax policies) **a typical representative of high bourgeoisie."**[1] [emphasis mine – B.E.]

1 Emanuel Ringelblum, *Kronika getta warszawskiego: Wrzesień 1939–styczeń 1943* (Warsaw: Czytelnik, 1988), p. 390.

In seeking a deeper insight into the moral issues present in the *Chronicle*, it is important to emphasize that, when I point out some moral aspects, it is a question of evaluation and judgments; I do not wish to discredit the objective character and historical value of the work. In his notes Ringelblum relatively rarely exceeds a factual, narrative way of accounting. The author of the *Chronicle* is quite an uncommunicative person, hidden behind a maximally objective description of reality, seemingly abstaining from own views and judgments. Of course, this does not mean that Ringelblum does not refer to morality at all. Quite the opposite: he refers to it relatively often, though generally indirectly. The record of events, though greatly impartial, is full of moral issues and reflects the author's outlook on life.

Ringelblum rarely uses the word "morality." On the whole, until July 1942, in the *Chronicle* – at least in the text I am now analyzing – the word appears only three times, and always in a social context. The first time it appears is in January 1940: "moral problem of wearing and not wearing armbands: solidarity."[2] Use of the word "solidarity" in this sentence emphasizes the social aspect of identification. Ringelblum does not see it as a problem of individual identity – often a dramatic personal choice between imposed identification and a feeling of affiliation – but rather as a question of loyalty, though obligatory, but still to a community.

Ringelblum refers to morality for the second time directly and in an intriguing way in March 1941, in these words: "Providing poor people with food during feast-days has a significant moral meaning."[3] It seems that the moral aspect in this sentence can be interpreted in many ways: it may refer to the necessity of helping the poorest; to the importance of the feast, as a particularly significant time; and also to the problem of social stratification in the ghetto. The ethical challenge of help is connected here with attributing importance to the experience of an existing community. I suppose that in a similar meaning the term "moral" is used by Ringelblum for the third time, one month later, in April 1941, when he writes:

2 Ibid., p. 78.
3 Ibid., p. 254.

"In many places for refugees Seders were organized.... For a moment the refugees forgot about their sad fate and loneliness. Seders were moral reinforcement to those exhausted homeless people."[4] The refugees' spirit was not raised only by the possibility of eating, but actually by being together, in a community.

I think that from these examples it is possible to recognize the key features of Ringelblum's concept of morality. *The most important moral criterion, according to him, is the attitude toward the community.* It is the community that is the source of morality for Ringelblum, who did not believe in God. His attitude toward religion – as befits a leftist intellectual – is critical. We can even talk about his disappointment with the behavior of religious people, which he expresses in November 1940: "religious Jews, and also rabbis did not show the slightest signs of readiness to Kiddush Hashem [consecration of the Name of the Almighty; martyrdom.] Only under pressure they burnt the houses of prayer in some cities in the provinces."[5] The interests of the community – in this case, the rule of collective responsibility applied by the Germans, where "disobedience to their orders could bring sad consequences to the community"[6] – were justification for acting against the rule of *Kiddush Hashem*.

Ringelblum finds the good of the community to be more important than religious rules. It is the attitude to the community – described, among others, in terms of categories of help, solidarity, loyalty, and responsibility – that is the source of evaluation and judgments of people and their behavior. The attitude toward one's own group, in my opinion, was at the source of Ringelblum's hierarchy of values and his views on what is good and what is bad, what is appropriate in time of war and what is not.

In such an attitude toward morality, we find not only a leftist ethos but also a tradition of Hobbesian social philosophy. This proposes a criterion for the division of human merits into virtues of citizens and virtues of human beings. The first – civic virtues, do-

4 Ibid., p. 268.
5 Ibid., p. 206.
6 Ibid., p. 282.

ing good, like altruistic help, justice, and goodwill –bring benefits to fellow citizens and are profitable to the state. The second – personal virtues, also known as honor virtues, like dignity, modesty, veracity, and courage – are not actually profitable to the community but grace those who display them. In the moral discourse of the *Chronicle*, the context of civic virtues definitely dominates.

The analysis of the moral narration shows that Ringelblum most frequently writes about what strikes him as incompatible with his system of values, what surprises him as something absolutely not obvious in the trial in which the community of Polish Jews was being tested. Ringelblum's attention is drawn by various acts that are noxious to the community and the behavior of those people who break loose from the common fate. Assimilated Jews and neophytes are the kind of people that Ringelblum comes down on most heavily. However, even though they break loose from the community, the community should treat them with justice. In June 1941, he wrote: "The Ghetto is not a Jewish state, but a territory in which converted Jews also live and that is why they ought to be treated equally."[7]

Ringelblum very often writes about demoralization and its various manifestations. The behavior of demoralized people strengthens social differences and, therefore, also injustice. As noted in May 1942: "Demoralization in the Ghetto is spreading wider and wider. At the same time, when the poor become paupers, covered with rags, there are girls wearing more and more elegant clothes, as if there was no war at all."[8]

More serious signs of demoralization were bribes, frauds, and corruption. The great danger in this area of demoralization is that it strikes the basis of social solidarity and causes serious harm to the community. Ringelblum condemns collaboration and denouncing and also the Jewish police, which clearly stood against the Jews as a whole, even before the deportation action. Deploring the scale of events of this type, he wrote: "Lately a plague of denouncing has spread. Leszno 13 has just opened [the dam], gave vent to evil in-

7 Ibid., p. 260.
8 Ibid., p. 387.

stincts and enabled [manifestation of] such tendencies."[9] This sentence contains a belief in the weakness of human nature, its inclination to evil, its susceptibility to the demoralizing influence of a situation, when there is no clear "social contract" and an individual is left to his own, in fact, imperfect moral intuition.

In a situation of tremendous pressure of circumstances, a human's weakness is perhaps not justified, but explicable. In May 1942, Ringelblum wrote: "I think that statement that demoralization has influenced us stronger than others is exaggerated, especially if we take into consideration our particularly difficult situation in which many face an alternative: follow the wicked path or die starving."[10] Ringelblum refers here to Kant's condition of free will, which means that only internally a free man can act "morally." Hungry, sick, frightened, dying people could not act morally, as their free will and possibilities of taking decisions were limited. The inability to make a free moral choice sometimes became a terrifying paradox. In May 1942, Ringelblum wrote: "Jews have the right to live provided that they work for the German army.... There has been no such tragedy in the whole history. A nation that hates Germans with all its senses can evade death only by helping the enemy in his victory, and this victory means an absolute extermination of Jews."[11] It was, indeed, as commented by the author of the *Chronicle*, a "tragic knot."

Among the ethical dilemmas present in the *Chronicle* until July 1942, is also one of the moral problems characteristic of socialism – the tension between justice and equality. During the war, in the ghetto, in the context of life-and-death choices, this clash became very dramatic. In May 1942, the author described the insufficient means of social help in the ghetto:

> A question therefore arises, wouldn't it be better to use that money only for the chosen, for the social activists, for the spiritual elite and so on?.... A **tragic problem** emerges: give everyone a spoon, and then nobody will survive, or give abun-

9 Ibid., p. 253.
10 Ibid., p. 375.
11 Ibid., p. 367.

> dantly, then there will be enough only for the few[12] [emphasis mine – B.E.].

Formulating the problem in such a dramatic way as did Ringelblum reflects a conflict among various values. Not only is there a dilemma of choice between justice and equality, but also we can find here an antagonism between justice and compassion. Justice has got to obey the rules, be absolutely objective, while compassion is completely spontaneous. Justice is not merciful, and mercy cannot be just. Any solution of this problem brings remorse of conscience.

The remorse and feelings of guilt – which are a sign of acting against moral norms – speak volumes about the author's ethics. Ringelblum writes about two situations in which his conscience could find no peace – and both these situations refer to the suffering of starving children. In August 1941, on a silent night, "screams of hungry begging children make a doleful impression. And no matter how tough you are, finally you toss them a piece of bread, otherwise you will find no peace in your house."[13] A few months later he confesses that he gives a few coins each evening to the children begging next to his house on the corner of Leszno and Karmelicka streets, which, still, however, "cannot bring peace to my conscience."[14]

Ringelblum writes a lot about children, but these are the only cases when he reveals his own feelings, writing directly that he is shaken. The children's misery in the ghetto, their loneliness, orphanhood, poverty, and death are proof of the community's helplessness, which should actually defend its weakest members. Maybe, when looking helplessly at children's death, Ringelblum was thinking about his son Uri? Maybe he was afraid for him when describing such a scene in August 1941: "Begging children often die in the street. I was told about a startling scene in front of the house at number 24 on Muranowska Street. A six-year-old child was dying there throughout the whole night and couldn't crawl to a piece of bread thrown from a balcony."[15]

12 Ibid., p. 389.
13 Ibid., p. 301.
14 Ibid., p. 347.
15 Ibid., p. 302.

Space limitations preclude showing the variety of moral issues present in Ringelblum's writings, so I will not at this moment continue to speak about children and the feeling of obligation, about passiveness, about the antisemitism of the Polish people, about "good Germans," and about many other moral issues that appear in the *Chronicle* until July 1942. I cannot, however, refrain from presenting here, at least briefly, one of the more interesting and particularly relevant moral issues during the war; namely, the problem of revenge.

Quite early – as it was already in May 1940, even before the closing of the ghetto and long before the beginning of the extermination – Ringelblum took part in a discussion about revenge. There is nothing unusual about that, as all difficult experiences often cause a lively moral reflection. According to the words of the author of the *Chronicle*, "during four and a half years of war the main topic of each and every discussion…was avenging the innocent victims of the Germans."[16] During the first discussion about revenge related by Ringelblum, "Mr. Yitzhak [Gitterman] tried to prove that revenge never leads to any sensible solution. A defeated nation will think again about revenge, and it will be unceasingly this way. It was stated, that the only way is humans' ennoblement."[17]

At the first stage of the war, this group was deeply under the influence of socialist ideas, and they still believed in the progress of humanity. They had not yet abandoned hope. They spoke about revenge in a completely different manner, in June 1942, when they knew about the actions of the Einsatzgruppen in the East, the extermination camps in Bełżec and Chełmno, and the deportation from Lublin. Ringelblum writes then about the joy of the ghetto inhabitants with the bombardment of Cologne on May 30, 1942. Cologne was an omen of revenge for millions of murdered Jews that must and would be taken on Hitler's Germany. And that is why Jewish people in oppressed Europe treated Cologne as their act of revenge. "After the history of Cologne my spirit was raised, I felt, that if they kill me, my death had already been avenged in advance!"[18]

16 Ibid., p. 521.
17 Ibid., p. 131.
18 Ibid., p. 402.

It is rare in the *Chronicle* that the author reveals his own feelings. Here there is satisfaction and a sense of personal dignity. A desire for retaliation, a lust for revenge is an emotional reaction to harm that has been experienced. Retaliation helps in rebuilding social prestige and self-value. It contains reference to the idea of justice, care for one's own welfare, for compensation for the harm; it enables one to retain the feeling of one's own value, and, therefore, it comes close to honor and dignity. The inability to retaliate directly causes anger, hatred, helplessness, and humiliation. With time the need for revenge becomes more popular; it spreads and gains momentum. Just after the deportation action, Ringelblum wrote:

> I have found many noble and delicate people, who would not hurt a flea, who swore that they were ready to smother with their bare hands the first German that they would come across. Even leftist Jews thought that Germans in general are a nation with criminal instincts and as such, they should be wiped out from Europe.[19]

Many meanings can fit into that "Even"! Ideas of brotherhood, a vision of equality, belief in progress, humanistic ethics all fall apart when confronted with martyrdom of the nation and individual suffering.

Stressing the attitude to community, which is, in my opinion, the key moral criterion for Ringelblum, and emphasizing the advantage of civic virtues over individual ones in the *Chronicle*, I would not like to leave the impression that the latter are omitted or absent in the text. Of course this is not the case. Ringelblum writes a few times about courage and heroism; for example, in November 1941, he speaks about the youth: "It is a must to emphasize the unusual courage of young people from Ha-Shomer ha-Za'ir. They hold conferences...; carry out widespread informative work, publish newspapers."[20]

Even here, however, individual virtues are employed in social

19 Ibid., p. 521.
20 Ibid., p. 339.

service, in activities for the community, similarly to such personal experiences as suffering. This word appears in the *Chronicle* only once, and there it also has a common, not individual, dimension. In April 1941, Ringelblum quotes Yitzhak (Ignacy) Schipper: "I have heard an interesting theory that was to give reasons for the martyrdom of Jewish people. Jews are waging a war, so they have to suffer casualties."[21] Individual sacrifice also serves the community, like in a note from August 1941: "I have heard about an activist of Jewish Social Self-help, who fasts one day a week to be able to donate for the poor."[22] To fast in the ghetto was indeed heroism.

Witness to the Holocaust: Notes from the Deportation and Afterward

A dozen or so pages of Ringelblum's notes from the deportation action and, subsequently, tens of pages until January 1943, make up a text fundamentally different from the previous part of the *Chronicle*. On July 22, 1942, the world as it had existed until then caved in. The structure of the text reflects this collapse, and the writing style changes completely – to the point of disintegration. Ringelblum now jots down unfinished sentences, short forms, feverish notes, and quick remarks – his own and those heard from others. The short elliptical sentences echo a sigh or a shout. In the amorphous text the experience of the *Aktion* reflects an immensity of impressions, disorientation, disorder of life at the bottom of the void, confrontation with the accidental character of one's own existence and impending death, helplessness, and despair. Face to face with chaos.

Every day brings a new wave of atrocities, murder, fear, and despair. The Jews live in a state of extreme stress, at the edge of insanity, at the very edge of existence. The bridge of life over an eternal abyss becomes more and more unsteady, insecure, and fragile. There is a feeling of an ultimately dramatic character of fever-

21 Ibid., p. 269.
22 Ibid., p. 311.

ishly-made choices; accidental and temporary salvation produces disorder and helplessness. Salvation is never final: each day means another day of trying to save oneself again. No one has any influence on the course of history. A person's life depends on accident and coincidence. On August 27, Abraham Lewin wrote: "We are drowning, and the water is already up to our mouths."[23]

How can one even presume to write about this? Everything that was happening was radically new, and the language was made up of only old, worn out, and inadequate words. Ringelblum, along with other inhabitants of the ghetto, knew the limits of written transmission, yet were absolutely aware of the necessity of preserving, of recording their own experiences. But where could they look for new, more precise words to describe the Holocaust?

Facing the limited ability to convey the message and the inadequacy of language, many people ceased talking. Already in the spring of 1942, Rabbi Klonymus Kalman Szapiro recalled two types of silence from the Bible:

> There is a distinction between the word *harishah* [silence] and the word *ilmut* [muteness]. The word *harishah* generally refers to someone who has the potential to speak freely, but nevertheless does not speak. On the other hand, when a Jew is so broken and crushed that he has nothing to say, that he does not feel, he has neither the head nor the heart with which to perceive or feel, it is not silence (*harishah*), but rather muteness (*ilmut*), like the mute, who has no power of speech.[24]

Emanuel Ringelblum – though drowning and mute – found enough strength to keep up his chronicle. In my opinion, there are two key moral issues in the notes from the deportation period: passiveness and fight. There is no place to write about other, albeit important issues, which include looking for help outside the ghetto,

23 Abraham Lewin, *A Cup of Tears: A Diary of the Warsaw Ghetto* (Oxford: Basil Blackwell, 1989), p. 169.

24 Nehemia Polen, *The Holy Fire: The Teachings of Rabbi Kalonymus Kalman Shapira, the Rebbe of the Warsaw Ghetto* (Northvale, New Jersey and London: Jason Aronson, 1994), p. 25.

Adam Czerniaków's attitude, or the role of the Jewish police during the deportation.

The Jews' passiveness is, for the ever-active Ringelblum, an "eternal enigma," not to be understood. "Why?" he asks rhetorically. "Why did it come so easily, so smoothly to the enemy? Why did they go to the slaughter like sheep? Why didn't the executioner suffer at least a single casualty?"[25]

In reflections written in the fall of 1942, he himself gives some reasons for the Jews' passiveness. First of all there are psychological causes, what Ringelblum calls "moral crushing during three years of war,"[26] tiredness, exhaustion, starvation, hopelessness, despair; in a condensed formula: "a slave, completely oppressed, can no longer resist."[27] The second cause is the bond with the community, "fear of common responsibility — fear that every act of resistance could cause punishment to the whole society."[28] What had served until then the good of the community — solidarity, loyalty, responsibility for others — worked since then against the chance of individual salvation.

The third reason for passiveness was the German policy that destroyed the solidarity of the community, following the principle: "Share and rule. They have poisoned relations between the Poles and the Jews and made any help from there impossible.... They opposed Warsaw citizens to the refugees... Afterward... they opposed one 'shop' to another."[29]

The German methods strengthened the Jews' passiveness. They were constantly being deceived, lured by false hopes. The Germans dangled before them the hope that, in a moment, within two or three days, the deportation would come to an end. Thus, the Germans took them by surprise: "They declared that all rumors about deportation are false, just to catch us unawares...and deprived...of the possibility to think it over."[30]

25 Ringelblum, *Kronika*, p. 409.
26 Ibid., p. 425.
27 Ibid., p. 422.
28 Ibid., p. 425.
29 Ibid., p. 424.
30 Ibid., p. 425.

Another important moral issue that appears in the deportation period is resistance. Ringelblum relates a discussion between activists in which he participated in August 1942. We do not know his opinion; all we know is a general statement that "it was decided to wait and make a decision later, as on the 1st the action would end."[31] Such a conclusion was an effect of fear and paralysis, but also a realistic evaluation of their own strength and possibilities. Even those who formerly had declared the necessity to fight changed their minds during the deportation. Ringelblum writes about Ignacy Schiper, who, in the spring of 1942, made a passionate speech about a need to try and resist in case of deportation from Warsaw: "…After a few months, after the liquidation action in Warsaw began, the same Schiper was however against defence, …he was the strongest supporter of passiveness, not resisting the enemy, as it could bring punishment to all people."[32]

A dramatic conflict of values is reflected in such an attitude: on the one hand, the responsibility for the community; on the other hand, the matter of honor and dignity of that community. This tragic ethical dilemma is also linked with a generational conflict, which Ringelblum clearly expresses:

> A paradox has emerged. The generation of adult people that had lived already half of their lives talked, thought, cared and were preoccupied about surviving the war; they dreamed about life. The youth in contrast…talked and thought only about an honorable death. They did not think how to survive the war, they did not equip themselves with Aryan documents, they did not have flats on the other side. They were preoccupied only with the most noble, *most honorable death, as was fitting for an old nation with a few thousand years of history*[33] [emphasis mine – B.E.].

In the above quotation we find evidence of the decomposition of a

31 Ibid., p. 446.

32 Ibid., pp. 550–551.

33 Ibid., p. 502.

traditional community — at least by negating its internal hierarchical structure. It was not the elders but the youth that were now the guardians of moral values. It was they who represented virtues that had formerly adorned individuals and now, according to Ringelblum, should become common virtues superior to civic virtues. A dying community does not need unselfishness or goodwill; there remains only courage and honor.

The moral atmosphere in the ghetto after the deportation action changed. Ringelblum wrote: "Nowadays, when people have recovered a little and calculate what happened, a feeling of shame arises, that there was no resistance."[34] Shame — an ethical experience — refers to negation of the norm of dignity, with the experience of humiliation, helplessness, and fear. "It cannot happen again.... Most people are willing to resist. I think they will not go now like sheep to the slaughter."[35]

The expression "sheep to the slaughter," used for the second time by Ringelblum, appears also in many other texts written in the ghetto, in survivor memoirs, and later in historiographical publications. Nowadays it most often carries a pejorative connotation, and it has became a symbol of "ignoble" behavior, humiliating and irrational death. We can, however, also interpret it in the context of the original, biblical references, to the words of the prophets Isaiah and Jeremiah. Isaiah says (53:7):

> Like a sheep being led to slaughter,
> Like a ewe, dumb before those who shear her,
> He did not open his mouth.

So this would rather refer to suffering in silence, contempt of the butchers, maintaining dignity when faced with martyrdom.

On the other hand, Jeremiah (12:1–3) emphasizes the innocence of the victim, God's injustice, and awaiting fair punishment for the killers:

34 Ibid., p. 429.
35 Ibid., p. 422.

> Why does the way of the wicked prosper?
> Why are the workers of treachery at ease? …
> Yet You, Lord, have noted and observed me;
> You have tested my heart, and found it with You.
> Drive them out like sheep to the slaughter,
> Prepare them for the day of slaying!

I do not know the context in which Ringelblum used the expression about sheep to the slaughter: was it to emphasize the innocence of the victims, or their silence, or the lack of dignity? Interesting, however, is the mere fact that this left-wing socialist, leftist intellectual, who finds moral sources beyond religion, refers here to biblical visions and language. Maybe it is in situations in which everyday language proves inadequate that this old tongue can express more?

Witness of Past: Portraits and Polish-Jewish Relations

The notes from the deportation period give testimony to helplessness, shock, and defeat that Ringelblum feels as a historian and as a human. I think that his attitude to his own role as a historian begins to change from that moment. The suffering exceeds the boundaries of history, and personal experience overcomes historic awareness. This change becomes clear in the text he wrote at the turn of 1943/1944, when he was already in a shelter on the Aryan side, in a bunker at 84 Grójecka Street. In a situation of mass extermination, a sense of the individual becomes a moral defense. From now on there is an evolution in Ringelblum's texts; there is a change in the proportions between what is objective and what is subjective, between the historic and the personal. The *Chronicle*, until July 1942, was the most objective; in later texts a balanced language of neutral record falls apart. Ringelblum reveals own opinions more directly; he judges others more frequently and more resolutely. It seems that methods of historical materialism and analytical skills are no longer sufficient. The value of an individual fate moves to the foreground, becoming in a way a defense against total murder.

It seems that the mere fact that Ringelblum wrote *Portraits* of particular people demonstrates not only his grief after losing them, but also perhaps a growing belief in the influence of individual people on the course of history. He does not look at events as an aspect of historic process; an existential perspective appears instead. In *Portraits*, apart from presenting particular deeds of characters he describes, there is a reflection of his personal, often very private, feelings of respect, admiration, love, and longing.

Polish-Jewish Relations is an attempt at a synthetic, retrospective expression, yet enriched with wartime experiences, of the mutual relations between the Poles and the Jews. They are a "hot document, they are an expression of few Jews' opinion who remained in Poland after Hitler's massacre."[36] However, the scientific synthesis is broken by the author's personal experience; there is an immense tension visible in the text between the need for historical objectivity and the shock of the Holocaust. Of course, as a historian, Ringelblum tells the malefactors and witnesses apart, distinguishing between Polish and German antisemitism, but, as a human being, he is particularly disappointed with the attitude of the Polish government and the Polish nation. His expectations from the Poles were totally different; he had hoped that "when faced with such an extraordinary suffering unknown by the history of the world [it will be possible to] forget about all divisions…overcome the abyss."[37] He is embittered by the attitude of the government of the state of which he is a citizen. He criticizes its indifference and silence during the Holocaust.

The moral issue of civic solidarity returns here. Ringelblum charges – rightly so – that the Polish people lacked it:

> What did our neighbors do when a heavily armed occupant stroke the most defenseless nation – Jews? Were the victims of Nazism who escaped ghettos given a shelter in spite of an existing terror?…The Polish nation and the government of the Republic couldn't drag away from Jewish citizens Hitler's

36 Emanuel Ringelblum, *Stosunki polsko-żydowskie w czasie drugiej wojny światowej* (Warsaw: Czytelnik, 1988), p. 176.

37 Ibid., p. 32.

> crushing roller. **But we have the right to ask whether the Polish nation's attitude was adequate to the magnitude of the disasters that touched the Jews?** Whether, when "death trains" ran through different regions of the country to Treblinka or other points of extermination, their last views had to be indifferent or even pleased faces of their neighbors?[38] [emphasis mine – B.E.].

Ringelblum is right when he accuses the Polish government of lack of help – even moral support – during the deportations and the uprising in the Warsaw ghetto.

Only class-conscious members of the working class are excluded from the general accusations against Polish society of indifference, antisemitism, and denouncing. They are the ones who "long before the war understood the class dimension of antisemitism as a tool of power of the local bourgeoisie.... Jews generally dream about getting to workers' flats, as it guarantees that they will not fall victim to abuse and blackmail."[39]

Unfortunately, even workers' flats did not guarantee salvation, and it seems that Ringelblum must have known that. However, for some reason, he stuck to his pre-war outlook on life. Maybe in this way he sought to preserve any remaining feeling of safety and orientation in the world? He still believed – or wanted to believe, in spite of what he must have been looking at every day – that "suffering clears, suffering ennobles, suffering brings together."[40] Maybe this defense of his own ideals, a belief in the value of suffering, was a self-defense against the destruction of his internal world?

Community – not only in the literary meaning, but also as a former source of morality – ceased to exist. What was left – some groups of friends, family, people in hiding – apparently was nothing to fall back on. In his writings the lost world becomes mythically perfect. The memory of lost community becomes holy. What is interesting is that Ringelblum again reaches for biblical language,

38 Ibid., pp. 29–30.
39 Ibid., p. 146.
40 Ibid., p. 143.

but, more enigmatically, to the language of the New Testament, in order to describe poetically the "Last Supper" of Poalei Zion-Left:

> I remember that last party meeting...before the deportation of Jews from Warsaw.... Almost 200 comrades had gathered in the room, of which 97%, just like from the whole city of Warsaw, ended in Treblinka or other extermination camps.... They ate together on beautifully laid tables.... For security reasons no speeches were made. However it was enough, that comrades met after a long period, for the unspoken words to become audible. **It was like in the Gospel. Where two meet, there I (Christ) am among them**[41] [emphasis mine – B.E.].

I do not know why Ringelblum used this particular comparison. Maybe it is an expression of the incapacity of everyday language? Maybe biblical language is the only one capable of reflecting the magical atmosphere of that moment? This beautiful memory, modelled on a miraculous legend, shows the strength of Ringelblum's longing, and how painful the loneliness must have been.

Witness of Memory: Letters from the Bunker

Emanuel Ringelblum's letters to Adolf Abraham Berman, written in a shelter on the Aryan side, are the most personal among the sources mentioned here. I want to write only a few words about them, in conclusion. What strikes the reader is a dominant sorrow. Ringelblum suffers a progressing depression, and he writes: "Indeed I do not know what to do in such conditions... Nerves fall apart" (Jan. 27th) "I fell under the weather. There is no end to suffering" (Feb. 7th) and, in the last letter: "E. suffers now a very heavy spiritual depression caused by this hopeless situation" (Mar. 3rd). What makes his depression deeper is his illness, which he mentions: "as I have already written You many times, illness of Trawniki [after the

41 Ringelblum, *Kronika*, p. 537.

camp in Trawniki – B.E.] has made me lose my memory" (Dec. 6th).[42]

Ringelblum suffered heavily from helplessness and dependency on others. He had been active, independent, and dynamic throughout his entire life; now he had to stick to the rules of life in a shelter, which he described: "a Jew is a small child that cannot make even one step on his own."[43] I think that the lack of independence and an obligatory dependence was one of the causes of his bad mood. In addition, he had financial problems, which, in the bunker, were critical. But even in such a bad situation Ringelblum cared first about others. He often asked in his letters for help for his colleagues, neighbors, and friends; rarely for himself.

Despite the bad mood and memory problems – which really had to be a curse of fate for a historian – Ringelblum worked all the time. It was then that *Portraits* and *Polish-Jewish Relations* were created. As a historian Ringelblum remained constantly impartial, loyal to the moral order of Spinoza about love of truth as the ultimate human ideal. A reflection of this attitude can be found in a sentence from one of the letters that refers to relating the story of the uprising in the ghetto. On December 13, Ringelblum writes: "Why there is no data about Ż.Z.W. [Jewish Military Union]? A trace of them should remain in the history, even though we do not find them likeable."

In this period of his creative activity – which is particularly clear in the *Letters* – a new quality appears: besides historic awareness, which is knowledge of facts, a clear feeling of tradition emerges, which is the issue of the memory of the past. Ringelblum remained loyal to the ethical order of engaging himself, but the area of his activity changed. Remembering the latest events, and especially people who perished, became almost his obsession. "This is apparently our holiest duty, as there is nothing else left of them," he writes on November 25, 1943.

42 See the letters in the Hebrew section of this volume. See also the Polish edition: *Zagłada Żydów. Studia i Materiały*, vol. 1, 2005 (Warsaw: Centrum Badań nad Zagłada Żydów, 2005).

43 Ringelblum, *Stosunki*, p. 157.

It sounds similar to an absolute biblical order of memory. Memory materializes in stories and rituals. A story, a historic transmission, appears in Ringelblum's texts. A need of a ritual appears in a letter from February 17:

> I would like to remind you that there is an anniversary of an important family ceremony soon (April 19). It is important to remind…the whole family about it. Our uncle deserves that the whole remaining family remembers him forever. Write him in advance, and propose to him to celebrate solemnly this memorable day for the whole family.

Ringelblum's concern about commemorating is a concern for the future, about the future meaning of history. Ringelblum as a historian had come a long way: from describing the past, through testifying to the present, to creating tradition.

What was his journey as a man? From a participant and an activist through witness to the role of victim. What did it mean for him? Did any of his ideals endure: belief in humanity, in justice, in progress?

I frequently think about the last three days of Emanuel Ringelblum's life, days spent in Pawiak prison: from his arrest on March 7, 1944, to his execution in the ruins of the ghetto on March 10. Most probably, along with his son and another man, he was separated from his wife. What did he think about? Three days of torment… Were they filled with fear, suffering, or maybe a hope of salvation? Did he assess his life? Did he find his mission complete?

He considered the underground ghetto archive as his mission, his life work. He expressed it in a beautiful essay about the activity of the *Oyneg Shabes* group, written at the beginning of 1943. He cared about the future of the archive. In his penultimate letter, on March 1, he wrote: "I would notify Rafael [Mahler] of the address of our collections. In case none of us survives the war…at least then this will remain of us."[44]

44 Israel Gutman, "Emanuel Ringelblum's Last Request, March 1, 1944," *Yad Vashem Studies*, 31 (2003), p. 9.

He was aware of the priceless value of the documents he had gathered. Creating the archive was a measure of his outstanding personality – not only as a historian; it was also a deed of a man – an idealist who more often acted morally than merely talked about it. This heritage was left to his "heir," who we all – as Holocaust researchers – somehow are.

Sociological Reflections on Emanuel Ringelblum's Work[1]

Nechama Tec

Emanuel Ringelblum's wartime contributions are vast, encompassing the political, cultural, social-welfare, and scholarly domains. This versatility also underscores Ringelblum's impressive, organizational and cooperative skills. My own determination to learn more about this humane, intellectual giant, who, under devastating circumstances, juggled his ever-expanding wartime pursuits, has been an exhilarating and humbling experience.

This paper explores two questions. First, to what extent, are Ringelblum's contributions – particularly the underground archival collection, also known as the "*Oyneg Shabes*" Archives – based on sociological methodology? Second, are there any connections between the findings in *Oyneg Shabes* about diverse categories of individuals and my recent research about gender differences during the Holocaust?[2]

Emanuel Ringelblum's life began in 1900, and ended with his execution in 1944. Already as a teenager Emanuel stood out among his peers due to his predisposition for hard work. His dedication to hard work was reflected in a lifelong commitment to aid the needy, to the study of Jewish history and Jewish literature, and to the study

1 I am indebted to Israel Gutman for his insightful comments about this paper.
2 Results of my research are summarized in Nechama Tec, *Resilience and Courage: Women, Men, and the Holocaust* (New Haven: Yale University Press, 2003).

of economics and sociology. Artur Eisenbach, a fellow historian, friend, and Ringelblum's relative, was convinced that "The German occupation strengthened Ringelblum's noble humanity, his love for freedom, social justice, and the Jewish people. It also strengthened his uncompromising opposition to Fascism and a disdain for the followers of Fascism." [3]

Most Holocaust scholars enthusiastically applaud Ringelblum's achievements. Assessing the value of the *Oyneg Shabes* archives, Israel Gutman is convinced that "Ringelblum's work forms, without a doubt, the most important and detailed source of information about the Holocaust period and its universal significance."[4] Another scholar concurs that, "this work, unparalleled in its range and its sense of responsibility for the truth in history as it really was, constitutes a testimony to human courage and a memorial for the Jewish historiography of that terrible period."[5]

Ruta Sakowska, a historian and expert on the *Oyneg Shabes* collection, is convinced that Ringelblum's exposure to sociological methodology affected his wartime research. She traces Ringelblum's knowledge of sociological research methods to his long pre-war association with YIVO, the Jewish Scientific Institute in Vilna. From 1925 on, YIVO had relied on avant-garde, sophisticated sociological methodologies. It seems that, through Ringelblum's guidance, the underground archivists were exposed to these methodologies. Indeed, Sakowska marvels at how much time these illegal chroniclers spent discussing each question and how it might fit into the

3 Artur Eisenbach, "Introduction," in Emanuel Ringelblum, *Kronika getta warszawskiego* (Warsaw: Czytelnik, 1983), p. 5.
The quotations are based on my "free" translation from the Polish in the hope that I have captured Ringelblum's spirit and the translation conveys the original intent.

4 Israel Gutman, "Emanuel Ringelblum, The Chronicler of the Warsaw Ghetto," *Polin: A Journal of Polish Jewish Relations*, vol. 3 (1988), p. 16.

5 Joseph Kermish, "Introduction, " in Joseph Kermish and Shmuel Krakowski, eds., Emanuel Ringelblum, *Polish-Jewish Relations During the Second World War* (Jerusalem: Yad Vashem, 1974), p. xxxix.

questionnaire, which was the actual tool for gathering much of their wartime evidence.[6]

An edition of Ringelblum's *Warsaw Ghetto Chronicle* appeared in Polish in 1983. This publication contains a wealth of wartime history, covering the years between 1939 and 1943; reports are chronologically divided into each of these years. The volume ends with over 130 pages of biographical portraits of different individuals and groups who perished while devoting their lives to the welfare of the Jewish people.[7]

From the summer of 1942, the Jewish Warsaw ghetto population in general, and particularly the ranks of the *Oyneg Shabes* archivists, were steadily shrinking. Ringelblum assumed the responsibility to record some of these losses. On January 18, 1943, SS men and Ukrainians surrounded the Warsaw ghetto. Early on that morning, Yitzhak Gitterman, an outstanding welfare activist, an archivist, and Ringelblum's close friend left his home to find the location of a recently completed hiding place. Close to his home he stopped briefly to exchange a few words with two friends. They heard a shot. Then they realized that a German bullet had ended Yitzhak Gitterman's life.

Gitterman's murder came as a shock to the Jewish people and to many, who, like Ringelblum, were his close friends and co-workers.[8] This tragedy reminded Ringelblum of Gitterman's earlier visit during which he looked at the list of the murdered Jews and added to it a few new names. Ringelblum writes:

> and now the list Yitzhak fixed will have his name. My hand shakes as I add it to the rest. Who knows whether a future historian, looking over this list will add to it E. Ringelblum. So what? We are accustomed to death, it makes no impression on us. If some of us will survive this war, they will appear to be

6 Ruta Sakowska, ed., *Archiwum Ringelbluma: Getto warszawskie* (Warsaw: Panstwowe Wydawnictwo Naukowe, 1980), pp. 13–14; idem, "Wstep," *Archiwum Ringelbluma* (Warsaw: Wydawnictwo Naukowe PWN, 1997), pp. 12–17.

7 Ringelblum, *Kronika*, p. 494.

8 Ibid., p. 522.

> creatures from another planet. Their survival will be at once a miracle and a mistake.[9]

Perhaps Gitterman's murder served as an additional wake-up call? Perhaps it added an extra incentive to preserve that for which so many had already died? Rather brief, the 1943 section of Ringelblum's chronicle is a clarification, an explanation, and an historical overview of the *Oyneg Shabes* labors, all wrapped into one.

Ringelblum reports that at the beginning of the occupation people were afraid to write because of continuous house searches by the occupiers and their collaborators. To write about their wartime experiences was dangerous. But eventually this changed after the Germans established ghettos. To be sure, in these special quarters the terror grew, but the terror was directed against certain groups or at different strata of society. The occupational authorities did not care about the Jewish activities inside their homes. Spurred by this development, the Jews began to write. Some of these writers were journalists, literary figures, teachers, social activists, young people and children. Most of the authors wrote diaries, which served as personal lenses through which they viewed an emerging tragic history.[10]

Ringelblum, the initiator, organizer, and moving spirit of the *Oyneg Shabes* Archives points to the autumn of 1939 as the start of this undertaking. He explains that,

> in the beginning, because of my participation in various welfare activities I had contact with many people, whatever I heard during the day, I would write down in the evening. I did it by myself. After several months I wanted to enlist the help of others. Without much success. Then I met the young rabbi Shimon Huberband, a self-taught historian. This is how I got one of my best co-workers. Unfortunately, Huberband wrote his observations and notes, in the form of comments, in various books. He wanted these to look like references about the

9 Ibid., p. 470.

10 Ibid., p. 471.

> text. Only much later did I succeed in persuading him that he should not be afraid, that he can now write, because we will hide the material anyway and nobody will find it.[11]

By May 1940, Ringelblum felt that he had to transform this data collection process into a collective undertaking. At this time he decided to select Hirsch Wasser, a refugee from Łódź, to be the secretary of the archives. During the day Ringelblum came into contact with many delegations of refugees, representatives of different communities, from various parts of the country. From them he amassed

> …information for hundreds of monographs about a variety of cities and smaller towns. And these materials became very valuable additions to our archival acquisitions. The creation of the ghetto also turned out to become a special turning point. At least initially, the Germans left the Jews alone in their private homes. The Jews were able to write and they did…[12]

Sociology, probably more than other social-science disciplines, is preoccupied with methodological issues. It appears that many of the *Oyneg Shabes* meetings were devoted to various methodological and procedural discussions. Many of Ringelblum's comments reflect sensitivity to the use of proper research methods. In part, this sensitivity originated in his enduring interest in sociology. He dwelled on a variety of methodological procedures, explaining that,

> occasionally we would collect information via coffee shop discussions.…At other times, to give a semi-legal status to our undertaking and evidence, we would announce a competition with monetary awards for writings about specific aspects of contemporary life… A contest, in itself, improved the quality of these writings… in addition often, several individuals

11 Ibid., p. 472.
12 Ibid., p. 473.

> would independently collect information about the same issues.[13]

During their gatherings the archivists would specify the themes to be studied and the appropriate research procedures. These decisions were guided by general commitments to non-judgmental, value-free objectivity. Mixed with these guidelines was an awareness about the complexity and diversity of life as it was evolving in the ghetto. That is, the archivists shared an obligation to report the evidence, as it was, regardless of whether it seemed ”ugly” or “beautiful.” Ringelblum commented that, in order to come close to an unbiased kind of research,

> they made an effort to examine the same events by as many researchers as possible. Besides, this procedure also promised to facilitate the task of future historians who by contrasting several reports would have a better chance to arrive at the historical truth about events that had actually happened.[14]

For example, if the chroniclers wanted to learn about a given occupation, they would ask several individuals to report about this topic. Among them might be a young person who would write about it, an older one, a religious person and a non-religious one. In this way the accumulated evidence would have been presented from a variety of perspectives, while, at the same time, reflecting the actual complexity of life.[15]

In the summer of 1942, the Germans began large-scale deportations. When these were halted, the Warsaw ghetto population had shrunk by about 90 percent. The work of the underground archives also came to a halt. Still, a few of the co-workers never ceased their work; they continued to write even while the deportations were going on. Others continued to collect evidence as usual.[16]

All along the *Oyneg Shabes* archivists were prodded to write in

13 Ibid.

14 Ibid., p. 479.

15 Ibid.

16 Ibid., pp. 475–476.

a clear, concise way; not to beautify what they saw, simply to stick to the facts. The reasoning behind this was that since life was so tragic, there was no need to beautify it with words. These researchers were determined to capture a full view of life in extremis – in all its objective and complex manifestations. [17]

Gradually and tentatively, changes in substance and mood began to invade Ringelblum's notes:

> …the deportations that started on July 22, 1942, established a new history about Warsaw Jews. This history imposed upon the *Oyneg Shabes* members an interruption of activities, extending over several months. In the end, only a few of us had managed to resume the research in modified ways. Under the emerging, oppressive circumstances it was impossible to engage in large-scale cooperative work.[18]

This 1943 section of Ringelblum's chronicle concludes with a moving tribute to the *Oyneg Shabes* members, describing them as a cooperative, loyal, brotherly undertaking, one in which all of them were ready to sacrifice their lives for a shared selfless service to humanity.[19]

A substantial part of the evidence collected by the *Oyneg Shabes* involved the accumulation of evidence about a wide range of categories of people. This translated into research reports about Jewish ghetto councils (Judenräte); about the ghetto police, known as the Order Service (Ordnungsdienst); the Polish policemen – many of whom collaborated with the German authorities; Polish blackmailers; and Poles who risked their lives to save Jews. Additional data appeared as an array of information about many traditional and newly emergent categories of people – refugees, beggars, smugglers, Nazi collaborators, orphans, street children, intellectuals, and many, many others.[20]

17 Ibid., p. 477.

18 Ibid., pp. 493–494.

19 Ibid., p. 494.

20 Jacob Sloan, ed., Emanuel Ringelblum, *Notes from the Warsaw Ghetto* (New York: Schocken Books, 1975) contains vivid descriptions of various categories

Within this wide range of categories of people were also Jewish women. Already in 1939, Ringelblum entrusted Cecylia Slepak, a historian and translator, with a research project about the wartime fate of Jewish women. He asked Slepak to diversify her sample by including women from various walks of life – poor and rich, intellectual and uneducated, and so forth. Hers was a longitudinal research that gathered information from a small sample of women, interviewing and re-interviewing them in depth, for several years. It was a qualitative study, interrupted only in 1942 by Cecylia Slepak's deportation to Treblinka. Slepak's research on the wartime fate of Jewish women forms an important part of the underground archives. Over the years Holocaust scholars have continued to benefit from her meticulously collected and carefully analyzed evidence.[21]

Slepak also left insightful summaries of these research findings. Accordingly, she found two kinds of wartime women. The first were those Jewish women who struggled for their self-preservation and for the preservation of their families. This group of women was propelled by feelings that it was their duty to concentrate on their own and their family's needs. The second type were women who were particularly challenged by the contemporary life-threatening disasters. The war, with its upheavals, pushed this kind of woman into activities that reached beyond their self-preservation and the preservation of their families. Some as independent, private individuals; others as employees of welfare organizations, devoted themselves to helping wide circles of people. Slepak felt that this type of woman had the will and ability to identify with the suffering of strangers and the community at large.[22]

As an example of the first kind of woman, Slepak identified Mrs. F.

Mrs. F. belonged to the group of those who struggled for life

of Jews and gentiles, how they coped with their own lives and with each other. Needless to say, Ringelblum's *Kronika* is richer in content. Artur Eisenbach, in his comprehensive introduction to Ringelblum's *Kronika*, repeatedly emphasizes the valuable contribution of *Oyneg Shabes* to the study of different categories of individuals.

21 Ringelblum, *Kronika*, pp. 474, 585.

22 YVA, JM/217/4, pp. 3–4.

because they were convinced that it was their duty to do so in order to take care of themselves and their families. She was a mother of two small children, married to an unemployed laborer. She had a modest business, which was transformed by the war into a black-market operation. Neither her unexpected pregnancy nor the birth of her third child interrupted her efforts to support the family. Then came the imposed move into the Warsaw ghetto. Following that, in the fall of 1941, the Germans introduced a law forbidding all unauthorized crossings between the ghetto and the Aryan side. Disobedience to this law carried the death penalty.[23] Concurrently Mrs. F.'s unemployed husband was incapacitated by a severe case of typhus. She felt that she had no choice but to disregard the threat of this new law.

Even though Mrs. F.'s appearance did not betray her Jewish background, a Polish policeman stopped her.

"You are Jewish," he said.

Her automatic, "No, no, I'm Polish," met with, "Let me see your papers."

But Mrs. F. had no papers to show. The policeman told her to follow. On the way she offered him a bribe of fifty złotys. The policeman demanded a hundred. All she had was fifty. He refused it. After her arrest, she was transferred to the ghetto prison. From there she was taken with the first group that was executed for illegally crossing over to the Aryan side. Mrs. F. was murdered during the early stages of ghettoization that signaled the accelerated pace of Jewish destruction.[24]

The women in the second group were those who rose to the challenge posed by life-threatening disasters on a broader scale. Wartime upheavals had pushed these women into activities that reached beyond self-preservation and the preservation of their families. Occasionally, some of them, as private individuals or as employees of welfare organizations, contributed their selfless services to a broad spectrum of individuals and groups of people.

23 Lucy S. Dawidowicz, ed., *A Holocaust Reader* (New York: Behrman House, 1976), p. 67; Nechama Tec, *When Light Pierced the Darkness* (New York: Oxford University Press, 1986), pp. 27–39.

24 YVA, JM/217/4, pp. 3–4.

Slepak recognizes these women as having had the strength to rise above their own sufferings in order to comfort other people or even entire communities which they perceived as being in need of help.

A professional librarian, identified in Slepak's survey as Mrs. B., serves as an example of this second type of Jewish women. In the Warsaw ghetto Mrs. B.'s paid job barely enabled her to meet her needs. Yet she ignored her own difficulties and devoted herself to creating a children's lending library. She began by collecting books and contacting potential helpers. Despite seemingly impossible obstacles she persevered. Eventually, her dream came true, and Mrs. B. became the director of the Children's Lending Library in the ghetto.

She shared her feelings about this accomplishment with Slepak:

> My library job has a wonderful psychological effect on me. It gives me life. I believe in the importance of this kind of work for the present and for the future. When I used to sort clothes under much better physical conditions, and then I had more strength, I frequently felt exhausted and sick. Now with my library work, although what I do is physically more taxing, with less agreeable surroundings... even though I am now undernourished, I feel healthy and invigorated. I feel fulfilled. My feeling of self-fulfillment must be strengthening my immune system.[25]

Independently, and in addition to Slepak's research, Ringelblum periodically observed and commented about Jewish women. In an entry during January 1940, he wrote:

> The Jewish woman sustains the family by standing for hours in dangerous food lines, by intervening with the authorities–German soldiers and the Gestapo — by accepting jobs, jobs

25 YVA, JM/215/3; my translation from the Polish. Slepak was deported from the Warsaw ghetto in the summer of 1942, so this statement must have been made before that time.

> that promise only meager benefits. Gone is the elegant lady with the fancy hats. We see instead simply dressed women with kerchiefs on their heads constantly searching for ways to support their families.[26]

Later, in 1942, in connection with a description of the conditions within the Warsaw ghetto, Ringelblum writes approvingly about the coping strategies employed by some of the Jewish women:

> …The future historian will have to devote an appropriate chapter to the wartime Jewish women. They occupy a prominent place in wartime Jewish history. Thanks to their persistent contributions, thousands of families have a chance to overcome these horrible times. Recently we have observed an interesting development. The men, exhausted by the strenuous labor, make room for women. Some House Committees are run by women. For our expanding welfare operations, we need new people. It is both fortunate and important that we can rely on these new sources of energy.[27]

Ringelblum also paid special tribute to an activist whose work on house committees spilled over into other important community needs as well. She was a distinguished woman and was noted for her innovative ways of extending aid. He refers to her as Mrs. Mokrska from Łódź. Mrs. Mokrska initiated several house committees. She also had a gift for finding women who were ready to sacrifice. Many of Mrs. Mokrska's co-workers became patrons of boarding schools, refugee centers, and public kitchens. The tireless Mokrska seemed to be everywhere, spreading her effectiveness in the most unexpected ways.

During the height of the 1942 deportations, she discovered a workshop that accepted laborers free of charge. At that point people were convinced that employment would shield them from deportations. In reality, work was either a temporary respite or an outright

26 Ringelblum, *Kronika*, p. 67.

27 Ibid., p. 394.

illusion. In the end Mrs. Mokrska herself fell victim to the 1942 deportations.[28]

Ringelblum again pays tribute to other women when he describes Jewish underground couriers.

> The heroic girls, Chajka [Grosman], Frumka [Plotnicka] and others – theirs is a story that calls for the pen of a great writer. They are venturesome, courageous girls who travel here and there across Poland to cities and towns, carrying Aryan papers which describe them as Polish or Ukrainian… Day by day they face the greatest dangers, relying completely on their Aryan appearance and the kerchiefs they tie around their heads. They accept the most dangerous missions and carry them out without a murmur, without a moment's hesitation. If there is need for someone to travel to Vilna, Białystok, Lwów, Kowel, Lublin, Częstochowa, or Radom to smuggle in such forbidden things as illegal publications, goods, money, they do it all as though it were the most natural thing. If there are comrades to be rescued from Vilna, Lublin, or other cities, they take the job on themselves. Nothing deters them, nothing stops them. If it is necessary to make friends with the German responsible for a train so as to travel beyond the borders of the Government-General, which is allowed only for people with special permits – they do it quite simply. They travel from city to city, where no representative of any Jewish institution has reached, such as Volhynia and Lithuania. They were the first to bring the news of the tragedy in Vilna. They were the first to take back messages of greeting and encouragement to the survivors in Vilna.
>
> How many times did they look death in the eye? How many times were they arrested and searched? But their luck held. "Those who go on an errand of mercy will meet no evil." With what modesty and simplicity do they deliver their reports on what they accomplished during their travels on trains where Christians, men and women, were picked up and taken away

28 Ibid., pp. 462–463. Mrs. Mokrska's first name does not appear.

> for work in Germany. Jewish women have written a shining page in the history of the present World War. The Chajkas and the Frumkas will take first place in this history. These girls do not know what it is to rest. They have hardly arrived from Częstochowa where they took forbidden goods, and in a few hours they would move on again: they do it without a moment's hestitation, and without a minute's rest.[29]

Just as Ringelblum and his co-workers had hoped for, evidence about the many categories of individuals and groupings have contributed to a broader and more meaningful understanding of the Holocaust and, more generally, to life in extremis.

The preoccupation of *Oyneg Shabes* with diverse categories of people resembles a basic sociological concept, central to sociological understandings of human interactions. Sociologists view individuals in terms of the kinds of associations they have. Thus, an individual is at once a mother, a professional, a Jew, a friend, and many, many other things. Each of these labels is referred to as a status, or as a position within a system of interactions to which certain shared expectations are attached. The different statuses a person occupies at a particular time are ranked. Some are considered more important than others. In the Third Reich the most important status was a person's "racial" affiliation. This was the so-called "master status," with all others being subservient to it. Next in importance was political status. A Communist was doomed; a Social-Democrat less so. But a Fascist was the most highly valued. At the two extremes were, first, Aryan, Fascist, males; and, second, Jewish, Communist, males and females.

I have recently completed a comparative study of Jewish women and men in a variety of Holocaust settings.[30]A part of this research relies on direct in-depth interviews with Holocaust survivors–women and men. When I asked these respondents to compare the experiences and coping strategies of women and men dur-

29 Yitzhak Arad, Yisrael Gutman, Abraham Margaliot, eds., *Documents on the Holocaust: Selected Sources on the Destruction of the Jews of Germany and Austria, Poland, and the Soviet Union* (Jerusalem: Yad Vashem, 1981), p. 239–240.

30 Tec, *Resilience and Courage.*

ing the Holocaust, some of them were reluctant to reply. When I probed, rephrasing the question differently, their discomfort grew. Some of them said that there were no differences in the fate and reactions of Jewish men and women. Additional attempts at probing only increased their uneasiness. Unable to dispel their unwillingness to deal with this issue, I moved on to other topics.

When I returned to the previously unresolved queries, I kept in mind a set of gendered pairs relevant to whomever I was talking: e.g., mother/father; brother/sister; male friend/female friend, etc. I invited the particular interviewee to describe what had happened to each sex during the Holocaust and how this person reacted to various situations. I first inquired about several persons of the same sex; e.g., father, brother, male friend, etc. Then I switched to the opposite sex, raising similar questions about mother, sister, female cousin, and so forth. This time I avoided making gender comparisons and inquired separately about the experiences and coping strategies of several individuals of both sexes to whom the respondents were personally connected.

In reaction to this new set of queries, most respondents offered vivid descriptions of fathers whose public humiliations led to serious depressions, or feelings of apathy that were often followed by illnesses and deaths. When attention turned to mothers, the survivors portrayed them as hard working; some of them had even become smugglers. More often than not, these mothers struggled to keep their starving families from death, at least for a while. Other accounts included uncles who, in order to save themselves, escaped into the Soviet-occupied part of Poland, while their wives who remained were busy searching for ways to feed the remaining family. Some stories included brothers who emigrated, while the sisters stayed on with the parents, only to perish later. Consistently, different coping strategies were apparent for each gender.[31]

When these interviews were coming to an end, I presented this latest set of information together with the interviewees' earlier reactions to questions about gender differences. I asked them to comment on their initial denial of differences and their subse-

31 Ibid., p.15.

quent vivid descriptions of gender-specific experiences and coping strategies. I wanted them to explain these discrepancies. Most of them were surprised. The majority changed their minds and recognized that discussions of male-female differences in themselves do not distort or trivialize the Holocaust. Most came to think that such comparisons could even lead to a better understanding of Jewish wartime experiences. Not I, but their reconstructed memories brought about these changes. Indirectly, too, when inquiring about female-male comparisons, by listening carefully to their answers, I might have suggested that these distant, yet valuable experiences deserve to be listened to. No matter how this happened, once these survivors had overcome their initial reluctance to deal with male-female diversity, they offered a range of rich gender-specific comparisons that led to fresh insights and understandings.[32]

Nevertheless, a few of them still insisted that they saw no problems in their contradictory answers. I wanted them to explain their position. I heard them argue that, after all, the Germans aimed at the annihilation of all Jews, women and men. Therefore, these differences or discrepancies did not matter. They were right about the Germans' aim to annihilate all Jews regardless of who they were. However, this still did not explain what was behind the inclination of these few to avoid dealing with gender-based comparisons and distinct reactions during the Holocaust.

Through further probes I learned that, behind the attitudes of this minority and even some scholars, lurked a fear that an undue emphasis on gender distinctions would overshadow the centrality of the victims' Jewishness in determining their fate. That is, those who were particularly hesitant and reluctant to dwell on gender differences felt that gender-oriented studies would lead to a neglect of the victims' Jewishness and eventually result in historical distortions and trivializations.

Surely students of the Holocaust know how central the Jewishness of the victims was in determining their fate. We know that the German policy of Jewish annihilation was fueled by racial ideology that defined all Jews as not human and a threat to the creation of an

32 Ibid., pp. 14–17.

ideal "Aryan world." As a result of these perceptions, all Jews were destined to be murdered.

We also know that this policy of Jewish murder could not be implemented at once. History indicates that different categories of Jews were targeted for destruction at different times with different degrees of ruthlessness. But whom the Germans had targeted for annihilation at what time was in part determined by the intricate relationship between racial, political, and economic ideologies. For example, at the initial stage of the occupation, mainly elite Jewish males were targeted for immediate destruction. In the eastern ghettos in particular, these assaults upon Jewish men continued as the Germans rendered them less capable to perform their traditional male roles of family protectors and supporters. However, by mid-1942, women and their children were targeted for speedy annihilation. At this stage, for Jewish women and their young children, deportations to concentration camps meant death by gassing immediately upon arrival.

In a sense, then, all Jews moved toward the destination of annihilation. The destination was the same, but the roads upon which they traveled were different.[33]

Being a woman or a man affects our self-image and influences our fate and behavior. Gender definitions and expectations are universal, and it is this universality that demands our attention. Under some circumstances whether one was a man or a woman could make a difference. But under German rule these difference were not as central as whether one was a Jew or an "Aryan." Variations in the experiences of Jewish women and men and their possibly distinct reactions to German assaults cannot be traced to the Jewishness they all shared. Instead, these variations might be better understood in terms of other special characteristics that differentiate Jews from one another. One of these characteristics is gender – societies shared definitions, meanings, and expectations about women and men.

Anthropologists and sociologists who pursue comparative studies of societies agree that gender distinctions are universal and

33 Ibid., p. 3.

important features in every society. They also agree that gender is one of the basic, distinguishing characteristics that affect people's lives in significant ways. Given the universality and importance of gender, objections, denials, and hesitancy about its effects during the Holocaust demand some attention. At the same time we must be sensitive to the issues raised by those objecting to gender studies. But by neglecting the distinct experiences and coping strategies of women and men, we miss an opportunity to broaden our knowledge about the Holocaust. Inevitably, too, by avoiding the study of gender, we miss an opportunity to widen our understanding of the implications for life in extremis.[34] Class affiliations, age categories, the degrees and kinds of prejudices that are attached to different groups of people, as well as other human attributes all call for attention. These, too, promise to provide us with fresh insights and understandings about people's relationships and coping strategies in a variety of social settings. My most recent publication is filled with such examples.

Although, at first, they were not as openly or as directly attacked, Jewish women, as well as other family members, inevitably experienced painful losses as fathers, husbands, and other men in their lives were forced to flee, were taken away, abused, or killed. For the men who stayed on, who avoided some of the most deadly assaults, their traditional world was shattered; and with it were gone important sources of their masculine identification and pride. Unable to fulfill their traditional roles as providers and protectors, many of the men broke down. For others, just watching these changes was painful. Women and other categories of Jews were all deprived of their freedom, rights, and properties. However, women, in addition to their direct suffering, were also stripped of the traditional emotional support systems they had come to expect from men. Inevitably Jewish women knew and often witnessed the abuses directed against men. This knowledge alone took its toll.[35]

Initially, accustomed to nurturing roles, women rose to the occasion and offered their support. Some tried hard to fill the exist-

34 Ibid., pp. 16–17.
35 Ibid., p. 35.

ing gaps. As Jewish women continued to protect men and provide for their families, they had to adjust to new situations – sometimes even without being aware of the changes. Of the men's two main roles, that of protector was totally obliterated, while the role of breadwinner, although severely impaired, was occasionally left with some slight room to maneuver. The overwhelming majority of Jewish men were forced to work for either no payment or for earnings that could not stop the chronic hunger. Some men were caught and forced into work camps or were murdered. Still others, anticipating danger, ran away from the areas occupied by the Germans. In contrast, women, relying on their traditional domestic and nurturing skills, tried to fill the gaps vacated by men. Equally barred from becoming protectors, women concentrated on being providers, caregivers, and nurturers. Adapting to the new, precipitous situations, some of them expanded their activities from helping their immediate families to aiding friends and the general community.[36]

Nearly seventy years ago, Emanuel Ringelblum felt comfortable and was deeply involved with precise, detailed research about a broad range of categories of individuals, including the study of women and men who tried to cope in a variety of Holocaust settings. Following in his footsteps and in the footsteps of the *Oyneg Shabes* archivists, we, too, ought to become involved in the study of different kinds of individuals, including women and men. Through comparisons of distinct categories of people in terms of their coping strategies and their relationships to each other, we can learn much about life in general and, more specifically, about life under extreme, oppressive circumstances. On the other hand, by neglecting to examine the effects of the diverse attributes that people have, including gender, we would inevitably miss an opportunity to expand our knowledge about the Holocaust and, more broadly, about life in extremis.

Rather than avoid issues that are difficult to study or are looked upon by some with suspicion, we would do well to remember Ringelblum as a shining light, as a humanist and intellectual giant who never avoided unpopular, complex problems for study.

36 Ibid., p. 74.

Throughout his brief life Ringelblum welcomed and even searched for complex, challenging issues for exploration. He never backed out of facing up to complicated, new, and difficult topics of research. Indeed, Ringelblum never viewed with suspicion or distrust the complex and seemingly impossible questions. Nor did he avoid unpopular, controversial research. On the contrary, he insisted on examining the most ugly, the most degrading behaviors – and the most beautiful. We would do well to rely on and use Ringelblum's research pursuits as a model for our own future scholarly explorations.

In tribute to Emanuel Ringelblum, rather than shy away from controversial, unpopular topics, we should listen to the whispering voices that continue to come from Ringelblum's painstakingly gathered underground contributions. These voices seem to be urging us on, never to give up traveling upon exciting, often bumpy, unexplored roads of research.

Contributors

Havi Dreifuss (Ben-Sasson), The Department of Jewish History, Tel Aviv University

David Engel, Greenberg Professor of Holocaust Studies, Professor of Hebrew and Judaic Studies, and Professor of History at New York University and a fellow of the Goldstein-Goren Diaspora Research Center at Tel Aviv University

Barbara Engelking, Professor of Social Sciences, Head of Polish Center for Holocaust Research – Institute of Philosophy and Sociology of the Polish Academy of Sciences

Israel Gutman, Emeritus, Institute of Contemporary Jewry, Hebrew University of Jerusalem; former Chief Historian, Yad Vashem

Samuel Kassow, Charles H. Northam Professor of History, Trinity College, Hartford, Connecticut

Lea Prais, Researcher, The International Institute for Holocaust Research, Yad Vashem

Nechama Tec, Professor Emerita of Sociology, University of Connecticut, Stamford

Feliks Tych, Professor of History; Director, Jewish Historical Institute of Warsaw